Returning to Judgment

SUNY series in Contemporary Continental Philosophy

Dennis J. Schmidt, editor

Returning to Judgment

Bernard Stiegler and
Continental Political Theory

Ben Turner

SUNY
PRESS

Published by State University of New York Press, Albany

© 2023 State University of New York

For information, contact State University of New York Press, Albany, NY
www.sunypress.edu

Library of Congress Cataloging-in-Publication Data

Name: Turner, Ben (Political theory lecturer) author.
Title: Returning to judgment : Bernard Stiegler and continental political theory. /
    Ben Turner.
Description: Albany, NY : State University of New York Press, [2023] |
    Series: SUNY series in Contemporary Continental Philosophy | Includes
    bibliographical references and index.
Identifiers: LCCN 2022023927 | ISBN 9781438492032 (hardcover : alk. paper) |
    ISBN 9781438492049 (ebook) | ISBN 9781438492025 (pbk. : alk. paper)
Subjects: LCSH: Political science—Philosophy. | Stiegler, Bernard—Political and
    social views. | Ontology—Political aspects. | Technological innovations—
    Social aspects.
Classification: LCC JA71 .T88 2023 | DDC 320.01/1—dc23/eng/20221101
LC record available at https://lccn.loc.gov/2022023927

10 9 8 7 6 5 4 3 2 1

For Úna

Contents

Acknowledgments

In the argument that follows, thought is as much collective as it is a result of individual volition. This book is no exception and was made possible by the support and contributions of many others. As PhD supervisor and colleague, Iain Mackenzie has been instrumental in this project's journey from fledging thesis idea to its final version in this book, which would not exist without him. Nathan Widder also provided advice and supervision at crucial junctures that was invaluable for the development of my position. As external examiners, Martin Crowley and Ian James gave me invaluable feedback and encouragement as I developed my PhD thesis into a book manuscript. Their generosity has been essential to the final form that this work has taken. I also thank the two anonymous reviewers for their extensive, and challenging, comments on initial and revised versions of the manuscript, which greatly improved the argument I pursue in the following. Last, I thank Michael Rinella for supporting this project as acquisitions editor at SUNY Press.

For engaging and lively discussions of my work and that of others, both of which I have learned much from, I am indebted to the graduate research student and staff communities in the School of Politics and International Relations at the University of Kent and Kent's Centre for Critical Thought. I am also grateful to everyone who has supported and inspired this work in some way over the space of almost a decade, whether as a colleague, collaborator, or participant in the smallest of conversations that have shifted and developed my thought. No list will ever be exhaustive, however; for playing one or several of these roles I would like to thank Nadine Ansorg, Jonjo Brady, Andy Brogan, Charles Devellennes, Maria Drakopoulou, Benoît Dillet, Conor Heaney, Kamila Kwapinska, Lucas Van Milders, Adrian Pabst, Connal Parsley, Marco Piasentier, Robert Porter, Sara

Raimondi, Victoria Ridler, and Hannah Richter. To anyone I may have missed, I deeply appreciate all of the discussions at talks, workshops, and conferences that shaped this work in some way.

I am grateful for the ongoing support of my parents, without whom this research would not have been possible. Finally, Úna McAuley's unstinting patience, kindness, and love were indispensable to this project's fruition, and for keeping me sane throughout.

Introduction

Totalization and Judgment in Continental Political Theory

> The most terrifying thing would be for The Human to exist.
>
> —*Technics and Time* 2, 162

> The great question of the twenty-first century will be finding the way . . . to invent new modalities of non-inhuman existence.
>
> —*Taking Care of Youth and the Generations*, 183

Continental political theory is commonly defined by its commitment to the overcoming of totalization. This is particularly true of poststructuralism, deconstruction, and postmodernism, which, while often conflated and misrepresented, are all defined by some version of a now familiar argument against totalizing theories. Enlightenment and humanist attempts to provide exhaustive, all-encompassing, and unifying accounts of social and political phenomena founded on the figures of reason, rationality, and nature fall at the hurdle of accounting for unpredictability, novelty, and difference. It is difficult to discern such differences from the viewpoint of a universal theory that applies to all, and therefore attempts to develop such frameworks inevitably exclude some individuals, groups, or ways of living. Criticisms of totalization are animated by the attempt to come to terms with the fallibility of reason in the face of otherness and often seek to account for how universal theories can support the domination of those who do not fit within their categories. This critical project is characterized by a move away from, or at least a tentative relationship with, explicit political judgments that might express or perpetuate unwarranted hierarchies and exclusions.

1

As a tradition, continental political theory consists of attempts to develop concepts that do not rely on judgments that legitimate domination by overlooking the innumerable, micro-political ways in which individuals differ from prevailing norms.

Before his untimely death in August 2020, Bernard Stiegler was a central figure in contemporary engagements with the legacy of this critique of totalization (James 2012). A student of Jacques Derrida and a reader of many figures within the continental canon, he was one of the first to develop a substantive continental philosophy of technology.[1] Technology is not so much a topic addressed by Stiegler's philosophy as the central organizing principle of his version of the non-totalizing project. This philosophy rests on the claim that the human is shaped by a constitutive relationship to technicity. Technics, in the form of material supports of memory, develops through interactions with human activity and, because it is subject to local interpretation and differentiation, acts as the source of human diversity. Neither the human nor the political can be totalized by universal concepts that apply to all because both are defined by their changing relationship to technicity, which differs historically, geographically, and culturally. Totalization is a problem for Stiegler because our perceptions of the human are tied to the historically and locally contingent way that technicity shapes our existence.

Understood in this way, Stiegler's philosophy is congruent with the continental critique of totality. He associates singular concepts of "The Human" that ignore technical differentiation with totalizing narratives that can lead to domination and endanger the diversity of forms of human existence. However, Stiegler's relationship to his precursors is more complicated than it first appears. He also breaks with the established continental legacy insofar as he claims that the political challenge incumbent upon denizens of the twenty-first century is precisely the task of making judgments on desirable forms of human existence, understood as the "non-inhuman." As technology changes, it poses challenges and problems that require solutions in the form of clear political judgments. These judgments can reasonably be considered as totalizing insofar as they stipulate ways of thinking and acting that might guide the future of humanity. Inevitably, this entails a shift from the micro-political to the macro-political level of general forms of political decision-making. If one finds value in the continental critique of totality, how should one make sense of the apparent inconsistency between Stiegler's critique of totalization, associated with universal conceptions of "The Human," and his advocacy of totalizing judgments regarding its future?

Rather than a contradiction, this book makes the case that Stiegler's simultaneous commitment to the critique of totalization and the advocation of totalizing judgment marks his importance for contemporary continental political theory. He contends that it is politically necessary to make judgments on the nature of the human while also recognizing that its openness eludes totalization. Failure to do so relinquishes the task of defining the human to those less concerned with its pluralistic, contingent, and open nature. Totalization is not just a vehicle for the constraint of diverse forms of thought and the perpetuation of exclusion and domination, but also a tool for articulating judgments that defend plurality from these ills. Stiegler advocates that we grapple with the problem of the necessity of totalization in political judgment rather than attempting to move beyond it. I claim that this issue motivates Stiegler's entire philosophy of technicity and argue that it presents a significant challenge to contemporary, ontological versions of the critique of totality in continental political thought.

The Critique of Totalization and the Legacy of Continental Political Theory

Why has totalization posed such a pressing and persistent problem for political theory in the continental tradition? Critical approaches to humanism represent a central example of this concern. For Judith Butler, "Universal conceptions of the human" characteristic of humanism "assume a substantive person who is the bearer of various essential and nonessential attributes" (Butler 1999, 14). While such attributes are intended to provide a clear rationale for political action, both radical and conservative, not all social and cultural forms line up neatly with them. One such attribute is the capacity of the human to exercise reason. Within enlightenment and modern conceptions of the human, the capacity for rational action has been deemed as a definitional, and therefore totalizing, element of human nature. Nevertheless, it has not always been seen as shared equally by women and non-European peoples. Totalization harms, in this instance, as it establishes a conceptual norm that justifies the ill-treatment of those perceived not to measure up to this standard (e.g., Butler 1999, 14–15; Eze 1997). Humanism totalizes insofar as it explicitly or implicitly demarcates those who are deemed to be more or less human along the lines of attributes that include (but are not limited to) race, gender, sexuality, ability, criminality, and intellectual capacity, justifying the domination of those who fall on the wrong sides of such categorizations.

Here totalization forms the central problem for continental political thought for theoretical and political reasons. Theoretically, totalization places strict limits on sociological and political concepts that stratify and constrain marginal ways of thinking (James 2012, 3; Watkin 2016, 3). Such concepts divert our attention from unforeseen and novel ideas that may be of significant theoretical importance, leading us to neglect other traditions and modes of thought. This theoretical perspective underpins the political critique of the ways concepts that guide action may be bound up with relationships of power and domination (Owen 2016). Without attention to the outside of the norms we take for granted, we might not comprehend the extent to which those norms legitimate unjust political situations. The continental critique of humanism rests on these two broader points about totalizing concepts: they direct us away from creativity and novelty in theoretical work and can justify the harm of those who fall into the cracks of the narratives that theories of totality establish. While it typically has focused on the philosophical content of such totalizing concepts, continental political thought is also motivated by the need to identify these malign influences within social and political life so that it can undermine the forms of authority that naturalize them (White 2011). In the wake of such developments, continental thinkers have been drawn to the advocation of forms of local and small-scale micro-politics to avoid legislating for social life with judgments that might repeat the problems of totalization.

Paradigmatic continental methods and concepts developed by thinkers such as Butler, Hélène Cixous, Derrida, Gilles Deleuze, Michel Foucault, Julia Kristeva, and Jean-François Lyotard, spanning performativity, deconstruction, difference in-itself, genealogy, and the differend, are all products of the attempt to uncover the contingency of these malign social structures and their susceptibility to critique, change, and transformation. Within the work of these thinkers and others, metaphysics, humanism, and universalism have been subject to continued scrutiny on account of their role in stymieing creative theorizing and within exclusionary conceptions of politics that underpin domination. In turn, they have been replaced with non-totalizing accounts of the political that attempt to do justice to the complexities and aporias of political concepts. Totalization must be challenged because these aporias demonstrate that, in Gavin Rae's words, "structure itself must be radically ever-changing and open-ended. All unity, consistency and stability must be questioned and undermined whenever and wherever it arises" (Rae

2020, 3). The methodological position shared across work that holds to this claim—particularly in the poststructuralist tradition—is that these complexities cannot be dissolved by conceptual rigor.[2] Political theory's task is not to provide definitions of concepts that would overcome the contradictions underlying them, but to press these problems further to account for how complexity, paradox, and impossibility act as underlying conditions of the political. Tidy gardening of its conceptual boundaries constrains and excludes other ways of thinking and acting politically, for no concept can fully exhaust the potentials of politics or escape the possibility of perpetuating relations of power, exclusion, and domination.[3]

Those who have followed in the wake of this critique of totalization have attempted to reconcile it with more substantive accounts of the nature of being. These approaches are committed to a post-foundational variant of ontological reasoning. This form of political ontology does not provide concrete foundations for social and political life but instead posits ontological conditions that do not act as a ground in a traditional sense. Being is not characterized by stable laws or structures, but is differing, in flux, or in constant becoming. Not only do totalizing political concepts lead to undesirable theoretical and political consequences, but they also misrepresent the very "nature" of being. If being is changeable, then our conceptions of politics must be adjusted to match this contingent, shifting, and non-totalizable understanding of reality. A variety of pluralist political projects have been based on these claims, which draw on the integration of critical reflexivity and the horizontalization of agency with the nature of being.[4] A question regarding the status of these post-foundational ontological claims lingers, however. To what extent does ontology, even if it is intended to be post-foundational, totalize the space of the political in the same way as the much-maligned categories of humanism, metaphysics, or universalism?

Stiegler's philosophy of technics allows us to formulate this question and provides an opportunity to rethink totalization as both a limit to political ontology and a necessary component of political theory. While he shares some of the motivations of those who develop the continental tradition's critique of totalization into more concrete political gestures, the turn to ontology for this task is complicated by two consequences of his philosophy of technics. First, because human existence is an effect of technicity, philosophical speculation is constrained by its technical context. At first glance this is not new. Post-Heideggerian continental philosophy has been committed to providing accounts of the finitude of thought that underpins the critique of totalization.[5] Stiegler's account of technical finitude is unique because he refuses to grant ontological speculation a privileged methodological position with respect to the diversity of ways that technicity shapes thought. Ontological reasoning occurs within a particular technical horizon and is therefore totalizing, as it cannot account for the diversity of thought that may occur in other such horizons. In this sense his work is "post-ontological" (Barthélémy 2012). Second, because of Stiegler's commitment to this post-ontological version of non-totalization within his philosophy of technicity, he is also concerned with the capacity of humans to judge, give meaning to, and totalize their circumstances. Totalization is not simply a constraint on the possibilities represented by the aporias, contradictions, and complexities that underpin concepts. It is also necessary to give meaning to human existence precisely because the technical condition renders humanity without essence, understood in either metaphysical or ontological terms.

Stiegler balances these two gestures by introducing the concept of the a-transcendental to continental philosophy as a new modality of totalization. The a-transcendental refers to the need to give meaning to the ever-changing technical foundations of social and political systems with totalizing judgments, on the condition that the "transcendental" ideas on which such judgments rest are inextricably tied to the contingent, empirical, technological horizons that act as their conditions. This modality of totalization substantially reorients continental political theory's critique of totality. The a-transcendental facilitates the exercise of totalizing judgment on the nature of social and political life without falling into the trap of articulating exclusionary claims about the timelessness of those judgments. Moreover, it leads Stiegler to stipulate that totalization is an unavoidable element of political judgment, as it responds to problems posed by the open and contingent human condition. Totalizing judgments need not be politically dominating if they are recognized as locally, historically, and geographically conditioned rather than universal. The a-transcendental radically situates philosophical judgment, curtailing the explanatory powers of ontology, while also necessitating the articulation of totalizing judgments in the absence of a-historical principles that might ground responses to problems posed by technological change.

I argue that the development of this position unifies the entirety of Stiegler's philosophy of technics. For Stiegler, the significance of the legacy of continental political theory lies in the need for an account of what it means to critically assess totalization in the absence of human essence. Totalizing judgments are compatible with the critique of totalization when they are understood as a-transcendental because they are both necessary, as they give meaning to the technical condition, and contingent, as their necessity is derived from their locality. Because of the necessity of these judgments in the face of the contingency of the technical condition, totalization is inevitable. Whether one is cognizant of it or not, judgment is always tied up with totalizing images of the human and of the nature of reality. Despite a reticence toward totalization inherited from the rejection of judgment in twentieth-century continental philosophy, political ontology, even in the form of post-foundationalism, cannot avoid these gestures.[6] Political ontology's limit, as seen from Stiegler's perspective, lies in its attempt to relinquish totalizing judgment and its simultaneous failure to recognize that ontological claims require totalization that short-circuit its pluralist intentions. The primary problem of political ontology, then, is the absence of a critical architecture to assess the degree to which it engages in totalizing judgment despite itself. Rather than avoiding totalization and falling into this trap, Stiegler's philosophy provides a set of tools for considering whether particular totalizing judgments maintain space for openness, critique, and diversity, or whether they totalize the political in a way that does not.

Totalization, Judgment, and Capitalism

Stiegler articulates his interest in the capacity of humans to judge, totalize, and give meaning to their technical contexts most clearly within his analysis of automation, machine learning, and algorithms under capitalism. An illustrative version of this concern is his critique of Chris Anderson's arguments regarding "the end of theory." In 2008, Anderson, then editor of tech magazine *Wired*, argued that data science has rendered the need for the posing and testing of hypotheses obsolete, and consequently that we can do away with "every theory of human behavior." Anderson advocated jettisoning the question of "why people do what they do?" and replacing it with the recognition that "the point is they do it, and we can track and measure it with unprecedented fidelity. With enough data, the numbers speak for themselves" (Anderson 2008). Out with human judgment and in with automated processing of data and the generation of correlations that predict behavior. Stiegler argued that this perspective poses a significant threat to the human capacity to judge, but also to the diversity of human life more broadly. The viewpoint that Anderson represents is responsible for a collapse in "noodiversity." If human behavior can be reduced to correlations among data points, then there is no need for originality, creativity, or independent judgment to give meaning to existence—it is simply fodder for the predictive machine.

Totalizing automated systems, Stiegler claimed, eliminate the space for the unpredictable and incalculable forms of critical judgment necessary for distinguishing a future that is actively desired from one generated from the mere "facts" of correlation. An increasingly global, complex, and integrated technological system facilitates this "*systemic* elimination of diversity," which "has everything to do, on the one hand, with *technology*, and, on the other hand, with *calculability*—technology being rationalized and through that inherently tied to calculation." According to Stiegler, the effects of this rationalization are exacerbated by capitalism. Computational capitalism rests on the assumption that certainty can be reduced to "instruments of statistics, measurement, simulation, modelling, observation, production, logistics, mobility, guidance, bibliometrics, scientometrics, marketing, self-quantification (the 'quantified self'), and so on" (Stiegler 2020b, 72). These metrics can then be deployed in the anticipation and prediction of human behavior in the name of profit. Calculation and capitalism are totalizing, insofar as all is calculable, but they do not provide meaning beyond the profit motive. Totalization here operates without critique, judgment, or a vision of the future.

The problem with capitalism in its algorithmic form is that "*industrial fiction overcodes* any question of ends" (Stiegler 2020c, 90). Capitalism systematically eliminates any local generation of meaning that might elude the profit motive while simultaneously totalizing the ends that humans might pursue, pushing out any purpose that doesn't fall within the boundaries of profitable calculation. It is in the context of Stiegler's response to capitalist totalization that the a-transcendental appears most starkly as a modality of totalization that can be reconciled with the contingency and plurality of technicity. That this mode of totalization is seen most starkly in contrast to capitalism should not detract from the extensive consideration of the relationship between technics, totalization, and judgment across his writings. Stiegler's political judgment on capitalism and automation is the fruit of a career-long attempt to rethink the question of ends in relation to technicity. Technological developments do not just pose new political problems of the kind found within automation. Responses to all political problems are shaped by technology, as the cognitive capacities, terms of reference, and normative expectations that inform judgment are constituted within the relationship to technics. If political judgments are conditioned by technological locality in this way, then they cannot fall back on a-historical, metaphysical, or ontological resources to make general claims about the nature of politics. Despite this, if technology poses dangers to institutions and norms in a way that threatens the very dissolution of political disagreement, as Stiegler argues it does within computational capitalism, then to defend politics requires critical judgment on precisely what is valuable. Political judgments will necessarily mobilize presuppositions that totalize their conditions because they answer the pressing question of ends in the face of human contingency. Such judgments are situated, conditional, and plural, because of the constitutive relationship between the human and technicity that renders the human without a-historical features, but also totalizing, insofar as they give meaning to the human future in the face of the very lack of any metaphysical, ontological, or teleological path.

While Stiegler's concern for judgment arises from his critique of twenty-first–century capitalism, which I touch on in the course of the argument that follows, I focus on the broader consequences that his philosophy of technicity and his conception of judgment have for the problem of totalization. This position on totalization arises within the context of a disagreement with continental political thought: by rejecting totalization, it is unable to articulate a vision of the future. Stiegler argues that reticence toward totality is untenable under the conditions of late capitalism, where futurity is totalized by the profit motive in a way that structurally constrains critique and restricts politics to the indifferent management of the economy rather than the articulation of criteria that would underpin the ongoing differentiating and discerning action of judgment.[7] Stiegler acknowledges that figures such as Derrida, Deleuze, Foucault, and Lyotard were all motivated by the need to defend small-scale and local forms of politics from being engulfed within capitalist totalization (Stiegler 2020c, 97). What they did not recognize, however, is the need to consider the dynamic and critical relationship between locality and universality that is established by the need for judgment in the face of the contingency of the human condition.

This evasion of totalizing judgment leaves continental political theory in a double bind. It cannot articulate a response to the problem of the erasure of the space for judgment within computational capitalism because it advocates local resistance to totalization while neglecting the need to invent new totalizing judgments (Stiegler 2015a; 2013e). However, it also unwittingly engages in totalization within its use of ontology without providing a critical framework for assessing it. Stiegler's wager is that totalization must be reconceived in a way that incorporates openness to avoid the twin threats of the abdication of judgment and the unintentional advocacy of totalization without plurality. Rather than focus on his critique of capitalist calculation, I provide an account of the framework that underpins Stiegler's attempt to break with his predecessors' positions regarding totalization, judgment, and ontology, for the problem of capitalism exacerbates this underlying theoretical tension that permeates the entirety of his philosophy of technics.

Totalization, Ontology, and the Human

This break leads Stiegler to diverge from two themes in contemporary continental political theory that attempt to further the critique of totalization: a turn to post-foundational ontologies of the political that integrate a concern for locality and difference with an account of being that is agonistic and constantly in flux, and to critiques of anthropocentrism that provide ontological accounts of nonhuman agency. In both cases, ontology is used to circumvent claims that human nature, metaphysical principles, or totalizing assumptions underlie the political (Viriasova 2018, 7). Totalization is the bête noir of both of these strategies, for it facilitates domination by constraining the diversity that underpins the political, and by restricting conceptions of agency inside humanist, and therefore exclusionary, limits. These ontological criticisms of totalization seek to remedy what Bonnie Honig referred to as the "displacement of politics" by recovering the ways that the political flourishes beyond the constraints of totalizing normative judgment (1993).

Within political ontology, post-foundational accounts of the political are contrasted with the totalizing tendencies of real-world politics. As mentioned above, this post-foundationalism represents a broad field that encompasses a range of ontological concepts and styles of argument opposed to totalization, ranging across weak ontology, lack, becoming, and antagonism (e.g., Marchart 2007; 2018; Mihai et al. 2017; Strathausen 2009; Tønder and Thomassen 2005; White 2000; Wenman 2013; Widder 2012). Many of these approaches distinguish politics from the political to grant the latter a degree of autonomy, superiority, and unpredictability. The political is only visible when it interrupts stable assumptions regarding the nature of the social represented by politics (Rancière 1999).[8] Two examples demonstrate the breadth of such approaches. In their adoption of a post-Heideggerian conception of ontology, Jean-Luc Nancy and Philippe Lacoue-Labarthe mobilize the philosophical essence of the political—a primordial state of being-in-common that cannot be reduced to a unitary identity—against the eradication of this contingency by the totalization of the social field by the static categories of politics. It is from this "retreat of the political that the political 'itself,' its question or its exigency, arises" (Nancy and Lacoue-Labarthe 1997, 131). Those influenced by Carl Schmitt, such as Ernesto Laclau and Chantal Mouffe, argue that the antagonistic differences between groups, represented by the political, are irreducible to politics (Laclau and Mouffe 1985). A translation of ontological antagonism into an agonism that recognizes difference but negates violence is necessary to counter liberal democracy's delusions of establishing a totalizing consensus that overcomes the ineradicable conflict at the heart of the political (Mouffe 2000; 2005; 2013). In both cases, a claim about the ontological nature of the political is leveraged against totalization.

A related but distinct tendency within continental political theory criticizes totalizing anthropocentrism by advocating for ontologies of immanence that account for the agency of nonhuman entities. Ian James and John Mullarkey have argued that much recent French philosophy has rejected ontological distinctions between the poetic and the scientific or the linguistic and the material (Mullarkey 2006; James 2012; 2019a; 2019b). Similarly, "new materialists" have adopted comparable principles to argue for the significance of nonhuman agency within political problems.[9] Both new materialists and proponents of immanence have developed monist ontologies that collapse the distinction between nature and culture into a single plane where nonhuman and human forms of agency intermingle. For William Connolly, this attention to ontological immanence "seeks to render us more sensitive to a variety of nonhuman force fields that impinge upon politico-economic life" by ruling out exceptionalist and totalizing conceptions of human agency (Connolly 2013, 9). In these perspectives, ontology is mobilized to highlight the political implications of nonhuman agency within an ethical attunement to materiality that escapes the totalization of politics. To engage in this attunement, Jane Bennett implores us to "*postpone judgment*" and "hold off the sorting discrimination often assumed to be the very essence of ethical action," a sorting that I am referring to as totalization (Bennett 2020, xvi).

Post-foundationalist and new materialist iterations of the ontological turn have been subject to criticism because of the consequences of their critiques of totalization. Both have been accused of focusing on ontological speculation to the neglect of real political problems (Lemke 2018; McNay 2014; Rekret 2016). Moreover, it can be argued that the attempt to incorporate epistemological reflexivity with ontological resources backfires insofar as the latter short-circuits the former (Turner 2019a). In the case of new materialism, Claire Colebrook argues that the decoupling of agency from the human and the attribution of agentic powers to a monist, flat, and vital ontological field leads to an "ultrahumanism" in which human capacities are simply expanded to being writ large—repeating the problems of humanism at the level of being in general (Colebrook 2014, 163). Such ostensibly egalitarian conceptions of agency fail to consider how our capacity to act is shaped in ways that are fundamentally unequal (McNay 2016). Ontological accounts of the political, for Clayton Chin, engage in a similar gesture by presupposing a level of argumentation that "subsists below conscious dialogue, conditioning our interactions, requiring a specialized form of theoretical access" (Chin 2021, 774).[10] While reflexivity regarding ontological questions is central to these theories, they conceptualize reflexive capacities within a particular ontology that is situated and thus subject to questions of power. Who gets to decide what the determining ontological principles of plurality are? In both cases, attributing necessity to particular ontological claims—such as the vitality of nonhuman agency or a specific conception of political ontology—leads to the conflation of being and normativity despite the intention of such claims being the untethering of ontological reasoning from totalization (M. G. E. Kelly 2018, 73–94). To borrow a phrase from Johanna Oksala, "ontology is politics that has forgotten itself" (Oksala 2012, 35).

Stiegler's skepticism toward the rejection of "'mastery'" that he sees in Derridean philosophy (Stiegler 2020b, 69) resonates with these criticisms of post-foundational and new materialist ontologies. As we have seen, he holds that totalizing judgments are a necessary component of any meaningful response to the problems posed by technological change *and* that totalization is an unavoidable component of any philosophical claim about the nature of politics. Rather than a rejection of mastery, the defense of plurality requires a critical assessment of possible modalities of totalization in order to reconcile judgment with contingency. It can be argued here that continental political theory does not reject concrete claims about politics. However, such claims are typically oriented toward the undoing of totalization and the rejection of judgments that might raise themselves to a macro-political level of generality beyond the micro-political and the local (e.g., Connolly 2017, 55). For Stiegler, this reticence toward mastery leads to the failure to articulate totalizing judgments that would both actively challenge the totalization of capitalism and engage in the task of critically assessing what counts as an acceptable modality of totalization. From the perspective he establishes, post-foundational, immanent, and new materialist ontological approaches to politics are too quick to withdraw from this challenge.

Because of his return to the questions of totalization and judgment, Stiegler's work resonates with attempts to resuscitate the figure of the human by considering its formation within a broader ecology of influences while simultaneously critiquing antihumanism for the "ultrahumanism" identified by Colebrook. Christopher Watkin finds in the work of Alain Badiou, Bruno Latour, Catherine Malabou, and Michel Serres a renewal of the concept of the human that is in line with, but nevertheless tries to overcome, its place within continental thought (Watkin 2016). Similarly, Martin Crowley argues that Stiegler develops a conception of agency that provides traction upon political problems in a way that responds to the new materialist rejection of mastery while also avoiding the exceptionalism of humanism (Crowley 2022). In this light, Stiegler's embrace of judgment does not entail throwing the baby out with the bathwater by rehabilitating the human and uncritically returning to totalization, humanism, and metaphysics. To the contrary, one finds a concern for the elimination of diversity by these three concepts across his work. The importance of Stiegler's contribution to continental political theory lies in his recognition that totalization is inescapable and must be grappled with in order to advocate for a pluralism that integrates local concerns with generalizable visions of the political.

The Philosophy of Technics
and the Problem of Totalization

I pursue this argument by drawing consequences from Stiegler's central philosophical claim: humanity is formed within a co-constitutive relationship to technical objects. Since its inception philosophy has, according to Stiegler, repressed the constitutive relationship between knowledge and technics by attributing necessity to the former and contingency to the latter (Stiegler 1998, 1). He develops this thought through readings of the continental canon of thinkers who influence theorists of political ontology, immanence, and new materialism—ranging from the phenomenology of Edmund Husserl and Martin Heidegger; the poststructuralism of Derrida, Deleuze, and Foucault; to the psychoanalysis of Sigmund Freud—while also stating the need to critique and overcome the shortcomings of these traditions (Stiegler 2013e; 2015a). This cast of figures is supplemented by the work of less prominent figures in continental philosophy, like Gaston Bachelard, Georges Canguilhem, and Gilbert Simondon, and those who do not explicitly fall within its boundaries, such as Alfred North Whitehead. Across his reading of these thinkers, Stiegler's consideration of technicity shares the concern for the underlying conditions of politics demonstrated by political ontology (Beardsworth 1998a, 71; Lindberg 2020, 385) and for the interaction between human and nonhuman agency within new materialism (Crowley 2013a; 2019; 2022; James 2012). His positive view of totalization both distinguishes him from these traditions and allows him to move beyond the vexed relationship between totalization and ontology within them.

Stiegler's interventions regarding the nature of technics are laid out in strictly philosophical terms in his *Technics and Time* series (1998; 2009b; 2011c) and form the basis of his engagements with politics across numerous books, series, and interviews. The most prominent of these include *Disbelief and Discredit* (2011a; 2013b; 2014b), *Symbolic Misery* (2014e; 2015b), *Automatic Society* (2016a), *Pharmacologie du front national* (2013c), *The Neganthropocene* (2018c), and *Qu'appelle-t-on panser?* (2018a; 2020c). Across these writings and his political interventions with organizations such as Ars Industrialis, Plein Commune, and the Internation Collective, Stiegler strove to develop a conceptual framework suitable for establishing new political futures from contemporary technical conditions.[11] In this work, one finds an understanding of politics that seeks to avoid the negative consequences of totalization (James 2015), understood as the elimination of diverse forms of human judgment, and an activism characterized by an attempt to put these ideas into practice.

The major consequence of Stiegler's understanding of technics that I pursue here is summarized in brief by Gerald Moore's claim that his work brings "an end to the philosophical overdetermination of the political" (G. Moore 2011, 199). Similarly, James sees Stiegler's writings as characterized by "an image of philosophy oriented toward an eclipse of totality and all horizons of unity and completeness" (James 2019b, 223). If ontologies and definitions of the human are tethered to the development of technical objects, then the conceptualizations of the political that arise from these claims are as varied as the technical contexts that support them. This insight curtails attempts to define and delimit the space of politics with reference to post-foundational ontologies precisely because ontology participates within the intellectual traditions of a particular technical context. Nevertheless, Stiegler argues that totalizing judgments are necessary precisely because the human lacks an overarching *telos* that would guide the political. While I concur with Moore and James regarding Stiegler's critique of totality and the philosophical overdetermination of politics, my account of his work emphasizes his commitment to a critical understanding of totality. As such,

I do not engage in a detailed account of the limits of the work of specific thinkers within the field of continental political theory, political ontology, and new materialism, although some of their work is discussed at crucial junctures. Instead, the limits to political ontology are developed within an account of the metapolitical consequences of the role that totalization and judgment play within Stiegler's philosophy of technics.

Three concepts in Stiegler's work are central to pursuing this argument. The first is the concept of the non-inhuman. This term represents Stiegler's attempt to retain the category of the human while evacuating any remnants of humanist totalization from it. At first glance, this appears to be contradictory. Is the human not among the most totalizing of philosophical concepts? Stiegler avoids this regression to humanism by conceptualizing the non-inhuman as a product of how what we have typically called the human is constituted, but also put into question, by technics: "humanism, as the question of knowing what humanity is, is not a true question if it is true that man is the one who individuates himself with technics such that he constantly *becomes other*" (Stiegler 2020a, 231). Humanism does not recognize that transformations in technical systems undercut the possibility of a-historical conceptions of the human. The non-inhuman is, by contrast, not a historical constant. It is a projection or judgment that responds to the question of the human posed by technics. Answers to this question are always provisional because of the lack of origin, and because our ideals are embodied only intermittently as a result of the presence of a counter-tendency toward inhumanity (Stiegler 2010e, 170). Intermittence prevents totalizing concepts of the non-inhuman from repeating the flaws of humanism, for we never fully embody our judgments on the nature of the human, and the possibility of inhuman totalization disregards this constitutive indeterminacy. Inhuman totalization in its universalist automated, capitalist form does not make space for this non-inhuman diversity (Stiegler 2019d, 44). The non-inhuman as a form of totalizing, yet non-transcendental, judgment is necessary to answer the persistent question of the human in a way that the inhuman totalization of capitalism cannot.

I introduce the non-inhuman by focusing on the question of why political judgment must recognize its particularity, locality, and contingency. This account rests on the second key concept in Stiegler's work: the a-transcendental. Stiegler did not dedicate an entire text to systematizing this term, yet he described himself as "an a-transcendental philosopher."[12] He continues: "Everything that precedes me in philosophy proceeds from what we call the transcendental, but at the same time I believe that I belong to an era that challenges the difference between what is transcendental and what is empirical, an era that says that this difference is not relevant" (Stiegler 2003, 165). Stiegler's scattered references to the a-transcendental articulate this co-implication of the empirical and the transcendental that permeates his entire oeuvre.[13] Any transcendental that regulates humanity's understanding of itself, its place in the world, and its political significance is mediated and produced by the technical objects that define the empirical contexts from which such concepts emerge. Speculation on human nature, metaphysics, or ontology always takes the form of an empirically conditioned transcendental. One might attempt to evacuate totalization from ontology or avoid making claims about the intertwinement of human nature and the political, however *all* political theory is situated within an a-transcendental, technical horizon and, as such, engages in judgments that are in tension with plurality. The a-transcendental allows a distinction to be made between totalizing judgments that recognize their situated character and those that do not, and makes it possible to articulate totalizing judgments regarding the nature of the political that are reconciled with their contingency.

A consequence of this position that must be resisted is a trajectory toward relativism that incapacitates politics. Without addressing this issue, Stiegler would fail to overcome the lack of critical purchase on politics that he identifies in his predecessors in continental political thought, and we might also argue characterizes the ontological turn and new materialism. The *pharmakon*, the third key concept in the argument that follows, represents Stiegler's response to this problem. By stipulating that technical objects are defined by both curative and poisonous tendencies, he provides a minimal definition of the political. Politics responds to the problems of a particular pharmacological field and must be defined in reference to the specific a-transcendental horizon in which these problems emerge. By pursuing this point, I expand considerably upon Stephen Barker's claim that it is "pharmaka on which 'the political' in general can be built" (Barker 2012a, 13). The difference between inhuman and non-inhuman forms of totalization rests on this pharmacological dynamic between poison and cure: "In order to think the possibility of non-inhuman beings requires the thinking of the possibility of the inhuman in the human . . . The non-inhuman is dynamically sensitive to this duplicity, which is endemic to human pharmacology" (Stiegler 2010e, 231, n.5). Politics navigates these two tendencies toward the non-inhuman and the inhuman and cannot be understood in abstraction from the pharmacological problems within which they are embedded. Totalizing judgments, such as the calculation endemic within capitalism, perpetuate inhumanity by negating the openness of the non-inhuman. By contrast, Stiegler advocates for political judgments that project a totalizing yet open vision of the non-inhuman in response to the pharmacological problems unique to a particular technical context.

The non-inhuman, the a-transcendental, and the *pharmakon* guide my account of totalization in Stiegler's work. Political judgments respond to the problems posed by the *pharmaka* distinct to a particular a-transcendental horizon, preventing any singular decision on the nature of politics from total-izing the possible permutations of the political. Nevertheless, such judgments are totalizing, as they presuppose an understanding of being and an image of the non-inhuman derived from that context. The task of political theory is to consider the pharmacological possibilities posed by these judgments and to determine whether they make space for the plurality of possible decisions on the nature of the political that might arise from other localities. This evaluative claim signals Stiegler's importance for thinking the limit to political ontology. If many have turned toward ontological judgments and away from the human to understand the nature of the political, then the a-transcendental limit to this approach represents the difficulty of turning to ontological reasoning for accounting for the diversity of forms of politics. Because of their situated nature, ontological claims are totalizing and there-fore must be subjected to a critique similar to those leveled at metaphysics and transcendental concepts of the human.[14] Thinkers of political ontology seek to avoid totalization, but in doing so fail to assess the pharmacological consequences of the judgments inherent within their ontological projects. Stiegler's work facilitates the recognition of this problem, as he provides a conceptual architecture for assessing whether judgments on the nature of politics are simultaneously open and totalizing.

This commitment to totalization is at odds with the ways that conti-nental philosophy has been used to underpin critiques of mastery, particularly within work on decoloniality (e.g., Singh 2018). My account of Stiegler's philosophy does not reject the necessity of this critique of mastery within ongoing relationships of coloniality and domination. However, rather than critique mastery qua totalization, I attempt to integrate this concern with the need to give credence to and support local forms of totalization that provide dignity for a plurality of ways of conceptualizing politics. Non-totalizing versions of political ontology are not up to this task, as they necessarily exclude other forms of politics because of the totalizing nature of ontolog-ical reasoning (Banerjee 2020, 8–12). With Stiegler, I make the case that the answer to this problem requires the support of a plurality of totalizing judgments rather than the rejection of judgment itself. In doing so, my account of totalization in continental political theory draws inspiration from decolonial and Indigenous perspectives in political thought that highlight the imposition of liberal political categories on other conceptions of politics (e.g., Coulthard 2014; Simpson 2014), comparative political theorists who challenge the primacy of Western presuppositions in political thought (e.g., Jenco, Idris, and Thomas 2020), those who argue that there is an exclusionary basis to the use of ontology within the Western tradition (e.g., Fanon 2008; Warren 2018; Wynter 2003), and anthropologists who stress the various ways in which the political is distinguished from the non-political across a plurality of ontological schemas (de la Cadena 2010; Candea 2011).

Uniting these diverse approaches to the problem of totalization, which should by no means be reduced to a single school or approach, is the presence, in some form, of the claim that a single concept of the political is insufficient to capture the plurality of possible understandings of politics that themselves constitute important judgments in their own right. To simply reject totalization as a political goal neglects the value of these political decisions. I do not have the space to engage with the above intellectual movements in detail, and I accept the shortcoming for the project of developing epistemological and political diversity presented by the fact that Stiegler did not engage with these traditions or the problems of colonialism, race, or racism.[15] However, I draw on some of the above perspectives at key points in my argument to both develop the implications of Stiegler's critique of totalization and make visible his engagement in totalization within his own political judgments in a way that many of these authors would be critical of. These developments in political theory and anthropology provide a critical mirror that shows how Stiegler both reconciles totalization with diversity but also relapses into totalization without openness.

Here my claims diverge from dominant understandings of Stiegler's work, for he is best known for his critique of contemporary capitalism. Put simply, my argument focuses on the consequences of his philosophy for concepts of the political rather than for capitalist politics.[16] Here his relevance for continental political theory lies in his provision of a way to formalize and assess the tension between ontological openness and the advocation of specific political goals. I suggest that Stiegler both articulates this problem philosophically and provides a clear example of how it operates. He makes it possible to conceptualize the tension between totalization and openness while also embodying it by presenting political judgments that close the space of conceptual plurality. His political judgments make totalizing claims regarding the nature of politics and of the human that, when viewed in terms from Stiegler's own work, do not always maintain a position of open totalization. By way of this immanent critique, I argue that Stiegler's work both makes the case for and demonstrates the need to engage critically with totalization if political judgments on the future are to resist placing unjustified constraints on the diversity of the political.

These two tendencies toward openness and closure, or the "unprincipled" and "principled" dimensions of Stiegler's philosophy (Colebrook 2017), can be perceived across the reception of his work. Some read him as committed to working through the complexities of a given pharmacological situation in a way that rejects the role of absolutes in political judgment (Abbinnett 2020; Colebrook 2017; Lampe 2017, 324). His return to ideology critique after its rejection by Deleuze and Foucault represents a clear example of where he grapples with this challenge (Turner 2017). However, others argue that he exhibits a tendency toward conservatism and the closure of pluralism within his analyses of capitalism (Davis 2013; Fuggle 2013; Howells and Moore 2013, 11; Hui and Lemmens 2017, 38–39; C. Turner 2010). A similar ambiguity can be found between those who see Stiegler as providing a conception of the human that rejects anthropocentrism (Crowley 2013a; James 2013, 72; Vesco 2015, 89) and those who see his claim regarding the co-constitution of the human and the technical as a traditionally anthropocentric gesture (A. Bradley 2011, 139; Vaccari 2009). There is also disagreement over whether Stiegler is a technophobe who clings to this latter anthropocentric image of the human (A. Bradley 2011, 135; Vlieghe 2014, 534) or whether he engages in a technocentrism that subordinates human becoming and ingenuity to the technical question (Hansen 2017, 185–86). These disagreements often find their motivation in dissatisfaction with Stiegler's argument regarding the co-implication of the empirical and the transcendental. His claim appears to be simultaneously positivistic, in the sense that technical objects are reduced to an investigation that is empirical and not philosophical (Bennington 2000, 162–79), and transcendental, insofar as it retains an anthropocentrism and idealism that an investigation of technics should displace (Hansen 2004).

I return to some of these disputes in due course. For now, suffice it to say that I do not seek to settle them by recourse to one position alone but to try and take stock of Stiegler's work in the terms set out by Arthur Bradley: "Stiegler's almost contradictory philosophical reception . . . where he is simultaneously criticised for being excessively transcendentalist *and* empiricist, or not empiricist or transcendentalist *enough*—might be a symptom that we have not quite come to terms with the central ambition of his thought: a re-organisation of the empirico-transcendental opposition" (A. Bradley 2011, 127). In developing an immanent critique of Stiegler's work, I do not seek to favor one of these tendencies but consider how they illuminate one another. Rather than settling for reading Stiegler as principled, because of his specific political commitments, or unprincipled, because of his account of the genesis of judgment, I pursue both of these claims and their consequences for a plural conception of totalizing political judgment, and for the future of the critique of totalization in continental political theory.

Brief Considerations on Method and Chapter Outline

To develop this argument, the following takes a methodological cue from Stiegler's consideration of what it means to practice philosophy in the second volume of *Symbolic Misery*. Because of his claim that thinking is conditioned by an a-transcendental, pharmacological horizon and its attendant problems, conceptual invention requires the re-composition of the ideas and concepts that preexist invention within the context where it occurs. Thinking generates new insights from its engagement with preexisting materials: "The consequences of a thought, if it is a genuine thought, which is to say a conceptual *invention*, always extends beyond the person who thought it" (Stiegler 2015b, 3). While I give an account of Stiegler's philosophy that will be useful to those unfamiliar with it, this is not a complete, chronological, or entirely faithful rendering. As such, there are some notable omissions concerning his influences in order to facilitate a focus on the problem at hand.[17] Instead of an exhaustive presentation of his work, I aim to engage in the conceptual invention advocated by Stiegler by folding his philosophy back upon itself to identify the wider consequences of the tension between totalization and openness within his understanding of technicity.

These claims are pursued as follows. The first five chapters introduce the reader to Stiegler's philosophy and the four limits to political ontology found within it. The concepts of the a-transcendental and the non-inhuman are introduced across these chapters on key elements of the philosophy of technics. Chapter 1 introduces the default of origin, or the claim that the human is without essence. Here I argue that ontology is limited by the fictional status of all concepts: conceptual decisions respond to the question of the origin that is, ultimately, unanswerable beyond a particular technical and empirical context. The first limit to political ontology is the inability of its explanatory powers to completely account for contingency because it *must* totalize in response to the lack of transcendental foundations. Chapter 2 introduces the *pharmakon* as a response to a challenge to the localism of the default. If there is no transcendental conception of politics, does it not lose all meaning? The concept of the *pharmakon* provides a negative answer to this question by presenting a minimal definition of politics: the political is defined in response to the poisonous and curative tendencies of a particular technological horizon. Through an account of Stiegler's reading of Derrida, I show that the openness of the human is conditioned by a particular technical context and its pharmacological problems. To define the political is to totalize these local conditions because such a judgment gives meaning to the non-inhuman in the face of the situated undecidability of the *pharmakon*. Political ontology's second limit is found in its inability to exhaust this local and pharmacological undecidability.

Chapter 3 gives a post-ontological account of the genesis of political ideas from these local conditions by way of an introduction to the concepts of individuation and general organology. I demonstrate how Simondon's concept of individuation is adopted by Stiegler to claim that thinking is situated within a set of pre-individual conditions that it participates in and recursively transforms. In the case of the human, cognition is conditioned by the interrelation between the individuation of biological, social, and technical organs. Conceptual judgments are framed by their genesis within processes of individuation, and therefore the third limit to political ontology is found in its inability to escape this conditioning and to account for locality in terms that do not totalize other conceptions of politics. A question that remains here is how individuals become attached to particular images of the non-inhuman. Chapter 4 gives an overview of Stiegler's understanding of libidinal economy and introduces his claim that desire should be understood as the binding of drives to ideas within an a-transcendental context. He argues that desire is produced by the attachment to interpretable and open ideas and that totalization without the potential for this openness destroys desire. The pharmacological problem of desire is that it requires totalization to function but that this totalization must operate in a non-inhuman manner. The fourth limit to political ontology is found within Stiegler's critique of the ontological politics of poststructuralism, which poses a form of desire that preexists and resists totalization and therefore cannot account for its destruction by the absence of meaningful political judgment beyond capitalism. However, here I also begin my pivot to a critical account of Stiegler's political judgments. I suggest that his understanding of proletarianization as the cause of desire's destruction relies on a universal image of the subject of capitalist totalization, an image that is totalizing and devoid of openness despite his criticism of such gestures.

This conclusion introduces the problem that motivates the immanent critique undertaken in the last three chapters of the book, in which I assess whether Stiegler balances totalization and openness in his own political judgments. Chapter 5 facilitates the transition to this immanent critique by unifying the limits presented to ontology by Stiegler's philosophy within an overview of his understanding of judgment. Judgment requires totalization to function because it engages with a technically supported tradition of local prejudgments that it transforms and contributes to. Stiegler is concerned with the pharmacological status of these totalizing judgments and whether they allow space for the diachronicity of future decisions on political problems. The final three chapters assess the extent to which Stiegler holds to these commitments. Chapter 6 gives an account of three of Stiegler's political concepts that all rest on the impossible, or the indeterminacy and unpredictability of the technical condition. *Otium*, the Antigone complex, and the amateur all present a critical relationship to a particular technical context. These concepts do not stipulate particular political conditions, but an attitude or sensibility that is open to transformation and suspension. In contrast, across chapters 7 and 8 I argue that Stiegler's turn to the language of thermodynamics in his analysis of the Anthropocene and his claim that the political finds its beginning in the ancient Greek *polis* both represent totalizing judgments without space for non-totalization. In conclusion, I consider the consequences of the preceding account and immanent critique of Stiegler's thought. After Stiegler, continental political theory must navigate the difficult task of making totalizing judgments about the nature of politics while also leaving these claims open to question. Ontology does not have to be abandoned absolutely, but it must be recognized as a constraint on conceptual plurality if increasingly global political problems are to be addressed with totalizing judgments that both respect and transcend locality.

1

The Default of Origin

The human is a much-maligned concept in continental political theory. To define the human is to engage in boundary work regarding where it begins and ends and to commit to a set of characteristics necessary for inclusion within the category of humanity. Continental critics of totalization have consistently highlighted the contingency of the human and the political consequences of mistaking historically and contextually situated understandings of humanity for universal or metaphysically secure categories. These consequences are most often seen to lie in the exclusion and domination of those considered to be on the borders of the human (Floyd 2016). Consequently, conceptions of humanity are treated with skepticism within continental political thought because of the consequences of the totalization they imply. Where humanity is drawn upon as a concept, it is defined as inseparable from the linguistic and social practices that constitute the multiplicity of modes of existence that characterize it, and is therefore beyond totalization (Lechte 2018). Stiegler continues this critique of the totalization implied by the human but also attempts to salvage it as a philosophical and political category, for the philosophy of technics compels us to address the question of what defines the human in perpetuity. Here I show that he adopts the critique of totalization while also advocating for the need to make decisions regarding the nature of the human in a totalizing yet open way. This chapter introduces this understanding of the human, how it underpins the concepts of the a-transcendental and the non-inhuman, and considers its consequences for the relationship between ontology and the political. These points form the beginnings of the framework that guides my later immanent critique of Stiegler's political judgments, insofar as he begins to make judgments that totalize without making space for the contingency of this vision of the human.

Stiegler's simultaneous continuation of and divergence from the critique of the human in continental philosophy arises from the keystone of his work, the default of origin. This default is a consequence of the guiding thesis of the philosophy of technics: humanity is constituted by its relationship to technics and is nothing more than this "pursuit of the evolution of the living by means other than life" (Stiegler 1998, 135). Humanity is a product of contingent, technical developments and is devoid of an a-historical essence. Philosophical answers to the question of the origin will always fall short, for they are articulated from within a particular technical conjuncture and lack direct access to the origin. Stiegler's entire philosophy rests on the claim that this default of origin necessitates the revisiting of "the founding concepts of philosophical thought in their entirety, but always on the basis of the technical question" (Stiegler 2017c, 35). Perhaps the most important foundational concept he seeks to rethink on the basis of this conception of the human is the division between the transcendental and the empirical. Rather than privileging either the a priori conditions of thought or a posteriori experience, he reconceives of the transcendental and the empirical as co-constitutive. The default of origin is a transcendental structure that defines human existence but has no direct content as it is expressed through specific, empirical technical objects. Concepts of the human, then, are "necessary fictions" that articulate their empirical conditions in transcendental but always provisional terms that give meaning to, but cannot resolve, the default (Stiegler 1998, 108; 2009a, 11).

This double movement between the questioning of the transcendental by way of a move toward the historical, empirical variations of technical objects and the simultaneous upholding of the transcendental in the face of its empirical grounding underpins Stiegler's understanding of both the a-transcendental and the non-inhuman. The a-transcendental refers to this intertwinement of the transcendental and the empirical, within which philosophical speculation is delimited by the technical constitution of the human. Similarly, any understanding of the human is shaped by the a-transcendental conditions in which it is articulated. By defining the human with reference to the permutations that it undergoes as a result of its constitutive relationship with technics, Stiegler pulls it away from the transcendental and toward a pluralization of the human condition (Lewis 2013, 65; Pettman 2006, 163). Within this "negative anthropology" that recognizes that it is "difficult to agree upon what is truly human," Stiegler argues that "what is important is to be non-inhuman," or to recognize that one's judgments on the nature of the human are provisional responses to the problem of the default (Stiegler 2010a, 472). These non-inhuman judgments are a-transcendental: totalizing yet contingent because of the default of origin.

Here I argue that the concepts of the a-transcendental and the non-inhuman have significant consequences for political ontology. Ontological explanations of the origin of politics, even if they are intended to be non-totalizing, are articulated within a particular technical horizon. Political ontologies will always be situated, partial, and unable to account for the indeterminacy of the origin that arises from the technical condition: they must totalize the origin to some extent. Without nature's guidance, the human must decide on the codes and norms that inform its existence—a set of decisions that constitute the boundaries of politics. If the default is irreducible to ontology, then the political cannot be reduced to a set of ontological conditions. This claim is particularly significant for political ontology, as it attempts to provide non-totalizing foundations for the concept of the political. Such accounts elide the task of reconciling non-totalizing political projects with the necessity of totalization, leading them to unwittingly totalize the space of politics. The necessity of totalization that arises from the default of origin constitutes the first limit to political ontology that I develop from Stiegler's work.

This claim is established in three steps. First, I introduce Stiegler's conceptualization of the default with an account of his critique of transcendental and empirical versions of the origin of the human represented, respectively, by Jean-Jacques Rousseau and André Leroi-Gourhan. Both present a second origin following the arrival of the relationship to technics that excludes it from the emergence of humanity proper. Nevertheless, Stiegler develops a consideration of the origin as a deviation from itself in dialogue with their work; the origin is a non-origin that can only be explained from a particular historical perspective. Second, the chapter then gives an overview of how this absence of origin underpins Stiegler's replacement of metaphysical accounts of the human with a tragic, a-transcendental, and non-inhuman perspective. His resolution of the default is presented in the form of his reading of the myth of Prometheus and Epimetheus, which provides a mythical account of the origin of the human that stipulates that it is caught within the tragic duality between divine and mortal, or transcendental and empirical, aspects of its existence. Third, this a-transcendental and non-inhuman account of the origin leads to a consideration of the consequences of Stiegler's conception of the default for political ontology. While ontologies of the political are intended to escape the totalization of politics, they define the political from within a specific historical conjuncture and with respect to a particular understanding of the human and of the origin. From this perspective, the value of Stiegler's position is a recognition that these totalizing gestures cannot be avoided, and that the political must be defined with an explicit image of the non-inhuman in mind. While Stiegler claims that the political cannot be reduced to a transcendental or totalizing category, I demonstrate that he also argues in favor of the necessity of accounts of the political in the form of non-inhuman fictions that regulate politics in an a-transcendental way. The political must be understood in terms that are simultaneously totalizing and non-totalizing, a task that, according to Stiegler, ontology cannot fulfil.

Rousseau, Leroi-Gourhan, and the Problem of the Double Origin

Stiegler's argument in defense of the co-constitution of the transcendental and the empirical rests on his reading of the origin in Rousseau and Leroi-Gourhan. By focusing on *either* the transcendental or the empirical, both end up positing a second origin that distinguishes between the beginning of humanity and the origin of the technical condition. Stiegler claims that the empirical and the transcendental must be understood as co-constitutive in order to argue that, while necessary, totalizing and transcendental accounts of the origin are mediated by their contingent empirical conditions. This claim forms the basis of the concept of the a-transcendental.

Stiegler sees Rousseau's *Discourse on the Origins of Inequality* as an exemplary attempt to define the origin in transcendental terms by shedding the baggage of history. Rousseau attempted to diagnose the ills of modern European states by turning back to the human "in his original constitution" as found in the state of nature, prior to the march of history and the problems of politics, and by trying "to disentangle what he owes to his own stick and from what circumstances and his progress have added to or changed" (Rousseau 1997, 124). For Stiegler, this exclusion of culture, history, and geographic locality leads Rousseau to rely on a distinction between origin and history, or "purity and corruption" (Stiegler 1998, 101). While it is widely acknowledged that this is a hypothetical understanding of human nature, this transcendental evidence provides a critical vantage point for assessing and critiquing the impurities of the present (Ellingson 2001, 83). Hypothetical or not, this critical definition of the human in the state of nature is explicitly outside the influence of technics. Rousseau strips away the historical aspects of the human in an attempt to avoid the anachronism of other social contract theorists' accounts of the state of nature. Rather than reflecting the problems or arrangements of European politics, in Rousseau's vision of nature humans are isolated from one another and can survive on what nature provides without technical intervention. This self-sufficient existence is characterized by a peaceful form of self-preservation, pity toward other living creatures, a form of natural goodness or a-morality, and the capacity for perfectibility. Perfectibility is potential rather than actual in the state of nature, and as such humans are "without industry, without speech, without settled abode" (Rousseau 1997, 157). In the state of nature, the human exists without the need for any technical supplements to facilitate its survival.

Despite his attempt to expel technicity from the state of nature, Stiegler contends that Rousseau reproduces elements of empirical, technical history within his a priori conceptual apparatus by assuming continuity in the human's anatomical structure. For Rousseau, there may be moral, social, and political differences between historical and natural humans, but nothing distinguishes them physically. According to Stiegler, this anatomical continuity implies the presence of technical manipulation within the origin because he holds that the hand necessitates manipulation: "to make use of hands, no longer to have paws, is to manipulate—and what hands manipulate are tools and instruments. The hand is the hand only insofar as it allows access to art, to artifice, and to *tekhnē*" (Stiegler 1998, 113). Within the state of nature, "this hand with 'everything close at hand' is no longer a hand, it no longer either manipulates or works" (Stiegler 1998, 114). By assuming natural humans stood upright and possessed the potential for manipulation characteristic of the hand, Rousseau repeats the social and political anachronism he wanted to banish on an anatomical level by introducing the possibility for technics into the otherwise pure origin. This is compounded by a slip in Rousseau's narrative that implies the presence of, and not just possibility for, manipulation. Rousseau states that "he who first made himself clothes or a dwelling thereby provided himself with things that are not very necessary" (Rousseau 1997, 139). Stiegler takes issue with the diminution of technicity here. Prostheses appear "if not unnecessary, *hardly so. Almost accidental and inessential, if not completely useless*" (Stiegler 1998, 118). This "not very" belies the absence of total denial of prostheses in the state of nature; they are *to some extent* necessary. The transition out of nature is the moment where nature is no longer enough, but Rousseau suggests that nature appears to have never been *quite* enough.

Rousseau could be seen to overcome this problem, as he emphasizes the accidental character of technicity. There is no necessity for these partial technical discoveries, and they cannot be passed on because of the absence of communication in the state of nature. Language is necessary to transmit such discoveries to others. For Stiegler, this merely exacerbates the problem by lodging an aporia within the exit from the state of nature: "what will have come first, language for the foundation of society, or society for a decision on language?" (Stiegler 1998, 127). Technics exists within nature, but symbolic expression to communicate technical discovery is absent. If technicity does not signify deviation from nature, then language must play this role. However, Rousseau leaves this fall from nature into society by way of language unexplained. He relies on a double origin, or an origin that follows the original state of nature. This "accidentality is witness both to the *quasi*-impossibility of explaining a second origin and to the fact that this second origin will have ended up being the *origin itself* while being but an *absence* of origin. It witnesses the impossibility of recognising, designating, and conceiving of any kind of beginning" (Stiegler 1998, 132). By inscribing technicity within the supposedly pure, non-supplementary origin, Rousseau is required to provide an alternative account for the transition out of nature, which comes up against the aporia of the origin of language.

Stiegler's reading suggests that while Rousseau's transcendentalism leads him to retreat from this aporia of origin, it also provides the opportunity to think of the origin as a deviation. Rousseau challenges us to think "in *a single movement* (the origin) of technics and (the 'origin') of the human" (Stiegler 1998, 133). The natural origin of the human is replaced with the co-originary status of humanity and the technical object. Ben Roberts has challenged this reading of Rousseau by asking whether Stiegler merely replaces the transcendentalism of the human in the state of nature with the transcendentalism of technicity (Roberts 2006). The difference separating these two transcendentalisms lies between Rousseau's attempt to define the human on the basis of a transcendental image divorced from its constitution through empirical events and Stiegler's attempt to show these realms to be co-constitutive. As Michael Lewis summarizes, any account of the origin "will not be completed if it does not enclose a historicity that is empirically conditioned," and therefore "the transcendental will never have been purely transcendental; its very constitution depends upon the empirical" (Lewis 2013, 61). The payoff of Stiegler's reading of Rousseau is that the aporia must be accounted for with fictions that are conditioned by the empirical history of technics. Beyond the first volume of *Technics and Time*, Stiegler says of the state of nature that "we need its fiction in order to think the human being, for Rousseau reveals to us that the human being is a process, and thus becoming" (Stiegler 2015d, 63). As the aporia of origin cannot be resolved, the human is subject to constant reinvention across the historical, empirical, and contingent unfolding of the transcendental deviation. While Roberts argues that this claim is transcendental, it is inconceivable without empirical, technical objects that condition the actuality of the constant deviation that constitutes the origin.

Stiegler turns to Leroi-Gourhan's materialist account of the human to think this empirical constitution of the human by technicity. Leroi-Gourhan critiques "cerebralist" accounts of the origin, like Rousseau's, in which humanity is "endowed with all the present human attributes" and invents technical and social order "from scratch" because of its own ingenuity (Leroi-Gourhan 1993, 10). Rather than enhanced cerebral capacity, technicity is the product of the gradual development of the upright posture that freed elements of the vertebrate structure of pre-hominids for the use of tools, making further cerebral development possible. According to Stiegler, in this account, "one much more readily imagines the human as what is invented" (Stiegler 1998, 134). However, despite Leroi-Gourhan's steps toward a technical account of the origin, Stiegler claims that, like Rousseau, he also posits a second origin by distinguishing between technical and symbolic intelligence. Where Leroi-Gourhan sees the emergence of linguistic capacities as a "qualitative shift" in the history of humanity, Stiegler argues that the emergence of the technical object is the sole causal factor in the inauguration of human existence (Johnson 2013, 39). If the human is to be co-constituted by technics, then it must be the primary driver of hominization.

Leroi-Gourhan goes some way toward establishing this position, for he argues that sapience is a product of the relationship between the evolution of the human skeleton and the use of tools. The erect posture that frees the hand for manipulation, which Rousseau took for granted, is the origin of the development of human cognition (Leroi-Gourhan 1993, 19). Stiegler locates the origin of both technics and language within this process: "The 'freeing' of the hand during locomotion is also that of the face from its grasping functions. The hand will necessarily call for tools, moveable organs; the tools of the hand will necessarily call for the language of the face" (Stiegler 1998, 145). Technicity and language find their genesis in the same evolutionary dynamic that replaces the human "rupture" with the gradual opening of space for cortical enlargement by the liberation of the hands within the upright posture. Human intelligence is not a prior condition of technicity but is formed by gradual anatomical transformations that are co-extensive with technical development. From Leroi-Gourhan's perspective, "the brain obviously plays a role, but it is no longer directive: it is but a partial element of a total apparatus" (Stiegler 1998, 145). By highlighting this form of "artificial selection" (G. Moore 2017), Leroi-Gourhan refuses to separate human and technical evolution.[1]

Stiegler also claims, however, that Leroi-Gourhan relies on a second origin in much the same way as Rousseau. This is found in his reliance on a divide between technical and symbolic intelligence. Stiegler argues that all human intelligence involves some form of anticipation and that within the coupling of humanity and technicity, "anticipation means the realisation of a possibility that is not determined by a biological program" (Stiegler 1998, 151). Symbolic and technical intelligence arise from the intertwinement of biological and technical evolutionary dynamics because they both represent forms of non-biological anticipation. To reduce anticipatory intelligence to a particular set of capacities is to face an aporia, for those capacities are formed within the historical relationship to technicity. Despite integrating biology and technicity, Leroi-Gourhan retreats from this aporia by reinstating the divide between technical and symbolic intelligence. He claims that "tools and skeletons evolved synchronously. We might say that with the Archanthropians, tools were still, *to a large extent*, a direct emanation of *species behaviour*" (Leroi-Gourhan 1993, 97). In contrast, Stiegler emphasizes that while technicity has its roots in the biological character of the species, the "nongenetic character of the tool" and its coupling with the human marks the point at which both technicity and language become socially and not simply genetically determined (Stiegler 1998, 155). Like Rousseau, Leroi-Gourhan's use of the phrase "to a large extent" belies a hesitance to make technicity constitutive of human intelligence, as he falls back on biology in a way that restricts its role in the development of the human.

According to Stiegler, Leroi-Gourhan does not just hesitate to link technicity with intelligence. He also actively distinguishes between technical and symbolic intelligence by arguing that the latter represents "the sphere of human thought proper" (Leroi-Gourhan 1993, 112). He claims that, on the one hand, "both are the expression of the same intrinsically human property," and, on the other hand, that early hominids are limited to a "language at a level corresponding to their tools" (Leroi-Gourhan 1993, 113–14). Stiegler argues that this endows early humans with a rudimentary, technical language, which shares a different set of causes to symbolic language. As such, Leroi-Gourhan claims that "technological evolution is essentially of zoological origin, and elsewhere there is 'nontechnical,' reflexive and symbolic 'intelligence'" (Stiegler 1998, 156). If the upright posture enabled the emergence of technicity and opened the path for expanded cerebral capacities, where does the origin of symbolic intelligence lie? Either it is a possibility as soon as anticipation occurs through technicity, or, as Leroi-Gourhan appears to argue, it constitutes humanity in the form of a break with technical intelligence, reducing solely tool-wielding forms of humanity to a pre-human status. For Stiegler, this divide is unavoidably Rousseauian and leads Leroi-Gourhan to institute a second origin that distinguishes between technical and symbolic intelligence (Stiegler 1998, 175). Despite providing an empirical account of technicity that undermines transcendentalism concerning the origin, Leroi-Gourhan ends up repeating the double origin.

Metaphysics, Myth, and the A-Transcendental

Stiegler's criticisms of both Rousseau and Leroi-Gourhan underpin his embrace of the aporia at the origin of the human. Technicity is not opposed to language, the product of human ingenuity, or a superfluous corruption of human nature but a constitutive component of our existence: "All human action has something to do with *tekhnē*" (Stiegler 1998, 94). Because human intelligence is formed by the use of tools, technicity encapsulates all human behavior as a form of collective memory that supplements biological inheritance and individual memories and supports individual and social activity. Stiegler calls this form of support epiphylogenesis, tertiary memory, and tertiary retention. I return to epiphylogenesis when discussing the relationship of the technical to the biological in more detail in chapter 2, but for now it is sufficient to define technics as a form of externalized memory that actively forms human behavior. Both Rousseau and Leroi-Gourhan distinguish between the emergence of technicity and the "proper" origin of the human with the birth of symbolic language, and by doing so relegate the constitutive role of the technical object to a pre- or quasi-human status.

Most significantly for Stiegler, their accounts lapse into totalization because they oppose humanity to technics in terms characteristic of metaphysics. In his accounts of Rousseau and Leroi-Gourhan, Stiegler argues that both define humanity in a way that distinguishes "between what it essentially is, what establishes it from the beginning and for all time as the human, and what it is accidentally" (Stiegler 1998, 95). The figures of the peaceful, self-sufficient dweller of the state of nature or the bearer of symbolic intelligence both relegate technicity to the status of an accident. In a gesture reminiscent of Derridean deconstruction, Stiegler claims Rousseau and Leroi-Gourhan lapse into metaphysical speculation regarding the human by trying to separate this accidentality from a clearly defined origin. Both distinguish between the transcendental and the necessary, understood as humanity proper, and the empirical and accidental, understood as technics. This totalizing gesture must be resisted as transcendental principles are generated within the accidental, historical, and empirical development of technicity. Accidentality is a productive, rather than negative, feature of the human condition: the technical invents the human and prevents totalization in the form of a recourse to metaphysics of origin or essence.

Beyond the first volume of *Technics and Time*, Stiegler refers to this contamination of transcendental questions by empirical and accidental circumstances as the a-transcendental. Stiegler's conception of the default underpins his assertion that he is "an a-transcendental philosopher," whose "reasoning is 'a-transcendental,' in the sense in which Bataille spoke 'a-theologically'" (Stiegler 2003, 161). In the notes for *The Unfinished System of Non-Knowledge*, Georges Bataille states that he draws on "the essentially atheist current of thought that has not renounced the wealth . . . of theology. An atheologism, in other words, a thought nourished by the experience of God" (Bataille 2001, 237). Stiegler repeats this gesture by claiming that "one must pass through the transcendental in order to get beyond the transcendental" (Stiegler 2007, 340). It is necessary to consider transcendental questions, such as the human origin, yet humans do so through capacities that are shaped by the accidental history of empirical technical objects. Within the a-transcendental perspective, regulatory transcendentals condition human existence, but they are deprived of any necessity beyond their role in a particular empirical context. While Stiegler did not fully work through the consequences of his oblique references to the a-transcendental, a clear statement of its implication for the relationship between the transcendental and the empirical can be found in the second volume of *Technics and Time*: "The transcendental field is thus a-transcendental—beyond empirical/ transcendental opposition, distinguishing them without placing them in opposition" (Stiegler 2009b, 222).[2] Humanity's origin is a non-totalizable aporia that demands a response, but in a manner that will never supersede the a-transcendental frame formed by technical objects.

This point can be clarified by considering Christopher Johnson's critique of Stiegler's reading of Leroi-Gourhan. Johnson argues that Stiegler neglects the gradualist account of the human origin in *Gesture and Speech* on the grounds that his claim that language and technicity emerge in the same *aporetic* moment repeats the originalist move that he criticizes in both Leroi-Gourhan and Rousseau (Johnson 2013, 45). For Johnson, Stiegler reiterates Claude Lévi-Strauss's reading of Marcel Mauss where he argues that humans "cannot have begun to signify gradually" and that language appears in a single moment (Lévi-Strauss 1987, 59). The same appears to be the case with technics. However, if one emphasizes the importance of the a-transcendental within Stiegler's work, then both transcendental "single moment" or empirical "gradualist" approaches to the origin of language or technicity occur within a technically determined horizon. All at once arguments bear the same risk of totalization as gradualist accounts of the human origin. Stiegler's point is that any account of the emergence of the human totalizes the non-totalizable default because it emerges from a particular a-transcendental horizon. The aporia of origin is not a single moment in history but a testament to the partiality of all explanations of the origin. One might argue, in defense of Johnson, that Stiegler does prioritize the transcendental within the a-transcendental by using philosophical rather than empirical methods to think the origin of the human (Ekman 2007, 56). Despite this, Stiegler's account of the a-transcendental conditions of philosophical problems leads him to redefine answers to these questions in terms of myths or fictions that are irreducible to metaphysical necessity. It is precisely because the default is aporetic and irresolvable that "the mythical and the transcendental *converge* when it comes to the question of man" (Lewis 2013, 55). The philosophy of technics sustains the aporia presented by the default of origin by engaging in transcendental speculation in the form of myth, in contrast to the "negation of the aporia" by metaphysics (Stiegler 1998, 100–1). Stiegler sees this latter gesture as constitutive of philosophy since Plato and defines his a-transcendental philosophical project as working against this tide (Stiegler 1998, 1; 2017c, 31). Hence, his focus on the transcendental side of the co-constitutive relationship between the transcendental and the empirical arises from his attempt to address the relationship between technics and metaphysics within philosophy as a discipline, which is later supplemented by a wider engagement with the empirical work of science (as I show in chapters 3 and 7).

This contrast between metaphysical and nonmetaphysical thinking is established by a comparison between the tragic thought of Socrates and its recuperation by Plato. The exemplar of metaphysical thought is found in Plato's *Meno*, within which Socrates's eponymous interlocutor presents him with the aporetic condition of knowledge: "a man . . . cannot search for what he knows—since he knows it, there is no need to search—nor for what he does not know, for he does not know what to look for" (Plato 1997a, 880, 80e). Socrates responds to this aporia by positing an originary knowledge, prior to bodily existence, which is recalled through learning as recollection: "cognition is recognition, a remembering—an *anamnesis*" (Stiegler 2009a, 15). *Anamnesis*, the remembering of originary truths, is opposed to the artificial and contingent learning of technique, or *hypomnesis*. This opposition between *anamnesis* and *hypomnesis* becomes more clearly transcendental in the *Phaedrus* where Plato has Socrates present the soul as existing before earthly becoming, leading to an opposition between *anamnesis*, memory of originary knowledge, and *hypomnesis*, artificial memory (Plato 1997b, 524, 245d–e).[3] According to Stiegler, this is a dogmatic reprise of the principle of the *Meno* in which "being is in reality opposed to becoming," establishing "the opposition between what will later be nature and culture, the human and the technical, as well as the question of technics *qua* writing" (Stiegler 1998, 100). Metaphysical opposition between the unchanging character of the soul and the contingencies of earthly existence correlates with the opposition between knowledge and technics.

Stiegler claims that a tragic perspective that is implicit in the *Meno* is covered over by the later *Phaedrus*.[4] Socrates demonstrates the existence of originary knowledge in the *Meno* by teaching a slave geometric principles despite his lack of any prior knowledge of geometry. In the dialogue, this serves as evidence of *anamnesis*; however, for Stiegler technical prosthesis, *hypomnesis*, is central to the transmission of this apparently originary knowledge (Stiegler 2010d, 74). As Christina Howells and Gerald Moore summarize, in the *Meno* "Socrates is tracing out the diagram of a square by way of demonstration, externalising his thought through technical prostheses, which serve in turn as the condition of Meno's intellectual awakening" (Howells and Moore 2013, 7). By highlighting how the technical object conditions the transmission of apparently transcendental knowledge, Stiegler claims that Socrates represents a pre-Platonic and tragic mode of thought that recognizes the mythical and conditioned status of thinking (Stiegler 2017c, 38–39). All knowledge is mythical because it is conditioned by its empirical supports and acts as a provisional response to the aporia presented by Meno. This a-transcendental claim underpins Stiegler's conception of the non-inhuman: "Because it is hybrid . . . what we call 'man'—the non-inhuman being that we should henceforth name *Neganthropos*—is *both in excess and in default of itself*: it is *never itself*" (Stiegler 2019d, 304). I return to the language of the "neganthropos" in chapter 7. For now, Stiegler claims that the human's knowledge of itself passes through technicity and that consequently this knowledge is conditioned by its locality. Humanity is non-inhuman because it rests on its empirical constitution by technicity, which means it is "never itself." Accounts of the human, and by association all forms of knowledge, take on the status of fictions in this tragic form of thinking. To think the non-inhuman is to take this tragic condition seriously.

Stiegler turns to the myth of Prometheus and Epimetheus to further his tragic understanding of philosophy with his own mythological account of the origin. He combines the Hesiodic accounts of the encounters between Prometheus and Zeus, in which the human appears as a tragic figure caught between gods and mortals, with Protagoras's account of the myth in the Platonic dialogue of the same name because of its inclusion of Prometheus's forgetful brother Epimetheus. Promethean foresight is constituted alongside Epimethean forgetfulness, which has itself been forgotten. The Platonic version begins amid Protagoras' demonstration that virtue can be taught. In his story, the Titan brothers Prometheus and Epimetheus were given the task of assigning qualities to the mortal beings created by Zeus. Despite begging his brother to allow him to take on this task, Epimetheus forgets to set aside a quality for humanity, leaving it "completely unequipped . . . naked, unshod, unarmed" (Plato 1997c, 757, 321c). To ensure that humans have the means for survival, Prometheus grants the human technicity by stealing fire from Hephaestus, the blacksmith god, and knowledge of practical arts from Athena, the goddess of wisdom. Zeus also judges that without the art of politics, humans "would scatter again and be destroyed," and therefore distributes the feelings of shame and justice among humans so that they can live together to avoid their destruction (Plato 1997c, 757–58, 322b–e). In the course of an argument establishing the teachability of virtue, Protagoras gives an account of the fault of Epimetheus, the Promethean theft as foresight, and the art of politics, or virtue, which is gifted as a result of the default.

Stiegler claims that the earlier Hesiodic account is key to interpreting the Protagorean version of the myth. Epimetheus's forgetfulness is accompanied by another transgression committed by Prometheus that is charted across both *Theogony* and *Works and Days*. In the *Theogeny*, before the distinction between divine and mortal realms, Prometheus tricks Zeus by dividing a meal into two shares, leaving meat and entrails for humans (usually reserved for the gods) while disguising Zeus's meal of bones in fat (Hesiod 1988, 19–21). In anger, Zeus banishes mortals from the divine realm and deprives them of fire to cook the food set aside by Prometheus, to which the latter responds by stealing fire back from Zeus for humanity. These events build up to the Epimethean fault of the *Protagoras*, where it is noted that Prometheus "no longer had free access to the high citadel that is the house of Zeus" as a result of his earlier transgressions (Plato 1997c, 756, 322d–e). Responding to the trickery recounted in the *Theogony*, in *Works and Days*, Zeus hides the source of human nourishment in the earth, which forces humans to labor for their survival (Hesiod 1988, 38). This toil signals the simultaneous connection and disconnection between gods and mortals: humans must work to survive, but with means stolen from the divine realm (Vernant 1986, 38–43). In this version of the myth, Zeus also responds to Prometheus's theft by sending Pandora to become Epimetheus's wife. Epimetheus accepts willingly, compounding his earlier forgetfulness by ignoring his brother's counsel not to accept gifts from Zeus. With the opening of Pandora's jar, crafted by Hephaestus and gifted to her by Zeus, all the problems of humanity are let loose into the world, with only *elpis* (hope) remaining inside (Vernant 1986, 39–40). Pandora unites the *Theogony* and *Works and Days* not only because she brings the mortal woes of humans into the world but also because she does so as part of the ongoing squabbles between Zeus and Prometheus.[5]

Stiegler highlights two themes that guide his reading of these three texts together, both of which are taken from Jean-Pierre Vernant's structuralist interpretation of the Hesiodic account. First, the human, both mortal and immortal, possesses a share of the god's powers. Vernant reads this as a tragic combination of transcendental and empirical realms—the human resides within both without any clear resolution of its place in the world (Vernant 1986, 27–30). Second, the play of theft, gift, and non-gift between Zeus and Prometheus introduces *eris* (discord, war, and distrust) into the origin of the human. Neither mortal nor divine, the human cannot fully resolve this tragic state and must manage the strife that arises from its conflicts with the gods. As Vernant summarizes, the human is perpetually "oscillating between the two without ever being able to separate them" (Vernant 1980, 184). This mythical account of the origin unites the tragic condition of the human, neither transcendental nor empirical and unable to resolve its place in the world. These two themes place uncertainty and hope at the origin of the human, as Pandora arrives as a result of *eris* but suggests *elpis* as the path to resolving this default (Stiegler 2010a, 460–61). The human can hope to change its place in the world, but it cannot do so with certainty because of the tragic duality between mortality and divinity.

It is worth noting that for Vernant, *elpis* is not just hope. It is a radical uncertainty internal to foresight that arises because of its intertwining with stupidity, theft, and trickery in the gift of Pandora (Vernant 1986, 85). According to Stiegler, *elpis* arises from the consequences of the fault of Epimetheus and is bound to Promethean foresight, uniting anticipation with the uncertainty of forgetting. In his words: "*Elpis* could be seen as (the relation) to the indeterminate, that is (the anticipation of) the future" (Stiegler 1998, 198). Any projection or anticipation of what the future will or should look like rests on the indeterminacy and accidentality of the human, both divine and mortal, transcendental and empirical. Here the myth of Prometheus and Epimetheus plays two roles in Stiegler's argument: a mythical narration of the origin that also makes space for the uncertain anticipation of the future in the form of new fictions regarding the place and meaning of the human.[6] Totalizing and metaphysical accounts of the human are replaced by a tragic and a-transcendental understanding of the origin, which Stiegler takes from the Socratic position in the *Meno* and develops with the myth of Prometheus and Epimetheus.

The Default of the Political

In addition to providing a mythical account of the origin of technicity that rejects totalization with respect to the origin of the human, Epimetheus's fault has consequences for totalization within conceptions of the political. By unpacking these consequences, I argue that when viewed from the a-transcendental perspective, ontological accounts of the political that try to avoid totalization also engage in totalizing explanations of the origin. Stiegler's rethinking of the human places a limit on the ability of political ontology to provide non-totalizing accounts of politics, precisely because this understanding of the human rests on the co-constitution of the empirical and the transcendental. The primary limit of political ontology lies in its simultaneous attempt to avoid totalization while also unwittingly providing a totalizing account of politics.

As demonstrated above, in the Protagorean account of the Prometheus myth, Zeus gifts humanity with the art of justice. This gifting of politics is "imposed by the lack of origin," as without it, the human is left to the whims of *eris* (Stiegler 2003, 156). Moving beyond this myth, one can argue that politics supplements the lack of origin and is experienced only through its default: there is no single form that the political takes other than the empirical variations of technicity through which it is implemented. In Richard Beardsworth's reading of Stiegler, this means that "the very condition of situating the political dimension in relation to philosophical reflection today lies in the development of the differentiations of arche-writing" (where arche-writing refers to technics) (Beardsworth 1998a, 79). It is the nature of politics to engage in a constant revision of its limits precisely because it shares in the tragic indeterminacy of the default. Stiegler makes this claim by referring to the political community engendered in the myth of Prometheus and Epimetheus as a "community of those who have no community," whose concepts cannot be reduced to "an 'ought' and can only have meaning for those for whom one has to decide, immersed as they are in activity. Each time, in every situation of decision, in every position of necessity that opens up at the same time a flaw, one has to invent their meaning" (Stiegler 1998, 201). Stiegler rejects deontological or transcendental "oughts" in the realm of politics by invoking the constitutive indeterminacy of the default to argue for the reinterpretability of political concepts. They cannot be totalized metaphysically, yet they must totalize to some degree because of the need for decisions that give them meaning. From this perspective, ontological explanations of the political are totalizing in a manner similar to the metaphysical totalization that they attempt to avoid precisely because they neglect their status as a-transcendental judgments that give meaning to the origin.

Before moving to this account of why both ontology and metaphysics engage in the totalization of the political, Stiegler's claim that concepts are caught between incompleteness and totalization must be accounted for. In his wider system, the term consistence signifies this coexistence of concep-tual pluralization and the need for totalization engendered by the default of origin. Consistence is "that which gives meaning (its direction and its movement, or its *driving force*) to what exists, without reducing itself to this existing. Existing is a *fact*. But existing only consists as that which *surpasses* its *factuality*" (Stiegler 2011a, 41–42). Consistence is distinguished from subsistence, which nourishes the living through immediate consumption that cannot be left to unpredictability, and existence, which orients the human into the future in a manner that cannot be predicted in the same way that consumption demands. Objects that consist act as transcendental ideas that guide the human's movement into the future by projecting a vision of what the future looks like from within a particular state of fact. Consistences unite a set of empirical conditions within these projections, but because of their relationship to the default, they do so in a way that is open to challenge and contestation. Ideas consist insofar as they arise from, give meaning to, and totalize technical existence within a particular context, but they cannot be reduced to the calculation and exactitude that characterizes technics, as they "surpass factuality." Tragedy is the nature of consistence: totalizing answers to the questions of the nature of the human or of the political face the aporia of the origin that prevents them from escaping accidentality. That concepts take on the status of these interpretable and contestable consistences is one of the central consequences of Stiegler's development of the a-transcendental: they totalize without taking on metaphysical necessity.

Stiegler adopts the concept of the quasi-cause from Gilles Deleuze to understand this relationship between consistence, totalization, and contingency. For Deleuze, the quasi-cause refers to the imposition of necessity on a contingent set of relations in the form of an idea or event, which he calls an incorporeal effect: "Incorporeal effects are never themselves causes in relation to each other; rather, they are only 'quasi-causes' following laws that perhaps express in each case the relative unity or mixture of bodies on which they depend for their real causes" (Deleuze 1990, 6). The meaning of an event depends on the "relative unity" of its connection to other events. For Stiegler, an event qua concept must be understood as quasi-causal because "its origin causes its defect, and it is the *necessity* of this defect *as* its origin, its source, its provenance, to which it must respond" (Stiegler 2011a, 161). The default of origin necessitates a response, but any such explanation is contingent on the a-transcendental context, or "relative unity of relations," in which it emerges. Yuk Hui provides an excellent summary of the philosophical importance of the quasi-cause for Stiegler's rejection of the metaphysics of absolute certainty within causal relations: "By suspending finality one suspends also the relation between the origin and fate . . . according to which the origin already contains its end. It is in this attempt to reject a sort of Aristotelian final causality that Stiegler adds to hominization and individuation the concept of *quasi-causality*" (Hui 2019, 206). In Stiegler's words: "Quasi-causality . . . is what takes up the default of origin so that it can become that which is necessary" (Stiegler 2018c, 205). The necessity of ideas does not exist within the origin but emerges across the course of the development of technicity. There is no "ought" within the community of the default because the concepts that would inform any such imperative are defined by this quasi-causal logic: they emerge within an attempt to grant finality to a human without transcendental essence. Because of their status as quasi-causal consistences that have a mythical relationship to the default, concepts of the political cannot escape the tragedy of the co-constitution of the empirical and the transcendental.

Stiegler's use of the term "community without community" in this quasi-causal way draws implicitly on a dialogue between Blanchot, Lacoue-Labarthe, and Nancy. However, his divergence from their work within his account of the origin of the human and its relationship to technicity is crucial for the critique of political ontology at stake here. Blanchot, Nancy, and Lacoue-Labarthe all criticize totalizing understandings of community and the political to redefine both as the shared experience of a lack of essence or unitary identity. Nancy understands community as the shared exposure or disruption of identity, founded on an ontology characterized by "interruption, fragmentation, suspension" rather than unity or essence (Nancy 1991, 31). Blanchot responds to Nancy by uniting community with its absence: "the absence of community is not the failure of community: absence belongs to community as its extreme moment or as the ordeal that exposes it to its necessary disappearance" (Blanchot 1988, 16). Community is not an enclosed, definitive, and exclusive group, but the shared relationship to something irreducible to totality. Blanchot and Nancy, like Stiegler, see the image of community as a singular entity that is fully present to itself as the product of myth. According to Nancy, this is a necessary deception, for "with myth, the passing of time takes shape, its ceaseless passing is fixed in an exemplary place of showing and revealing" (Nancy 1991, 45). Myth totalizes by explaining community's absence but is nevertheless always partial, unfinished, and subject to the interruptions of the indeterminacy of community that escapes metaphysics.

This co-articulation of narrative and indeterminacy within the critique of totalization is also present in Nancy's joint considerations of the political with Lacoue-Labarthe. They distinguish the empirical condition of politics from the ontological and philosophical question of the political, treating "the questioning of the philosophical *as* the political" (Nancy and Lacoue-Labarthe 1997, 109). Politics mythologizes the social while the political forms a non-totalizable ground that interrupts these myths. This duality is threatened by what Lacoue-Labarthe and Nancy understand as the modern expansion of politics, which subjects all of social life to one particular myth, leading to "the disappearance of all 'political specificity' in the very domination of the political" (Nancy and Lacoue-Labarthe 1997, 126). These totalizing conceptions of the political are found in both totalitarianism and liberalism, for it is not the content of the myth that matters so much as the reduction of politics to a single mythological narrative (Nancy and Lacoue-Labarthe

1997, 115). This retreat of the political in the face of politics leads Nancy and Lacoue-Labarthe to propose a re-treatment of the political that would recover its philosophical essence, which Nancy refers to as the "in-common" and "being-*together*," a shared exposure to the incompleteness of identity (Nancy 1997, 88). It is these incomplete conditions that foreclose the possibility of accounts of politics totalizing the political.

Stiegler repeats this gesture insofar as the default of origin prevents the human condition, and therefore the political, from being totalized. However, his approach is distinct from Nancy and Lacoue-Labarthe's because of his commitment to situating all philosophical speculation within the a-transcendental conditions of the default. Nancy and Lacoue-Labarthe define the political in terms of incompleteness, but also ground the distinction between politics and the political within a post-Heideggerian conception of ontological difference that rests on the ontic-ontological distinction.[7] Politics refers to the ontic realm of particular entities, relations, and attempts to ground the social, whereas the political refers to the ontological sphere that underpins, and ultimately frustrates, these attempts at grounding (Marchart 2007, 7–8). The re-treatment of politics requires the retreat of the ontic to allow for the disclosure of the essence of the non-totalizable political. This commits Nancy and Lacoue-Labarthe to a particular ontological framework when conceptualizing the incompleteness of the political (James 2006, 109). Stiegler understands philosophical speculation of this sort to be constrained by the a-transcendental condition. Even when it is postmetaphysical and intended to be non-totalizing, the practice of ontology provides answers to the problem of incompleteness on which images of the political are subsequently built. Hence, any ontology engages in totalization from within a particular technical context that conditions its response to the default.

Nancy's response to criticisms such as this, that the ontology of the political must be totalizing, consists in highlighting its incompleteness. Not everything is encapsulated by the political because of the incompleteness of the ground it forms, and therefore it is not a totalizing concept: "politics is the place of an 'in common' as such—but only along the lines of an incommensurability that is kept open" (Nancy 2010, 50). The political cannot be everything precisely because its essence is defined by an incommensurability that would have to be negated to establish the equivalence implied in the claim that all is political.[8] Nevertheless, as Inna Viriasova has argued, the political maintains the status of a totality, for it is articulated within a philosophical system that provides "*a priori* conditions" for the thinking of politics. For Viriasova, "The political is the totalizing condition of possibility of relationality insofar as it admits of no other principle that could offer the space for the encounter of beings" (Viriasova 2018, 54). Even though such an ontological position is defined through openness, it nevertheless maintains the position of an ontology that can do nothing other than determine the conditions of openness—no matter how aversive it may be to such an enterprise.

Here it is clear why an account of the origin of the human, a concept that has been subject to much criticism on the grounds of its totalizing nature, can underpin a critique of totalization within political ontology. If the human, as non-inhuman, is constituted across its historical relationship to the technical object, then ontological explanations of politics cannot account for the incompleteness within the default at the origin of this relationship. Like metaphysical claims, ontological speculation is formed within a particular a-transcendental context that conditions philosophical thought. Postmetaphysical accounts of the political that remain within the Heideggerian conceptualization of ontological difference, like those of Nancy and Lacoue-Labarthe, cannot come to terms with the way that technics shapes philosophical concepts because "Heidegger, like Plato, rejects *hypomnesis*" (Stiegler 2011a, 91). As Hui has noted, Stiegler rejects the ontological difference as its privileging of the ontological neglects how the ontic, or technics, is constitutive of thinking (Hui 2022).[9] By doing so, thought of the ontological difference forgets that it is simply another way of responding to the default of origin as opposed to a way of accounting for the differentiation induced by the origin itself. By making this claim about the nature of ontological difference Stiegler draws close to Blanchot's response to Nancy's account of community. Blanchot argues that community is not constitutively incomplete because of the ontological difference so much as a result of "the unfinishedness or incompleteness of existence" itself (Blanchot 1988, 20). I return to Blanchot in chapter 5, where I argue that he is an important yet under-recognized influence on Stiegler's work. Here it is useful to note that Blanchot's response to Nancy rests on the claim that the incompleteness represented by community is irreducible to ontological conditions because it exceeds the totalization of ontology, even if that ontology has non-totalization as its goal. Stiegler's critique of the ontological difference rests on a similar claim. Technics forms the need for consistences because it leaves the human without essence, and as such no consistence can escape this a-transcendental conditioning. In Stiegler's words, "this hypomnesic fact . . . can now no longer remain concealed and is not thinkable within the framework of an ontology" (Stiegler 2010e, n.3, 209). Conceptions of the human, and by association the political, cannot be ontological *and* completely non-totalizing.

It is crucial to highlight the implicit link between definitions of the human and ontological claims within Stiegler's argument here. Accounts of the political cannot rely on ontology if they are to be non-totalizing because they are situated within a particular a-transcendental frame, which is itself a product of the co-constitutive relationship between the human and the technical. Even though they often attempt to avoid the totalization of the concept of the human, postmetaphysical accounts of the political must rest on some form of assumption about the nature of humanity. Stiegler is by no means the first to establish a link between ontology and conceptions of human nature. Critics of colonialism, coloniality, and racism have long demonstrated that claims about "being" relegate some to the status of "non-being" in a totalizing fashion. Frantz Fanon and Sylvia Wynter, for example, have both argued that colonial subjects stood outside of the onto-logical categorizations of the human within European modernity (e.g., Fanon 2008, 83; Wynter 2003). Stiegler does not address issues of race, racism, or colonialism; however, a potential contribution to these discussions lies in his conceptualization of ontology from the perspective of the problem of total-ization engendered by the philosophy of technics. Philosophical speculation is always caught up in claims about the nature of the human, whether it intends to make these claims or not, because philosophy itself arises as a result of the co-constitution of the human and the technical. Totalization will not necessarily involve the exclusions perpetuated by colonialism, but political concepts will nevertheless always be totalizing. Stiegler's relevance for critical discussions of the relationship between race, coloniality and ontology lies in his claims that all ontological reasoning is necessarily totalizing, and that a critical account of the modalities that totalization might take is necessary to mitigate its harms. To do so one must reconceive of this relationship as part of the open, ongoing and revisable formation of the non-inhuman.

There is not space here to explore the full significance of Stiegler's relevance for debates around the relationship between concepts of the human, ontology, race, and colonialism. However, it is worth highlight-ing the resonance between his account of ontology and Calvin Warren's critique of postmetaphysical thought. For Warren, the significance of postmetaphysics for the critique of antiblack racism lies in its attempt to subject metaphysical constraints on the nature of the human to constant hermeneutical reinterpretation. If being is post-foundational, then accounts of being that underpin antiblackness are in no way essential. In Warren's words, "The postmetaphysician understands antiblackness as a problem of metaphysics, especially the way scientific thinking has classified being along racial difference and biology. The task of the postmetaphysical project is to free blacks from the misery metaphysics produces by undermining its ground." The limit of this perspective, for Warren, is that the language of ontology underpinning postmetaphysics emerges alongside antiblackness. As Fanon and Wynter argue, the very nature of European ontology is to relegate the colonial subject, or the black individual for Warren, to the status of nonbeing: they exist outside of ontology. Postmetaphysical ontology does not repeat this gesture explicitly but it does not grapple with it, as it "still posits being universally" as if it applies to all without exception (Warren 2018, 5). This lack of an explicit attempt to grapple with the unequal distribution of ontological status leads post-foundational political ontologies to place similar totalizing constraints on the conception of the human, by failing to consider how these inequalities of recognition impact the efficacy of the methodology represented by ontological reasoning for establishing non-totalizing and non-exclusionary understandings of politics.

While he does not use the language of colonialism or anti-Blackness, Stiegler shares several assumptions with Warren's critique of postmetaphysical ontology. In particular, ontological claims are, in Stiegler's terminology, subject to a-transcendental limits. They may be made in an attempt to overcome totalization, but they nevertheless engage in totalizing gestures because ontological claims are articulated universally. This is despite their status as consistences that arise from a particular technical context. While the ontological difference, articulated as the political difference, may attempt to account for a diversity of forms of politics, it nevertheless sees a particular understanding of the political as their condition. The very notion of the priority of the political emerges within particular historical circumstances and therefore must totalize the way that politics is perceived to some degree (Banerjee 2020, 6–9). As Warren highlights, to try and escape this gesture without recognizing its centrality to ontology is to reify the totalizing conditions of ontological claims and the exclusions that they perpetuate. When viewed from the perspective of the originary default, the challenge is not so much to escape totalization as to recognize the totalizing status of all responses to the lack of origin. The limit of political ontology is not that it is not non-totalizing enough, but that it fails to recognize that ontology must on some level engage in totalization.

Conclusion: The A-Transcendental and the Political

It is on the basis of this claim that I argue Stiegler attempts to unite the question of the definition of the human with the problem of ontology, understood within the broader scope of philosophical answers to the default of origin. The a-transcendental and quasi-causal status of philosophical concepts prevents them from fully explaining or accounting for the origin, and thus they are non-totalizing, yet they must transform the contingency of an accidental a-transcendental horizon into necessity by totalizing it and giving it meaning. This dual status of consistences underpins Stiegler's commitment to the concept of the human as the non-inhuman. As consistences, philosophical claims answer the origin in a way that "may be inaccessible" but that "nevertheless guides all non-inhuman behaviour" (Stiegler 2019d, 197). The political acts as one such guiding concept: it consists only insofar as it is formed quasi-causally within the a-transcendental horizon that is made possible by the technical default. Affirming the undecidability of the default is a central component of politics, for "*Political* belief is precisely belief that affirms this *indetermination* as a *principle*, and in a way as the *principle of principles* . . . instead of concealing it in an origin myth that is always also a predetermination" (Stiegler 2013b, 74). This commitment to indetermination must be reconciled with the need for totalization in the face of the absence of meaning engendered by the default. Political ontology's account of this indeterminacy is limited by its failure to recognize that its attempts to develop non-totalizing accounts of the political *require* this totalization, and that ontology rests on a set of a-transcendental assumptions about the nature of the human. Stiegler's reading of Rousseau and Leroi-Gourhan is of paramount importance for this argument. He finds in both figures' work the undecidability of the origin and the necessity of mythical accounts of the human that curtail the explanatory powers of both transcendental and empirical definitions of humanity. The myth of Prometheus and Epimetheus represents Stiegler's attempt to provide a narrative of the origin that accounts for the co-constitutive nature of the human and the technical, and the impossibility of reducing the tragic duality of the empirical and the transcendental to a single account of the origin of the human.

This discussion has two consequences for the concept of the political. The first arises from Stiegler's emphasis on the formation of the human by its changing relationship to technicity. Politics cannot be investigated outside this transcendental-empirical complex or grounded in a particular ontology. Instead, it emerges within the mythical, fictional, and quasi-causal resolution of the default of origin, and must be understood in a non-inhuman manner that balances both totalization and openness. Stiegler hints at the extent of this position when he states that tool-using precursors to *Homo sapiens* "were 'social' and in this sense already idiomatic, having a language in the fullest sense of the word, even though that language and social sense remain for us radically inconceivable, foreign" (Stiegler 2009b, 66). When read in tandem with his mythical account of the origin, it can be suggested that politics is a defining aspect of the human that exists in forms inconceivable within current conceptual understandings of the political, precisely because it is a transcendental that is modified by its technical, empirical circumstances.[10] Stiegler makes it possible to conceive of a formative relationship between anthropological context and the political by way of the co-constitution of the empirical and the transcendental, which also opens the possibility of a definition of politics irreducible to ontology or metaphysics. The totalizing role of fiction constitutes the first limit to political ontology, as it cannot account for forms of politics that are irreducible to its concepts qua fictions.

The second consequence is the need for a clearer sense of how to delineate between, and assess the desirability of, different modalities of totalization. Across this chapter, I have argued that Stiegler seeks to reconcile the non-totalizing status of the origin with the need for totalizing consistences that give meaning to a particular a-transcendental context. At the same time, it has been argued that the concept of the a-transcendental places limits on the efficacy of political ontology's attempts to account for indeterminacy because it engages unwittingly in totalization. The issue here is not so much totalization itself but the extent to which the contingency and partiality of totalizing political concepts are avowed and recognized. The next chapter turns to Stiegler's concept of pharmacology to suggest that it provides a methodological tool for critically assessing totalization. This perspective underpins my immanent critique of Stiegler's own political judgments that assesses the extent to which they manage to balance totalization and openness, which is articulated in the final three chapters. In conclusion, a precursor to this discussion can be highlighted here. In the above quotation, Stiegler refers to the presence of the "social" as opposed to the political in technical existence prior to *Homo sapiens*. This hesitation to use the word politics means that he only hints at the existence of a political tendency before *Homo sapiens*. By making this claim in a highly attenuated manner, one can already see the possibility of Stiegler retreating from the radical consequences of his work: the political is formed alongside technicity and must be considered as an a-transcendental concept. In contrast, Stiegler's emphasis on the social suggests the possibility of a second origin with respect to the political. Technical pre-humans are social but not political. This is a claim I return to in more depth in my discussion of Stiegler's account of the origin of the political in chapter 8. For now, it is worth noting that while Stiegler makes it possible to conceive of a radical pluralization of the concept of the political that eludes all ontology, he also engages in totalization without openness when considering the nature of the relationship between the human and the political.

2

The *Pharmakon*

A common criticism leveled against the claim that everything is political is that it leads to conceptual indistinction. If everything is political, then nothing is, as we are left without categories to adjudicate on the difference between the political and the non-political (Apter 2018, 1). Put otherwise, the critique of totalization with respect to the political leaves one unable to demarcate the space of politics in a meaningful way. Chapter 1 noted the presence of a similar issue when the political is considered from the perspective of the default of origin. Stiegler uses the indeterminacy of the origin to critique the totalization of the human but also to argue for the necessity of totalizing judgments regarding the nature of the political, as the default leaves it without a-historical meaning. The problem here is twofold. Not only does the political appear absent of meaningful content, but it also seems to be impossible to judge upon whether a particular totalization does justice to the indeterminacy of the origin. I have claimed that theorists of political ontology come up against this indeterminate origin when attempting to define the political in a non-totalizing manner, as ontological accounts of politics must totalize the default in some way. How is it possible to avoid this negation of the necessity of totalization within non-totalizing conceptions of politics while remaining able to distinguish between forms of totalization that may or may not do justice to their incomplete character?

This chapter argues that the concept of the *pharmakon* plays this role in Stiegler's work. For Stiegler, "*all technical objects are pharmacological*: they are both poisonous and curative" (Stiegler 2013c, 421). By exploring how he expands his definition of the technical object by way of the poisonous and curative tendencies of the *pharmakon*, I show that Stiegler defines

49

politics as the need for judgments that respond to the pharmacological problems of a particular a-transcendental horizon. This, in turn, expands my account of Stiegler's relationship to the problem of totalization. From the pharmacological perspective, totalization can be non-inhuman, open, and curative; or inhuman, closed, and poisonous. This latter tendency presents a negative form of totalization that forecloses the questioning of political judgment. The political challenge posed by the *pharmakon* is that it renders the ability to make totalizing yet open judgments uncertain. Consequently, those critical of totalization within political theory cannot abdicate the task of making totalizing decisions without the risk of surrendering to judgments characterized by the absence of further questioning.

I introduce this conception of the political through a reconstruction of Stiegler's relationship to the work of Jacques Derrida. Stiegler adopts the concepts of the *pharmakon* and *différance* from Derrida to imbue technics with two forms of undecidability: one derived from the poisonous and curative tendencies of the *pharmakon*, and one that associates the origin of the human with the aporetic and non-totalizing concept of *différance*. By defining technical objects as pharmaka that are the condition of the non-inhuman, Stiegler claims that technicity transforms the general condition of undecidability represented by *différance*. Life in general is subject to undecidability, yet the *pharmakon* initiates a new relationship to this condition in which the undetermined is accessed through the conditions of technical supports. The undecidability and interpretability of technicity's relationship to the human is not, in Derrida's terminology, a quasi-transcendental, a condition that escapes totality. Instead it is a-transcendental, as it is a non-totalizable condition that is itself conditioned by particular totalities within the historicity of technicity. Where Derrida sought to provide an account of undecidability that undermined totalization in general, this chapter shows how Stiegler ties the indetermination represented by both the *pharmakon* and *différance* to the specificity of totalizing empirical contexts that make this transcendental undecidability possible.

I show that there is a political reason for this philosophical gesture. As *pharmakon*, the technical object supports both non-totalizing, non-inhuman judgments and inhuman judgments that totalize without the recognition of the open and undecidable nature of the human. Non-inhuman, quasi-causal, and local judgments on the nature of the human and its problems are not guaranteed. Recognizing this problem was particularly important for Stiegler, as he claimed that "non-inhuman-kind in its totality, composed of pharmacological beings, that is, potentially inhuman beings, must disintoxicate itself" because of what he saw as the inhuman nature of totalization that presented itself at the outset of the twenty-first century (Stiegler 2013f, 55). The *pharmakon* presents a pressing political problem insofar as it can induce totalization that prevents productive questioning of the problems faced by the human and results in the exclusionary claims of the inhuman. Pharmacology allows us to see how Stiegler conceives of the non-inhuman as a critical political concept leveraged against inhuman forms of totalization that also requires a critical embrace of totalizing judgment. Moreover, it will lead to the conclusion that the second limit to political ontology lies in its inability to exhaust the problems posed by the local undecidability of the *pharmakon*. Ontological accounts of politics are limited by both the situational nature of the problems posed by pharmaka that escape the constraints of a single ontology, and the undecidability of the *pharmakon* itself, which cannot be totalized within a single understanding of politics underpinned by a position on the nature of being.

This position is outlined in several steps. The chapter first reconstructs Derrida's and Stiegler's readings of Plato's *Phaedrus* to distinguish between their understandings of the *pharmakon*. Second, it shows that the full significance of the *pharmakon* is to be found in establishing connections between Stiegler's later understanding of this term and his earlier reading of *différance* in the first volume of *Technics and Time*. By claiming that the indetermination and deferral represented by *différance* are differentiated by the historical development of technical objects, I show how Stiegler claims that it is the *pharmakon* that underpins the rupture between deferral within life in general and within the human-technical coupling. The chapter then, third, considers several variations of the accusation of human exceptionalism that has been directed at Stiegler's reading of Derrida. To respond to these claims I demonstrate that, for Stiegler, technicity is not an anthropocentric tool but something that invents the human. The payoff of this intellectual move is a conception of the political defined by its relationship to specific technical organizations with their own pharmacological problems and tendencies. Fourth, to clarify the nature of these tendencies, I define them as two distinct types of totalization that characterize political judgment: inhuman stupidity and non-inhuman quasi-causal transformation. Not only is politics conceptually undecidable, but as a form of non-inhuman judgment, it is only experienced intermittently because it struggles against stupidity. Politics represents the attempt to grapple with these two pharmacological tendencies within the local limits and constraints of a particular a-transcendental horizon. This duality between poisonous and curative forms of totalization provides the political with minimal criteria that are nevertheless differentiated by changes in the relationship between the human and the technical object, changes that a single ontology cannot account for.

The *Pharmakon* in Plato, Derrida, and Stiegler

To understand how the concept of the *pharmakon* underpins Stiegler's conception of the political, Derrida's use of the term must be established first. In "Plato's Pharmacy," Derrida deconstructs what he sees as an opposition between philosophical reason and writing within Plato's *Phaedrus*. According to Derrida, Plato argues that writing has a poisonous impact on memory. Writing is a pharmaka and is treated as a pharmakos, a scapegoat for the contamination of philosophy with misleading and sophistic rhetoric concerned with persuasion rather than truth. However, he also argues that Plato uses the concept, and not just the practice, of writing to make this claim and therefore that it cannot be expelled from philosophical method. Derrida shows that the variety of meanings attributed to the term *pharmakon* renders its role in the dialogue undecidable: it is not just "poison" but also "cure," "potion," and "drug" (Brogan 1989, 9–10). Writing and truth are inseparable, as the *pharmakon* signifies an undecidable relationship between them. Here one finds the classic themes of deconstruction: the impossibility of a totality that would allow the distinction between the inside and the outside of truth, the problem of undecidability within philosophy, and the negation of writing by metaphysics. For Stiegler, these themes become a part of his critique of totalization as the impossibility of totalizing the nature of the human, the undecidability of the poisonous and curative tendencies of technical objects, and the repression of technics by philosophy.

While Plato's explicit meditation on writing appears at the end of the *Phaedrus*, Derrida argues that the entire dialogue attempts to establish an opposition between philosophy and writing.[1] The dialogue begins from Socrates's insistence that Phaedrus recite a speech on love, given by the speechwriter Lysias, from memory. Despite his claim to have memorized it, it transpires that Phaedrus has written the speech down and hidden it under his cloak. Their discussion leads Socrates to distinguish between the rhetorician's ability to "toy with his audience and mislead them" and the philosopher's aim of establishing truth (Plato 1997b, 539, 262d). It is not until the final passages of the dialogue that Socrates engages in an explicit evaluation of the written word in an account of an Egyptian myth regarding the invention of writing by the God Theuth and its denunciation by the God-King Thamus. On the basis of this myth, he concludes that writing is incapable of facilitating access to truth, as written words "are as incapable of speaking in their own defence as they are of teaching the truth adequately" (Plato 1997b, 553, 276c). The earlier discussion of rhetoric preempts this later consideration of writing, meaning that, as Derrida claims, "the *trial of writing* . . . is rigorously called for from one end of the *Phaedrus* to the other" (Derrida 1981, 67).

As there is not room here to engage with the entirety of Derrida's reading, I focus on totalization, undecidability, and the rejection of writing in favor of speech, for these themes are the most pertinent to Stiegler's use of the term *pharmakon*. Derrida addresses the problems of totalization and undecidability together, as the *pharmakon* frustrates Plato's attempt to secure a boundary between the inside and outside of philosophical reason. This problem appears at the opening of the dialogue, where the reader finds Socrates traveling outside the city. Phaedrus notes that Socrates rarely sets "foot beyond the city walls," to which he responds that Phaedrus has "found a potion to charm me into leaving" (Plato 1997b, 510, 230d–e). The written speech is presented as a *pharmakon* in multiple senses here. Socrates wishes to engage in philosophical discussion, which acts as a kind of drug, while Phaedrus has written the speech down, which acts as a poisonous influence on his memory. The *pharmakon* tempts Socrates out of the city, and the lure of philosophical discussion turns out to be a deception because of the presence of writing. In both cases, the totality and security of the interior of truth are compromised by the written *pharmakon*. Derrida claims that this leads to a kinship between writing and "going or leading astray" that undermines totality and certainty and that Plato wishes to repress (Derrida 1981, 71).

This "leading astray" occurs because of the undecidable nature of the *pharmakon*. Consequently, writing, as a *pharmakon*, is a drug that must be used well. For Socrates, "It's not speaking or writing well that's shameful: what's really shameful is to engage in either of them shamefully or badly" (Plato 1997b, 535, 258d). Socrates's reference to use could be seen to represent a more pragmatic understanding of writing than that suggested by Derrida in his hyperbolic presentation of Plato's oppositional structure. However, Derrida's strategy is not so much to show that writing is consistently condemned by Plato, but to show that he resists its undecidability in favor of a particular form of use that assigns it a supplementary status to philosophy. This occurs in an account of the myth of Theuth's presentation of writing to the God-King Thamus. Writing is described by Theuth as a *pharmakon*, a potion that can improve memory. Thamus's response is damning, however, as he sees it as a poison for memory rather than a cure. This leads Plato to conclude that writing "is external and depends on signs that belong to others." Rather than promoting memory, writing provides its users "with the appearance of wisdom, not with its reality" (Plato 1997b, 552, 275a–b). Despite the polysemy of the *pharmakon*—in the myth it is gift, potion, and poison—Plato judges it to be opposed to philosophical knowledge, even if it can be used prudently. Writing is totalized and opposed to speech despite its undecidability.

According to Derrida, this is evidence that "what Plato *dreams* of is a memory with no sign. That is, with no supplement" (Derrida 1981, 109). Because writing weakens memory and can be manipulated through shameful use, it takes on an undecidable status and must be expelled from philosophical truth. Derrida's strategy is to show that this is, indeed, nothing but a dream and that philosophical truth relies on writing. Key to this argument is Socrates's description of truth as "written in the soul" (Plato 1997b, 554, 278a). Derrida highlights this gesture to argue that instead of acting as a "pure" cure, philosophy is simply "a more effective *pharmakon*" (Derrida 1981, 115). Philosophical reason is a *pharmakon*, for it is produced through inscription, even if this is "in the soul," and therefore its borders, foundations, and truths are characterized by the same undecidability as writing. Here Derrida attempts to undo Plato's rejection of writing by emphasizing the impossibility of properly totalizing and distinguishing the interior of truth from its outside. Platonism resists this conclusion and attempts the "restoration of internal purity" to philosophy by defining the *pharmakon* as that which diverts reason from its path toward truth (Derrida 1981, 128). This requires the expelling of the very thing that truth requires; an undecidable component that both enables philosophy and prevents its purity. Consequently, the *pharmakon*'s undecidable play is transformed by Platonism into a game with defined rules.

Stiegler adopts the critique of totality, the concept of undecidability, and the undermining of the opposition between writing and speech from Derrida. He develops the opposition between philosophy and writing into a separation between *ēpistēmē* and *tekhnē*, where *ēpistēmē* refers to knowledge concerning philosophical truth and *tekhnē* refers to skilled or practical knowledge. Stiegler argues that Western philosophy has defined technology in a manner similar to the Platonic rejection of writing by opposing it to philosophical truth, or *ēpistēmē* (Stiegler 1998, 1). Here Stiegler enlarges

Derrida's understanding of writing so that it encompasses all technical entities: writing is inferior to *ēpistēmē* insofar as it is *tekhnē*. Stiegler expands on this distinction through the terms *anamnesis* and *hypomnesis*, first introduced in chapter 1. In *What Makes Life Worth Living*, Stiegler claims that Plato defined *anamnesis* "by opposing it to hypomnesic memory, that is, artificial memory, the *pharmakon*," whereas Derrida demonstrated that "the hypomnesic appears as that which constitutes the *condition* of the anamnesic" (Stiegler 2013f, 18–19). Here Stiegler considers the constitution of truth within philosophy to be conditioned by the empirical and shifting nature of *tekhnē* or *hypomnesis*, rendering it radically undecidable because of the changing nature of its empirical supports. Stiegler thus goes beyond Derrida in establishing a constitutive relationship between technicity and thought, for "Technics does not aid memory: it *is* memory" (Stiegler 2009b, 65). The three themes of Derrida's quasi-transcendental reading of the *Phaedrus*—totality, undecidability, and the repression of writing—are transformed into an a-transcendental claim regarding the relationship between technical objects and philosophical speculation. *Pharmaka* act as the supports of human memory and therefore constitute the undecidable and non-totalizable relationship between interiority and exteriority, or the transcendental and the empirical.

Stiegler's reading of the *Phaedrus* further differs from Derrida insofar as he hews more closely to Plato because of his concern for the problem of use. The *pharmakon*'s status as gift, drug, potion, and poison emphasizes Stiegler's view that it is characterized by two curative and poisonous tendencies: it can both support and poison memory. He does not view, as Plato does, the *pharmakon* as an imposition on philosophical truth but as a condition that can nevertheless threaten it. More fundamentally, if the technical object invents the human, then these curative and poisonous tendencies constitute the human's very existence. In Stiegler's words, "anthropogenesis must be understood as pathogenesis to the strict extent that it is technogenesis" (Stiegler 2013f, 28). Because of this pharmacological status, "technicity must be understood as bringing about a new 'infidelity' of the milieu" (Stiegler 2013f, 29). Technics forms an a-transcendental horizon that is open to change and is subject to both undecidability and indetermination, for there is no totalizable set of reasons for why a particular set of technical objects needs to be used to underpin social life in a specific way. Nevertheless, the conditioned and contingent status of the non-inhuman is not always recognized, and it is this failure of recognition that forms the poisonous dimension of the relationship between pharmaka and philosophy.

These two pharmacological conditions can be understood as tendencies toward openness and closure. The curative dimension of the *pharmakon* is represented by the transformation and translation of pharmacological uncertainty into a quasi-causal image of the non-inhuman that acknowledges its contingency and recognizes the perpetual question of the nature of the human. In contrast, the poisonous dimension of *pharmaka* is represented by a foreclosure of openness that *"prevents the possibility of posing questions"* (Stiegler 2013f, 105). Politics should concern itself with judgments that tend toward this open, curative tendency and do not close the space for the posing of questions. The urgency of the need to associate openness with the possibility for questioning arises from the infidelity of the technical milieu. Pharmacological problems are characterized by the technical objects of a particular context, and the openness of responses to those problems is necessitated by the process of adjustment required when technical systems change. In Stiegler's words: "The disadjustment to which the appearance of a new *pharmakon* always gives rise is the historical reflection of this instability, and it is what the knowledge of how to live, do and conceptualize formed within social systems takes care of: these forms of knowledge are always therapies for . . . the pharmacology of each particular epoch" (Stiegler 2019d, 39). This means that, for Stiegler, political judgments act as a therapeutics for properly integrating technical and social systems. Understood in this way, politics *"must* confront the irreducibly pharmacological character of . . . the non-inhuman being. It must do so by constituting therapies and therapeutics that we commonly call forms of knowledge" (Stiegler 2019d, 222).

Here Stiegler takes on a question that Plato himself was attempting to tackle in his consideration of writing: the negative effects of technicity on a particular non-inhuman milieu. He seeks to understand how technicity enables the *"construction* of rationality's critical space" while also possessing the potential to be that which *"poisons* this critical space" (Stiegler 2010e, 151). Here it is clear that political judgment must be resolutely critical. A truly political judgment is totalizing yet open, for it sets limits for the non-inhuman while recognizing its "improbable and non-predestined" condition (Stiegler 2014d, 96). It is this type of judgment that represents a "cure" for the sophistic closure of knowledge. In making this claim, Stiegler sees himself as continuing the Socratic tradition, for "Socrates argued that those teachers who were the sophists were abusing the *pharmakon* that is literal tertiary retention, and that they were doing so by ceasing to make the transmission of knowledge the moment of its re-elaboration" (Stiegler 2015a, 164). To make totalizing political judgments that do not include space for their reinterpretation is to engage in the sophistic and pharmaco-logically poisonous closure of the critical space opened by technicity. This point underpins my articulation of the second limit of political ontology, for it attempts to avoid totalization rather than interrogate the totalizing judgments that statements regarding the nature of being represent.

I return to this criticism and to the therapeutic understanding of the political below. For now, it is important to note that this political understanding of the *pharmakon* divides Stiegler from Derrida. For Der-rida, deconstruction resides within the undecidability of the reception of a text: "When I try to decipher a text I do not constantly ask myself if I will finish by answering *yes* or *no*" (Derrida 2004, 47). Stiegler also sees technicity as irreducible to a simple yes or no. Nevertheless, the poisonous character of the *pharmakon* necessitates a decision between one alternative and another. For Stiegler, Derrida did not address this problem of " 'cura-tivity' " (Stiegler 2019d, 157), and "never envisaged the possibility of such a pharmacology" (Stiegler 2013f, 4). As other commentators have noted, while Derrida emphasizes the deferral of the decision, Stiegler affirms the decision's necessity (Kouppanou 2015; Mui and Murphy 2020), a position that some have referred to as "post-deconstructive" (Ross 2013; de Beistegui 2013, 181–82). This shift marks the difference between the *quasi*-transcendental and the *a*-transcendental. Stiegler does not focus on the general conditions of undecidability represented by the former but on the conditioning of the unconditioned represented by the latter. The duality of the *pharmakon* means that the space for the indeterminate, and by association the space of politics, is shaped by the curative and poisonous dimensions of the technical object.

The Two Regimes of *Différance*

Stiegler's reading of the *Phaedrus* indicates that he is simultaneously invested in the critique of totalization and the advocation of a form of political total-ization that leaves space for the questioning of its judgments. This rests on an associated rereading of *différance*, insofar as technicity is seen to transform the quasi-transcendental nature of this term into an a-transcendental form of undecidability. Across the next two sections of this chapter, I introduce this reading of *différance* and consider some critical debates surrounding it before returning to the political consequences of the *pharmakon*. Stiegler's understanding of *différance* underlies both his critique of totalization, inso-far as it resists reduction to metaphysical completeness, and his break with

Derrida on the politics of decision and undecidability. By tying *différance* to the a-transcendental transformations of technical objects, Stiegler claims that it underpins the need to make decisions regarding the nature of the human and of the political: "The lack of origin is also a lack of purpose or end. It is in this way that technics *constitutes* the *problem of decision* . . . it calls for a capacity to make a difference, a capacity imposed by the lack of origin, by our original default. The feeling for such a difference . . . arises from this '*différance*'" (Stiegler 2003, 156).[2] By linking technicity and the decision, Stiegler transforms the relationship between the *pharmakon* and *différance*. For Derrida, the *pharmakon* and *différance* are but two iterations of the undecidability that serves as the "complex 'origin' of space and time and meaning" (Bennington 2000, 12). By defining the relationship between the human and technics as mediated by pharmaka, Stiegler transforms the quasi-synonymous relationship between these two terms. He argues that the pharmacological invention of the human causes a transformation of the logic of *différance*: technicity alters *différance* so that undecidability depends on the a-transcendental horizon within which it occurs.

To make this claim, Stiegler argues that there are two definitions of *différance* in Derrida's work: the *différance* between the human and its technical supplement (the *pharmakon*) and a more general form of *différance* operating at the level of life. According to Stiegler, Derrida expresses an "indecision" regarding whether *différance* refers to "the history of life in general" or to the articulation of the living upon the non-living through technics (Stiegler 1998, 139). The former understanding is found in "*Différance*," where Derrida introduces this term as a radicalization of the understanding of the sign in structuralist linguistics. If within structuralism signs establish their meaning through reference to other signs then, for Derrida, there can be no self-sufficient origin that fixes the meaning of any linguistic system. *Différance* is not a metaphysical or ontological principle precisely because it tries to name this deferral of meaning and, therefore, "the name 'origin' no longer suits it" (Derrida 1982, 11). Derrida expands this principle beyond signs to refer to the conditions of space and time in general, or "the becoming-space of time or the becoming-time of space," which he calls "archi-writing, archi-trace, or *différance*" (Derrida 1982, 13). It is this description that Stiegler sees as emblematic of the definition of *différance* as the quasi-transcendental conditions of life in general that defer totality.

A contrasting understanding of *différance* is found in the account of the *grammē* and the trace in *Of Grammatology*. Here Derrida claims: "*The trace is the différance* which opens appearance and signification. Articulating the living upon the nonliving in general, origin of all repetition, origin of ideality" (Derrida 1976, 65). Stiegler contrasts this definition with the previous understanding of *différance*: "To articulate the living onto the nonliving, is that not a gesture from after the rupture when you are already no longer in pure *phusis?*" (Stiegler 1998, 139).[3] If in *Of Grammatology différance* refers to the articulation of the living on the non-living as signification, then it does not refer to a general condition but to one that is articulated in stages. For Stiegler, the conflict between the first quasi-transcendental understanding of *différance* and this second, historical iteration of the term announces the possibility of thinking technical memory as something that transforms *différance*. Hence, he seeks to combine the understanding of *différance* as a general principle of deferral with this emergence of a history of forms of differentiation via the technical supplement.

This account of *différance* is found in the first volume of *Technics and Time*, but Stiegler refers to its consequence continually. Derrida hesitates to endorse the historical understanding of *différance* while also making it possible to conceive of a "history of the supplement" (e.g., Stiegler 2001, 252; 2009e; 2019d, 280). This transformation of *différance* is a condition of Stiegler's claim that the *pharmakon* is constituted by the historical articulation of its tendencies toward openness and closure because to embody these two tendencies technicity must mediate the relationship to the undecidable. This move inflicts an unavoidable violence on the Derridean understanding of *différance*. If the terms used to "signify" this logic are quasi-synonymous, then the designation of the *pharmakon* as that which invents the human and transforms *différance* limits the non-totalizable signifying chain that relates them. Some commentators have argued that this represents a fundamental transformation of Derrida's work into a new set of philosophical categories that puts it into communication with concerns unaddressed by deconstruction (Alombert 2020; Hui 2020; Pavanini 2022), while others claim that Stiegler's reading has unacceptable consequences for the Derridean position. Both Geoffrey Bennington and Ben Roberts have argued that Stiegler reduces the investigation of technics to a positivist, rather than philosophical, task and that he reifies life as "pure," or outside the logic of deferral that *différance* represents. By considering these criticisms, and possible responses to them, I show how Stiegler attempts to simultaneously reject the purity of life and the positivity of technics.

Bennington argues that Stiegler's reading of Derridean *différance* reifies the difference between humanity and life. Stiegler's position regarding "the passage from the genetic to the non-genetic and thereby from the animal to the human" assumes that "physis is or could be a pure presence subsequently affected by *différance*." This "force[s] the whole philosophical argumentation of Derrida through the "passage" of the emergence of mankind" and "commits [Stiegler] to a certain positivism about difference" (Bennington 2000, 169–71). This positivism is also at stake in the disagreement between Derrida and Stiegler in the televised interviews published as *Ecographies of Television*. Derrida resists Stiegler's positing of technics as the source of knowledge because of his commitment to the quasi-transcendental status of *différance*, as "the origin of sense makes no sense . . . that which constitutes sense is senseless" (Derrida and Stiegler 2002, 108–9). Roberts argues that this challenge forms a question that strikes at the heart of Stiegler's project: "how is theoretical and historical knowledge of "technics" possible, given that as you yourself argue technics is first of all what makes theory and history possible?" (Roberts 2005).

I first consider the claim that Stiegler treats the origin of sense in a positivistic manner before moving to the question of the purity of life. To treat Stiegler as a positivist implies that technicity is reducible to a single account of its relationship to the human. As argued in chapter 1 and in the account of the *pharmakon* presented above, this is not possible. If the origin of sense is the *pharmakon*, which is itself subject to the default of origin, then knowledge of it is subject to undecidability. Technicity both grounds and challenges systems of meaning and is therefore irreducible to positive knowledge. In Stiegler's words: "Technicity unfurls as the process of *différance* and as the conquest of time and space. It is thus that which uproots from the ground, that which does violence to one's home, that which thrusts outward the intimate, and that which corrodes idiomatic differences. But this violence is also the possibility of idiomatic differentiation, that which *constitutes* one's home in the first place by opening it to what is other than oneself" (Stiegler 2001, 260). We "know" technics in a provisional manner that can never be fully totalized, for "the elaboration of knowledge is the production of difference in its utterances" (Stiegler 2014d, 99). Attempts to "fix" the meaning of technicity engage in an interpretation and decision on the nature of the human and of the origin. It is impossible to fully know technics, because of the undecidability of the origin, despite the need to totalize and understand it. Stiegler does not reduce *différance* to a positivistic principle but tries to consider how undecidability is conditioned by the historical relationship between technicity and our perpetual attempts to give it meaning. It is this undecidable relationship that underpins Stiegler's attempt to reconcile totalization and openness within the non-inhuman.

With this established, the criticism that Stiegler reifies life before technicity as "pure" and outside the logic of *différance* can now be considered. Stiegler does not posit a radical break between "pure" and technical forms of life so much as claim that the relationship to technicity is representative of a particular form of *différance* gaining hegemony over human existence. This point rests on the presupposition that biological and technical life both represent programmes of memory that inform behavior. Technicity is a form of externalized experience and memory that humans inherit and that conditions their behavior in a manner similar to genetic or biological memory (Stiegler 1996). Humanity is distinguished from animality by this additional influence on its behavioral programmes. To make this claim, Stiegler distinguishes between genetic memory (memory of the gene), epigenetic memory (memory of the individual), and epiphylogenetic memory (exteriorized and manipulable technical memory) (Stiegler 1998, 140). The two prefixes that make up the neologism epiphylogenesis, epi- and phylo-, refer, respectively, to the experience of the individual and the inheritance of species characteristics that are passed down genetically. Epiphylogenesis forms the hegemonic influence over human existence, insofar as it allows the contingent epigenetic memories of individuals to be passed onto the species beyond the death of the individual organism. This inheritance conditions the expression of phylogenetic memory.

Stiegler's conception of the relationship between epiphylogenetic memory and the behavior of organisms is taken from Leroi-Gourhan's understanding of the programme. This is "the essential concept in allowing equally for the animality/humanity and the humanity/technicity divisions to be transcended" (Stiegler 2009b, 72). For Leroi-Gourhan, behavior in the animal is regulated by an inherited set of programmes, which might otherwise be called genes: "as one generation succeeds another the same sequences . . . are reproduced from individual to individual" (Leroi-Gourhan 1993, 222). In Derrida's reading of Leroi-Gourhan, as Francesco Vitale has demonstrated, this understanding of the behavioral programme is subject to *différance*. Genetic inheritance is never reproduced in identical form, and hence *différance* "is the condition of the possibility of the living: as a condition of possibility it structures the life of the living as a text" (Vitale 2018, 106). Understood in this way, genetic memory and epigenetic variations in the duplication of that memory subject the reproduction of biological life to undecidability and inexact repetition. Biological, genetic, and programmatic memory determine behavior while also being open to the unpredictability of *différance*.

Bennington's criticism is directed at the first volume of *Technics and Time*; however, Stiegler clarifies his position in later texts in a way that accords with the reading of Derrida presented by Vitale. In the third volume of *Technics and Time*, Stiegler states, "The reproductive capacity of living things is a prolific source of diversity precisely because a reproduction is never a simple copy but the trans-formation of the (re)produced" (Stiegler 2011c, 215). In *Automatic Society*, Stiegler expresses this point with explicit reference to Derrida, for whom "life in general is *already* the process of such a différance—which occurs, for example, through the replication of DNA, which is already a trace" (Stiegler 2016a, n.73, 260–61). Here it is apparent why Stiegler can both hold to and break with the Derridean understanding of life as *différance*. Technicity intervenes within the play of differentiation in genetic inheritance by preserving the contingent epigenetic experiences of individuals in material form and allowing them to be inherited. Stiegler draws on the work of the biologist François Jacob to develop this point. For Jacob, the central axiom of genetics is that the "programme does not learn from experience" (Jacob 1973, 3). This limit marks the difference between the *différance* of life and the *différance* of technical objects. The differentiation of the genetic programme is not subject to intentional modification on the part of the organism or species, whereas technicity allows the preservation of epigenetic experience in epiphylogenetic form. The logic of deferral that constitutes life is altered by the emergence of the human capacity to pass on experience and have its behaviors shaped by this collective memory: "Epiphylogenesis engenders the proliferation, in life, of a type of memory as irreducible to zoology" (Stiegler 2009b, 71). Humanity is defined by the capacity to externalize, reproduce, and retain individual memory within technics, which intervenes within the differential unfolding of the genetic and transforms the nature of *différance*.[4] Life is not understood as pure by Stiegler but is instead contrasted with this process of technical differentiation that takes precedence within the formation of human behavior.

Human Exceptionalism and the *Pharmakon*

This response to Bennington's and Roberts's criticisms allows me to expand on Stiegler's commitment to non-totalization and his rejection of metaphysical accounts of the difference between the human and life in general. Technics cannot be totalized in a positivistic manner because knowledge of it is subject to *différance*, and technicity and life represent two different relationships to undecidability represented by genetic and epiphylogenetic forms of inheritance. The point at which life becomes technical life is mediated by the *pharmakon* and is, therefore, not totalizable within a single metaphysical or ontological system; it is this that constitutes the *pharmakon*'s limit to political ontology. This point provides an opportunity to consider some issues within Stiegler's conception of the relationship between the genetic, the epigenetic, and the epiphylogenetic. The evidence presented above shows that he does not stray as far from Derrida as Bennington and Roberts suggest; however, it may be argued that when moving from philosophical to biological forms of reasoning, Stiegler comes close to expressing a form of human exceptionalism by limiting the hegemony of technicity to humanity. This issue needs to be considered before turning to the relationship between the non-inhuman, the political, and the *pharmakon* in more detail, for if Stiegler falls prey to totalization regarding the relationship between biological and technical life, then this would undermine the balance between totalization and openness that he wishes to develop.

One form of potential human exceptionalism can be found in Stiegler's understanding of the genetic. While he thinks life through the concept of *différance*, he also assumes a border between the genetic and the non-genetic, implied by his reliance on François Jacob's axiom that the programme does not learn lessons from experience. This is corroborated by Stiegler's insistence on an absolute barrier between somatic, or epigenetic, memory; and germinal, or genetic, memory, which he describes as follows:

> From Weismann to contemporary molecular biology, the living sexed being is constituted by two memories: species memory, which is replayed each time one has a fecund sexual life and which recombines chromosomes, thus remixing the genetic patrimony of the species (and each living being is a carrier of that memory), and the individual nervous memory of that living sexed being . . . the nonhuman life form relies on the structural impermeability between genetic memory—*the germ*—and somatic memory, that is, the nervous memory of the individual animal (Stiegler 2009a, 67).[5]

This understanding of the genetic as separate from the differential character of the somatic or the epigenetic conflicts with the claim that life is characterized by *différance*, where environmental and non-living influences impact the non-identical repetition of the genetic. Indeed, some have argued that work in molecular biology has rendered the concept of the "gene" as a self-contained unit obsolete, claiming instead that one should posit "hybrid conceptual constructions, which would be more rigorously designated without using the term 'gene'" (Gayon 2007, 92). Because he invokes a "structural impermeability" between the gene and epigenetic memory, Stiegler veers toward a crude understanding of genes as homogenous units that possess powers of determination in and of themselves, which are subject to *différance* in their reproduction but are not influenced by non-genetic factors.

This critique is compounded by Stiegler's use of a limited conception of the epigenetic as superfluous to the operation of the genetic. Michael Haworth argues that recent work on epigenetics poses a significant challenge to Stiegler's distinction between epigenesis in life that is lost to death and the preservation of epigenesis in technical life (Haworth 2016). Haworth draws on research in molecular biology to suggest that if genetic influences on behavior are modified by epigenesis, then the latter are in some way selected, retained, and passed onto the species because they modify the occurrence of reproduction. Epigenetics is not just integral to the differential unfolding of the genetic but also an influence on the way it is reproduced and perpetuated, and therefore a strict separation between the two is impossible (Dupré 2012, 158–59). It is on this basis that Haworth argues that the link that Stiegler claims technicity establishes between the genetic and epiphylogenetic is already present in the relationship between the genetic and the epigenetic (Haworth 2016, 164). Because he bases technics on a logic already present in life, the preservation of epigenetic differentiation, Stiegler repeats the mistake of Rousseau and Leroi-Gourhan by placing a second origin between humanity and life in general.

This also means that Stiegler risks human exceptionalism. Despite his vehement opposition to metaphysics, the claim that the retention and transmission of epigenesis are limited to technicity contains elements of anthropocentrism that some argue are resolutely metaphysical. In the words of Tracy Colony, for Stiegler: "The only form of exteriority that *articulates* life in relation to what is beyond life, i.e., beyond the tautology of "life by means of life," is the technical materiality that is opened in the anthropogenetic rupture" (Colony 2011, 84). Colony maintains that Stiegler does retain the Derridean claim that life itself is subject to *différance*, but, along with many other commentators, argues that the relationship to the non-living is exclusively human.[6] Here anthropocentric possession of technics naturalizes life, conflicting with the rereading of *différance* as subject to "living" and "technical" articulations.

My consideration of these criticisms leads toward conclusions about the relationship between the *pharmakon* and the contextual nature of the political. In response to Haworth's criticisms, I argue that Stiegler's philosophical commitment to a principle of *différance*, and hence non-identity, at the level of the living and at the level of the technical suggests that he does not hold completely to a deterministic understanding of the genetic. Here I invert Bennington's and Roberts's criticism somewhat: Stiegler's philosophical commitments vindicate his lack of reference to positivistic evidence from the biological sciences. In contrast to his adoption of the distinction between germ and soma, Stiegler understands the difference between the living and the human in terms of how technicity opens up and extends the degrees of freedom, or indetermination, that exist within the biological programme (Stiegler 2009b, 71–96; 2016a, 35–36). As Nathan Van Camp highlights, this is how Stiegler attempts to avoid metaphysical and ontological commitment to either strict continuity or separation between human and animal. The behavior of both is formed by the level of indeterminacy within the genetic programme, but this margin of indeterminacy is altered by technicity (Van Camp 2011, 69–70). This gesture allows Stiegler to unite the human and the animal while also separating them through the human's relationship to technical objects. His focus on the genetic appears self-contained and deterministic, but when understood in the terms of his wider philosophy it is clear that he understands the living as a system that unfolds according to differing degrees of determination and indetermination. This point is more forcefully emphasized by Stiegler's claim that the human is a product of the technical. He claims that "transmitting individual experience beyond the individual's life" is the condition of "the possibility of a sur-vival in which 'the human' is merely an 'effect'" (Stiegler 2009b, 160). Technicity preexists the human, and the emergence of the latter represents "a sudden hegemony of the epiphylogenetic within the developing process of differentiation. 'The human' is precisely this hegemony" (Stiegler 2009b, 161). Viewed in this way, technicity does not double the passing on of epigenetic experience to the gene, as Haworth suggests. Instead, it establishes hegemony over the process of inheritance that characterizes the human and establishes a relationship to the already existing differentiation of the genetic by epigenesis.

This hegemony of the technical is also central to challenging the accusation of human exceptionalism with regard to the relationship to the non-living. There are two possible ways to reconsider this point. First, Stiegler does not rule out the possibility of other forms of technical life emerging.

Technicity is anterior to the human, occurring "before the human not only in ape societies but perhaps much earlier in the pre-history of animality" (Stiegler 2009b, 161). Epiphylogenesis is hegemonic within human life but not exclusive to it. In Martin Crowley's words: "Species difference here (despite those residual suggestions of hierarchy) need not reduce to species privilege" (Crowley 2013a, 57).[7] Second, Colony criticizes the claim that it is the human alone that pursues life through inorganic means. Here Colony misreads Stiegler somewhat, for he also articulates a distinction between the inorganic, or the non-living, and the organized inorganic, or technics. The human does not have a special relationship to the inorganic, but it does have the capacity to transform it into organized inorganic supports of memory in the form of technics (Stiegler 1998, 17). For example, when Stiegler states that "territory itself constitutes the first collective memory support" (Stiegler 2011c, 105), he does not suggest that animals do not have a relationship to the inorganic fact of geographical location. Instead, the very notion of "territory" requires the articulation of an idea of ownership over physical space supported by techniques, practices, and rituals. Nonhuman animals have a relationship to the inorganic but of a different kind to that within the hegemony of the organized inorganic. Technicity represents neither a human privilege with respect to epiphylogenesis nor the inorganic in general.

Quasi-Causality, Stupidity, and the Political

Why is this rebuttal of the accusation of human exceptionalism so central to the relationship between the *pharmakon* and the political? If Stiegler was to articulate human exceptionalism regarding technicity, it would be impossible to form a politics that is committed to an open form of judgment, for the human would be subject to metaphysical totalization. I argued above that the political significance of the *pharmakon* lies in its capacity to support two kinds of judgments: those that recognize this constitutive openness and those that do not. This detour through Stiegler's interpretation of *différance* and the potential for exceptionalism within it has demonstrated that curative and open judgments cannot fall back on an a-historical understanding of the difference between the human and life in general. Instead, political judgments must be articulated in relation to the pharmacological tendencies of a particular a-transcendental context and in a way that projects a particular image of the non-inhuman. I now expand on my earlier definition of these two tendencies to more closely link the *pharmakon* to the non-inhuman condition.

Stiegler's focus on pharmacological context situates him within what Beardsworth refers to as a "left-Derridean" political tradition that affirms the need to derive political claims from an examination of the intertwinement of humanity and technicity rather than a "right-Derridean" focus on quasi-religious messianism (Beardsworth 1996, 156; 1998b).[8] Stiegler's left-Derrideanism lies in the claim that politics is constituted by the pharmacological tendencies that arise from the establishment of a threshold between animal and human life by technicity.[9] This leads to two related tasks: the articulation of totalizing judgments regarding the nature of the human, understood as non-inhuman; and the incorporation of openness within these judgments. Judgments that fail to balance totalization and openness do not recognize that the *pharmakon* puts the human into perpetual question. By short-circuiting such questions, poisonous judgments prevent the adjustment of political commitments in response to the shifting nature of technicity, a critical problem that political ontology does not provide the intellectual tools to assess.

Stiegler expands on the two dimensions of the *pharmakon* with reference to two concepts that he takes from Gilles Deleuze: quasi-causality and stupidity. In chapter 1, I demonstrated how quasi-causality underpins the relationship of concepts, or consistences, to their a-transcendental horizons. Here I expand on this further by exploring two elements of the "quasi-causal logic of the *pharmakon*" (Stiegler 2019d, 202). Responses to pharmacological problems are defined by quasi-causality, for they cannot fully totalize and exhaust the undecidability of any particular technical object or context. They nevertheless represent an attempt to totalize and respond to those problems in a curative manner. According to Stiegler, if "invention is in Deleuze what creates an event and bifurcation starting from a quasi-causality that inverts a situation of default," then "quasi-causality is clearly a kind of therapeutics within a pharmacological situation" (Stiegler 2016a, 61). The myth of Prometheus and Epimetheus informs this interpretation of Deleuze. For Deleuze, "the event is subject to a double causality, referring on one hand to mixtures of bodies which are its cause and, on the other, to other events which are its quasi-cause" (Deleuze 1990, 94). It is the ambiguity of this link between bodily causes and the quasi-causal meaning attributed to them that Stiegler takes to refer to the Promethean and Epimethean, or curative and poisonous, dimensions of technical conditions. Technics is pharmacological "because of *Epimethean quasi-causality* which is also the law of the primordial *pharmakon*" (Stiegler 2013c, 206). It is Epimetheus's accident that Prometheus responds to and makes necessary by stealing fire and gifting it to humanity. Stiegler sees the necessity of quasi-causal responses to all pharmacological problems in this mythical account of the primordial *pharmakon*.

Humans respond to technicity with concepts and judgments that render its accidental status necessary by making sense of pharmacological undecidability. Consistences that give meaning to a particular a-transcendental field are "offered *by* the *pharmakon*, against the *pharmakon*, and as its quasi-causality" (Stiegler 2018c, 198). Stiegler claims that the strength of Deleuze's notion of quasi-causality is that it is "a position with respect to life that consists in positing that what wounds me, what weakens me—if it does not kill me—is also my chance" (Stiegler 2018d, 142). Quasi-causality does not just respond to the default of origin by filling in for its absence. It also underpins judgments that act as curative responses to the pharmacological problems of a particular technical context. Such an image of pharmacological judgment as care or cure is necessitated by the concept of the non-inhuman, precisely because it rests on the claim that there is no necessity underlying a particular technical situation: "To take care, to cultivate, is to dedicate oneself to a cult, to believe there is something better: the *non-inhuman* par excellence, both in its projection to the level of ideas (consistencies) and in that this 'better' *must* come" (Stiegler 2010e, 178–79). If they are to be curative, these caring projections cannot totalize without recognizing their contingency, for they are subject to a set of a-transcendental conditions that cannot be reduced to an "'ontology' or any theology" (Stiegler 2018a, 109). Curative judgment cannot be expressed in a way that totalizes the human or being in general, for to do so would be to neglect the pharmacological undecidability that underpins the quasi-causal nature of consistence.

It is this undecidability that underpins the need for such quasi-causal decisions as well as their contingency. Because responses to the question of the non-inhuman are quasi-causal, they do not possess ontological or metaphysical necessity and can be prevented by the poisonous dimension of the *pharmakon* that Stiegler understands as stupidity. This term, the second concept taken from Deleuze, is not defined as "error or a tissue of errors" but as "a base way of thinking." Deleuze continues by doubling down on the distinction between error and stupidity, as both falsity and truth can be articulated as stupidity: "In truth, as in error, stupid thought only discovers the most base—base errors and base truths that translate the triumph of the slave, the reign of petty values or the power of an established order" (Deleuze 2006, 105). Stupidity represents a reactionary form of thought that does not perceive openness or contingency in a particular set of judgments, for it reduces judgment to "the power of an established order." In *Difference and Repetition*, this definition of stupidity is translated into "the faculty for false problems; it is evidence of an inability to constitute, comprehend or determine a problem" (Deleuze 1994, 159). A true problem eludes commonsense solutions and generates its own evaluative criteria: " 'solvability' must depend upon an internal characteristic: it must be determined by the conditions of the problem" (Deleuze 1994, 162). Stupidity is the tendency to provide reactive solutions that do not inquire into the transformative qualities of the logic internal to a particular problem.

Stiegler's understanding of stupidity hews closely to this definition. He defines it as that which "obstructs, as *stupidity*, the passage to the critical, noetic act" (Stiegler 2014b, 33). Stupidity is the inability to conceive of a solution to a problem beyond existing solutions. This condition arises because technicity forms a changing, infelicitous milieu that both underpins and challenges existing quasi-causal judgments. Stupidity is "induced by the interruption . . . of hypomnesic programmes" insofar as it leads to a misalignment between those programmes and new technical objects (Stiegler 2018a, 321). This experience is engendered by transformations in technical systems, for "the appearance of a new *pharmakon* always produces stupidity" (Stiegler 2012a, 181). To act stupidly is to apply existing conceptual frameworks to the new pharmacological problems posed by those objects. Crucially, stupidity is internal to, rather than distinct from, knowledge. The experience of stupidity is a necessary preliminary for the production of a solution to a particular problem: it represents the originary "*impropriety* of knowledge" (Stiegler 2015a, 47). Stupidity has a structural relationship to *pharmaka*, and as such Stiegler rejects the possibility of eradicating it. Stupidity "is not what can *at times* affect thought, but what affects thought *first of all*, precisely insofar as thinking only 'is' intermittently" (Stiegler 2013b, 77). Changes in technical systems induce stupidity by posing new pharmacological problems to which the non-inhuman must respond. The *pharmakon* is the source of political questions, as it requires both a critique of existing concepts and the constitution of new ones in response to technical change: "Faced with stupidity, the question arises of the second pharmacological moment—which can clearly only be considered through a critique of the first moment" (Stiegler 2013f, 132). Consequently, the questions that the *pharmakon* poses can only be derived from the changes within the a-transcendental field that supports a particular mode of existence. Here Stiegler adopts Deleuze's claim that "Stupidity and baseness are always those of our own time, of our contemporaries, our stupidity and baseness" (Deleuze 2006, 107). Political responses to the *pharmakon* must engage with a distinct field of stupidity to think quasi-causally.[10]

The necessity of stupidity within knowledge also underpins the relationship between the non-inhuman and the *pharmakon*. The fictions that form conceptions of the non-inhuman exist primarily as responses to pharmacological problems. In Stiegler's words: "This relation, stupidity/ knowledge, is what is at stake in what . . . I have to [sic] tried to think as the *pharmacological condition* of knowledge, that is, of *noēsis* as that existence which is possible for non-inhuman beings faced with the fact of being-inhuman" (Stiegler 2015a, 47). The non-inhuman is faced with the possibility of being inhuman, or of expressing stupidity, and must struggle against this condition. Again, as with knowledge, this is not an aberration but instead the very condition of the non-inhuman. Non-inhumanity "is possible only as the experience of that which is small, that is, of what Deleuze called *baseness*—which may sometimes cause shame, that is, provoke thought" (Stiegler 2015a, 129). This pharmacologically poisonous tendency toward inhumanity is the cause of non-inhuman reflection, but it is also present in totalizing judgments that do not recognize the quasi-causality and conditionality of their concepts and cannot respond to the questions posed by the transformations of *pharmaka*.

This duality between quasi-causality and stupidity underpins Stiegler's conception of the political. This is demonstrated clearly by the second manifesto issued by the political group Ars Industrialis, of which Stiegler is a founding member and whose philosophy provides the theoretical basis for its programme. Here politics is defined as "a system of care that con- sists in establishing ways of life (and a culture) that knows how to deal with the given pharmacological (technical and mnemotechnical) state" (Ars Industrialis 2014b, 20). With this definition established, I now conclude by returning to the problem of finding appropriate criteria for demarcating the concept of the political within a philosophy characterized by the default of origin. Stiegler's definition of the political as a system of care that responds to pharmacological problems provides minimal criteria for delineating the space of politics. These criteria must be elaborated within a particular set of a-transcendental conditions to give them meaning quasi-causally, but also to avoid the inhuman totalization characteristic of stupidity. This resistance to stupidity is urgent for Stiegler because non-inhuman judgments only occur intermittently. Because of the undecidability of the *pharmakon*, "most of the time we tend not to be not-inhuman-*in-action*: we *tend* toward not-humanity . . . this is the 'tragic condition' of being-only-intermittently" (Stiegler 2010e, 170). Intermittence motivates Stiegler's commitment to a modified form of totalization. He claims that it is necessary to give meaning to the pharmacological condition in a way that cultivates and encourages non-inhuman forms of being because these political judgments are not guaranteed. To pose non-totalization as a political good in-itself fails to provide traction on political problems because of the need to provide meaning to the undecidable nature of pharmaka.

Pursuit of this goal in ontological terms totalizes the ultimately undecidable and intermittent nature of the human relationship to the *différance* of the *pharmakon*. Political ontology cannot exhaust this undecidability. A positive pharmacology is constituted by a form of knowledge that "knows that *this condition of impossibility is the condition of a contingent positivity*, one that is accidental . . . that is, a *possibility arising from out of* [sic] *impossibility*, and as the *necessity of a fault*" (Stiegler 2021a, 367). Ontology, as a discourse on being, cannot encompass this accidentality, for it provides a totalizing conception of openness that is not open to the permutations of pharmaka. This constitutes the second limit to political ontology. It attempts to avoid totalization, leaving it unable to decisively respond to the pharmacological problems that characterize politics, but it also totalizes the political in a way that cannot exhaust the infidelity and changeability of pharmacological objects. Stiegler's left-Derrideanism, by contrast, consists of a delicate balance between totalization and openness: it is not enough to pose the undecidability of the human's relationship to technicity as the condition of an open conception of the political. Stiegler's distinction between the *différance* of life and the *différance* of technical systems is integral to this claim insofar as it constitutes the basis of his shift from a quasi-transcendental to an a-transcendental philosophical position that necessitates a critical engagement with totalization.

Conclusion: The Pharmacology of Political Judgment

I can now answer the question that opened this chapter: how to give meaning to a conception of the political derived from the concept of the default? Two key principles have been developed in the above that demonstrate Stiegler's commitment to a form of totalization that incorporates the aims of the critique of non-totalization. First, technicity structures human existence and allows the human, as non-inhuman, to change, critique, and transform those conditions, but it also has the potential to destroy this quasi-causal capacity for questioning through stupidity. Totalization is present in the basic structure of the political, as it is a form of judgment that responds to these pharmacological threats. In this sense, the political is universal, insofar as all forms of non-inhuman existence are structured by a set of pharmacological problems. Second, this universal conception of the political has no meaning beyond its formation by the pharmacological conditions of a particular technically supported milieu. It is in this sense that Stiegler proposes a contextual understanding of the political that combines totalization with non-totalization. Political judgment is intermittent and is never guaranteed because of the pharmacological constitution of political problems.

On the basis of this pharmacological intermittence, I have established that the political is universal but does not exist as a constant or an abstract principle outside the a-transcendental horizon in which the two pharmacological tendencies are actualized. The scope of the political is a product of a specific set of pharmacological problems. Pharmacology represents Stiegler's attempt to balance the tendency toward non-totalization represented by *différance* with the totalization necessary to give potentially poisonous pharmaka meaning. This gesture leads him to propose a pluralization of the concept of the political that renders it irreducible to ontology precisely because it can only ever partially totalize a specific, contextual set of problems. The second limit to political ontology posed by Stiegler's work is its inability to exhaust the problems posed by the local undecidability of the *pharmakon*. In the next chapter, I explore how these concepts of the political are generated from a dynamic relationship with this undecidable sense of locality.

3

Individuation and General Organology

A problem that faces the non-totalizing conception of the political derived from pharmacology is whether pharmacological problems overdetermine politics. To what extent are political judgments characterized by a degree of indeterminacy or dynamism with respect to their conditions? Here I respond to this issue by developing an account of the dynamic relationship between the political and its conditions from Stiegler's reading of the work of Gilbert Simondon. Simondon's understanding of individuation allows Stiegler to further his reading of Derridean *différance* by providing a way to conceptualize the forms of indetermination within different regimes of individuation and to account for the interaction between biological, social, and technical regimes of individuation within human existence. General organology is the methodological tool Stiegler uses to understand the relationship between these three types of "organs." In this chapter I argue that within the organological perspective, the political is generated within specific a-transcendental contexts and in response to particular pharmacological problems while maintaining a recursive and indeterminate relationship to those conditions.

Stiegler's work has contributed to a growing interest in Simondon's philosophy.[1] While Simondon already played an important role in the history of non-totalization within continental political thought because of his influence on the work of Gilles Deleuze (e.g., de Boever et al. 2012, vii), Stiegler rethinks the relationship between Simondon and the problematic posed by the critique of totalization. Simondon's work plays two methodological roles for Stiegler. First, his principles of individuation and transduction underpin Stiegler's non-totalizing understanding of the human, the political, and the concept of the a-transcendental. Simondon rejects explanations of individuation that rest on general principles that do not account for the genesis of the individual in terms derived from the conditions of particular processes of individuation. In doing so, he develops a transductive mode of thinking that focuses on the co-constitution of the individual and its milieu in relation to pre-individual tensions that are never fully exhausted by a process of individuation. Consequently, individuation is conceptualized as an ongoing and non-totalizable process that is irreducible to ontology. For Stiegler, both individuation and transduction place limits on universal accounts of the genesis of the non-inhuman that would subsume all aspects of its individuation within a single philosophical position. It is in this way that transduction forms the basis of his a-transcendental method.

Second, Stiegler draws on this concept of individuation to form his own methodological principle in the form of general organology. Stiegler develops Simondon's typology of regimes of individuation to argue that the non-inhuman is constituted by the transductive relations between biological, social, and technical individuation. This organological method is central to understanding and responding to pharmacological problems insofar as it "constitutes the paradigm of transdisciplinarity without which no critique of pharmacological reason, and no positive pharmacology, are conceivable" (Stiegler 2015a, 187). Moreover, this transdisciplinary method is necessary for understanding how a "new *pharmakon* carries new possibilities of psychic and collective individuation" and for responding to it with "'therapeutic' prescriptions" (Stiegler 2018c, 34). Simondon's work provides the basis for understanding how these totalizing prescriptions are generated from within a particular process of individuation as opposed to being applied to them from the outside, while maintaining that they are also non-totalizable because of the dynamism of individuation. It is this interplay between totalization and non-totalization within individuation that underpins Stiegler's development of a "post-ontological" theory of the human, technicity, and the political (Barthélémy 2012). As a post-ontological position, general organology forms the third limit to political ontology: all concepts are generated within a particular process of individuation and cannot account for all eventualities of the dynamic and recursive development of that locality, or the problems posed within the localities of other processes of individuation.

Stiegler's adoption of Simondon's work allows us to conceive of the political as a response to pharmacological problems generated from within a particular process of individuation and the degree of freedom accorded to thinking within that organological context. Stiegler is not the only thinker to use Simondon's philosophy to conceptualize this conditionality of the political. For Jason Read, Simondon's work provides a method that examines the "processes through which individuality and collectivity are constituted and transformed" and that forms a "precondition for a new practice of politics" (Read 2016, 12). Similarly, for Yuk Hui, Simondon provides a way of thinking the conditionality of moral and political concepts. Following Stiegler, he argues that technics is *"somatically* and *functionally* universal" but "not necessarily *cosmologically* universal" (Hui 2016, 217).[2] All humans possess technicity, but the concept of technicity itself is not present within all processes of individuation. Hui proposes "cosmotechnics" as a method that analyzes the range of understandings of technicity across the moral and conceptual frameworks of different groups, societies, cultures, and their philosophies (Hui 2017). Following this proposal, one might say that the political is functionally but not cosmologically universal. When we deem a judgment political, we do so from within an organological context by making sense of the threats posed to psychic and collective individuation by a particular set of pharmacological problems.

I develop this argument in several steps. First, the chapter reconstructs Stiegler's adoption of the concept of individuation and unpacks Stiegler's use of this context to conceptualize the relationship between individuals and collectives on the basis of their technical, a-transcendental context.[3] This leads me, second, to consider how Stiegler develops the concept of general organology to claim that technical, social, and biological forms of individuation are intertwined within human existence. Stiegler refuses ontological or metaphysical exhaustion of the political because he situates political responses to the *pharmakon* within the a-transcendental and post-ontological frame provided by organology. Third, I then give an account of how the concepts of individuation and general organology frame the production of concepts in an a-transcendental manner through reference to Stiegler's use of the concepts of automatism and repetition. Individuation allows Stiegler to reconcile totalization with non-totalization by defining a process of individuation as reliant on a priori conditions that are the a posteriori result of an ongoing ontogenesis and its associated automatisms and repetitive practices. Fourth, and finally, I conclude by considering the consequences of this account of the nature of knowledge for concepts of the political. For Stiegler, political concepts emerge from and guide a particular process of transindividuation by totalizing their a-transcendental horizon while undergoing recursive alteration by the ongoing individuation of their locality. As one such concept, political ontology's third limit is its inability to exhaust this conditional and recursive understanding of the political.

Individuation and Transduction in
Stiegler's Reading of Simondon

To demonstrate the centrality of Simondon to Stiegler's philosophy of technics, I first introduce the methodological significance of his concepts of individuation and transduction. This can be seen most immediately in Stiegler's connection of the principle of individuation to the work of Derrida. Like *différance*, individuation represents an attempt to name indeterminacy without subordinating it to metaphysical or ontological principles. The difference between Derrida and Simondon lies between the former's quasi-transcendental conception of indeterminacy and the latter's attempt to understand how the genesis of individuals is conditioned by the indeterminacy of a particular process of individuation. This mirrors Stiegler's understanding of *différance* as conditioned by its relationship to the determinate conditions of technicity, which I introduced in chapter 2. When following this line of thought, "we must *think différance as individuation*" (Stiegler 2015a, 63).[4] Stiegler seeks to think *différance* as individuation to account for the indeterminacy and undecidability of the ongoing genesis of the human-technical coupling, as part of his broader shift from a quasi-transcendental to an a-transcendental perspective.

Simondon's starting point for developing this concept of individuation is the rejection of philosophies that begin from existing individuals when accounting for their genesis. He argues that "it is necessary to reverse the search for the principle of individuation by considering the operation of individuation as primordial." This leads Simondon to adopt an ontogenetic perspective, within which "the individual would then be grasped as a relative reality, a certain phase of being which supposes a pre-individual reality prior to it and which, even after individuation, does not fully exist all by itself, for individuation does not exhaust in a single stroke the potentials of pre-individual reality, and, moreover, what individuation manifests is not merely the individual but the individual-milieu coupling" (Simondon 2020, 3). Before defining the concepts of the pre-individual and the individual-milieu coupling, it is worth noting that two central elements of Simondon's philosophy can be seen in this quotation. First, individuation is ongoing because it does not exhaust the potentials from which it emerges, and, second, that individuation understands individuals to be relational. Individuals are relative to the context in which they emerge and to the phase of being that they represent. The presence of both totalization, insofar as individuation occurs from a set of determinate conditions, and non-totalization, the inexhaustibility of pre-individual reality, signifies the importance of Simondon for the reading of Stiegler developed here.

Pre-individuality is the primary concept within Simondon's ontogenetic account of individuation. Individual entities are the product of processes of individuation that represent partial actualizations of a pre-individual field of potentials and tensions. Simondon gives two physical analogies that help define this pre-individual state. The first is a supersaturated solution in which a crystal can form upon the addition of a germ or solute seed. Before the addition of this germ, the potentials represented by the pre-individual milieu of the solution are metastable, or only apparently stable. The addition of the germ disrupts this metastability and engenders the individuation of the crystal from the potentials within the solution (Simondon 2020, 6). A second example is found in the wave-particle duality within quantum physics, which holds that quantum objects may be observed as either waves or particles but not both at the same time—either form is the expression of a metastable pre-individual state undergoing a process of individuation. In Simondon's terms, "the individual can sometimes play one role and sometimes the other of two possible roles in relation, but not both at the same time" (Simondon 2020, 110). While brief, both of these physical examples help define Simondon's concept of the pre-individual; individuation begins from the introduction of new information into a metastable set of potentials and tensions that represent the unactualized possibilities of a particular context, whether that be the addition of a chemical element or the presence of an observer.

A situated form of indeterminacy and the transductive method are two basic consequences of this theory of the pre-individual, both of which have ramifications for the nature of ontogenesis. The pre-individual field that underpins ontogenesis is irreducible to predictability because it is only after a process of individuation has been engendered that it can be subject to scrutiny. Pre-individuality is structured by possibilities that are subject to degrees of indeterminacy, and it is not certain how the tensions of a metastable system will be resolved by a particular process of individuation, for "at the critical instant . . . there is a sort of relative indetermination of the result" (Simondon 2020, 258). For Simondon, an individual is simply a stage in a process of individuation that represents a partial and indeterminate actualization of the potentials of the pre-individual engendered by the accident of an unpredictable critical instant. Consequently, relations between the pre-individual and the individual are metastable: they are only temporarily, rather than perpetually, stable. An individual is a metastable, rather than stable, reality because these potentials and tensions can be subject to further individuation.

Simondon understands these metastabilities to be transductive because individuation necessitates a relationship between two or more distinct elements, which he refers to as the individual-milieu coupling. Individuation is relational because it is engendered by the introduction of new information into an existing metastable state. In Simondon's words: "The veritable properties of the individual are at the level of its genesis and, for this very reason, at the level of its relation with other beings, since, if the individual is the being that is always capable of continuing its genesis, this genetic dynamism resides in its relation to other beings" (Simondon 2020, 84). Simondon refers to this relational methodology as transduction, which he distinguishes from both deduction and induction. Deduction fails to grasp individuation because it explains the genesis of individuals in terms of pre-existing theories and concepts, whereas induction understands the various components of a particular system to take the form of discrete elements that are then related (Simondon 2020, 15). In contrast, Simondon takes the relationship between elements of a metastable relationship to be constitutive of that process of individuation and the individuals that are individuated. Within this perspective, the coupling between an individual and its milieu is a primary consideration for attempts to understand a particular process of individuation. Transductive methods demand that distinct processes of individuation are understood in terms of the transformations undergone by a field of pre-individual potential that constitute an ensemble of individuals within a particular milieu, themselves the product of existing processes of individuation.

Stiegler's adoption of pre-individuality and transduction from Simondon provides him with a way to think the genesis of particular individuals while deferring totality, incorporating indeterminacy into the origin of those individuals, and by considering the individual-milieu relation as the condition of individuation. This requires the recognition of distinct regimes of individuation particular to these transductive relationships, a perspective that Stiegler draws on in his development of general organology. To clarify how, I briefly summarize Simondon's distinction between physical, vital, and psychic and collective regimes of individuation. The distinction between physical and vital regimes of individuation can be understood in terms of the relationship between the interior and exterior of the individual. Simondon takes the example of the individuation of a crystal as a paradigmatic example of physical individuation. A metastable solution acts as a field of potential for the individuation of a crystal by a germ of new information. This individuation occurs at the boundary between the crystal and the solution, expanding the limits of the crystal at its edges until the metastable potentials for that particular individuation are exhausted. In contrast, vital individuation establishes a permeable barrier between the interior of an organism and its exterior that maintains potentials for further individuation: "in the living being, there is a more complete regime of *internal resonance* that requires ongoing communication and that maintains a metastability, which is a condition of life" (Simondon 2020, 7). Vital individuation prolongs an organism's genesis by regulating its metastable relationship to its environment across this barrier. This activity distinguishes it from physical individuation: "The living being resolves problems, not just by adapting, i.e. by modifying its relation to the milieu . . . but by modifying itself, by inventing new internal structures . . . inside the living individual the interior is also constitutive, whereas in the physical individual only the limit is constitutive" (Simondon 2020, 7–8). Living beings actively negotiate with their environment to maintain their individuation.

This relationship between interior and exterior undergoes a further transformation because of two shifts that condition the emergence of psychic and collective individuation. First, psychic individuation involves the capacity to consciously intervene as a subject within individuation (Simondon 2020, 8). The maintenance of metastable relations between the psychic individual and its milieu takes place not just through vital individuation but also through deliberate action. Second, in psychic and collective individuation, the collective pole of this relation forms a part of the environment of the psychic individual that is integral to its individuation. This relation is transductive: there are no isolated individuals that form a collective, nor a collective that imprints individuals with a particular identity. Instead, the collective forms the pre-individual fund of potentials from which psychic individuation occurs, which is itself constituted by a multitude of psychic individuals. Both form and shape the other. Changes in the collective fund alter the path of psychic individuation while this fund is transformed by the processes of psychic individuation of which it consists (Simondon 2020, 9). Unity between these two poles is constantly deferred because both the psychic individual and the collective participate in the ongoing maintenance of a metastable set of pre-individual tensions from which individuation begins and which it transforms.

It is here that Simondon is of most interest to Stiegler as he addresses the shift from vital to human individuation. Stiegler adopts the concept of psychic and collective individuation to conceptualize this transformation, often referring to it as the relationship between the I and the We. This can be seen clearly in Acting Out: "If every *I* is inscribed in the *we* that constitutes it, and that it constitutes, if the *I* and the *we* are *two faces of the same process of individuation*, at the core of which develops their *tendency* to become-indivisible, ceaselessly projecting their accomplished *unity*, this projection is never concretized except by default, in other words by ceaselessly *deferring* this completion" (Stiegler 2009a, 4). Stiegler emphasizes that this transindividual relationship contains both diachrony and synchrony: the collective informs psychic individuation, but this occurs in a diachronic and indeterminate manner. Hence, "synchrony is only possible through a diachronic indetermination" (Stiegler 2011c, 96–97). This tension is maintained by disindividuation, disconnection from the collective We in which psychic individuation responds to a shock or unexpected encounter—which Stiegler also understands as moments of stupidity—engendered by encounters with new information or with pharmacological changes to a process of individuation. Through its attempts to maintain a metastable relationship with its environment, an individual responds to disindividuation by integrating it within its process of individuation, by resolving the tension it establishes with pre-individual reality, and by inscribing this resolution within collective individuation. Consequently, the disindividuation of the I is a necessary moment in the transformation of any process of psychic and collective individuation (Stiegler 2015a, 60–61). This means that individuation is not purely volitional: "A process of individuation is what *happens to me* in such a way that when something or other happens to me, I in a way arrive to myself through that which happens, of which I become the quasi-cause" (Stiegler 2020a, 119). Stupidity and quasi-causality ensure that the individual and the collective relate to each other in a diachronic and dynamic way that recursively integrates the indeterminacy of disindividuation, or what "happens," into the ongoing production and maintenance of a set of synchronic pre-individual potentials for future individuation.

For Stiegler, it is of paramount importance to be able to identify the role that pharmacological technical objects play in the disindividuation of psychic and collective individuation. General organology is the method he uses to think this form of analysis. However, Stiegler develops this concept in response to what he sees as a lacuna in Simondon's work. He argues that Simondon does not see the technical object as the condition of psychic and collective individuation and therefore fails to think the political challenge posed by the pharmacological status of technics. While there is a tendency within Simondon's work to make this link explicit, Stiegler argues that there is a countervailing tendency within his work that renders it a-political (Stiegler 2019a). Both of these perspectives can be found within Simondon's *On The Mode of Existence of Technical Objects*. In the first, he suggests that there is an irrevocable link between psychic and collective individuation and transformations in technical objects: "A change in technics entails a modification of what one could call the political constellation of the universe . . . Social and political thought becomes integrated into the world according to a number of outstanding points, problematic points that coincide with the points of integration of technicity envisaged as a network" (Simondon 2017, 231). In Stiegler's terminology, "the technical milieu . . . is the condition for the encounter between the *I* and the *we*" (Stiegler 2014e, 51). This transformation of the conditions of the social and political alongside the technical corresponds to what Hui refers to as the cosmotechnical dimension of Simondon's thinking, where conceptions of technicity are integrated with ethical, moral, and political presuppositions (Hui 2017). Here I refer to this cosmotechnical relationship with the concept of the a-transcendental, which also corresponds with Stiegler's understanding of the production of the link between the technical and psychic and collective individuation by grammatization.

The concept of grammatization underlies the claim that psychic and collective individuation requires a technical pre-individual fund.[5] Grammatization makes individual memories accessible to others by discretizing them in technical form. More extensively: "Grammatisation describes all technical processes that enable behavioural fluxes or flows to be made discrete . . . and hence to be reproduced, meaning all those behavioural flows through which are expressed or imprinted the experiences of human beings" (Stiegler 2013a, 32). These externalized memories and "behavioural flows" form the pre-individual fund from which both the collective and the psychic individual find the potentials that engender their processes of individuation (Stiegler 2014e, 53–54). These potentials are found in all forms of externalized experience, such as "mental images (cave painting), speech (writing), gestures (the automation of production), frequencies of sound and light (analogue recording technology)," and algorithms that predict and model behavior (Stiegler 2016a, 19). Stiegler adopts Simondon's concept of psychic and collective individuation on the condition that this relationship relies on a grammatized pre-individual fund of technical objects that reproduce experience to inform future individuation.[6]

The second tendency in Simondon's work resists this gesture by dissociating the pre-individual fund and technics. He posits a phase of psychic and collective individuation preceding technicity, which he refers to as a magical unity between the human and the world: "Primitive magical unity is the relation of the vital connection between man and the world, defining a universe that is at once subjective and objective prior to any distinction between the object and the subject, and consequently prior to any appearance of the separate object" (Simondon 2017, 177). Stiegler identifies in this claim a separation between technical and non-technical modes of human existence akin to the second origin that he finds in Rousseau and Leroi-Gourhan. He links the above position in *On The Mode of Existence of Technical Objects* with a statement in *Individuation in Light of Notions of Form and Information* that distinguishes between pre-individual and transindividual components of psychic individuation: "The subject being can be conceived as a more or less perfectly coherent system of three successive phases of being: the pre-individual phase, the individuated phase, and the transindividual phase, all of which partially but not completely correspond to what is designated by the concepts of nature, individual and spirituality" (Simondon 2020, 348–49). Stiegler's understanding of the role of grammatization within psychic and collective individuation gives a clear indication of why he finds fault with this passage. Both the presupposition of a stage of magical unity preceding technicity and the separation between the pre-individual and transindividuation undermine the necessity of technicity within the pre-individual tensions that constitute psychic and collective individuation, for Stiegler sees technicity as the condition of both pre-individuality and transindividuality in psychic and collective individuation. According to Simondon, "technics is only one moment in psychical and collective individuation, and does not play any role in the constitution of pre-individual milieus" (Stiegler 2019a, 586).

Consequently, Stiegler argues that Simondon is incapable of conceiving of the political problems that face psychic and collective individuation as they are found in the disindividuating tendencies of pharmacological, technical objects. Above I introduced how disindividuation disrupts an established set of metastable relations and in doing so transforms an existing, or engenders a new, process of individuation. To individuate as a psychic individual who is part of a collective process of individuation, one must quasi-causally make this accident one's own by incorporating it into a process of individuation. Chapter 2 demonstrated that the pharmacological opposite of quasi-causality is stupidity, or the incapacity to respond to a problem on its own terms and in an open-ended manner. Within the Simondonian perspective adopted by Stiegler, stupidity is understood as the perpetuation of disindividuation, a state where this quasi-causal transformation of a moment of disruption is impossible. While disindividuation can engender individuation, it can also lead to the encompassing of the individual's process of individuation by the collective, the reduction of their individuation to preexisting metastabilities, or the eradication of one's capacity to judge by its externalization in technicity (Stiegler 2015a, 59–61). I return to this latter possibility in chapter 4 when introducing the concept of proletarianization in Stiegler's work. For now, it is sufficient to note that, for Stiegler, Simondon's position is fundamentally a-political because he does not recognize that technicity constitutes psychic and collective individuation in the form of non-inhuman existence while also threatening it through the possibility of stupidity and disindividuation (Stiegler 2012e, 198–99; 2014e, 51).[7] If technics is to be political, it must be constitutive of psychic and collective individuation.

Some have questioned Stiegler's reading of Simondon. This involves a defense of Simondon's claim that, in Mark Hansen's words, "the technical object is emphatically not a quasi-transcendental condition for transindividuation" (Hansen 2012, 49). For example, Muriel Combes argues that Stiegler's divergence from this position flattens Simondon's distinctions between the ways that human action is conditioned, and therefore precludes any non-technical form of social invention. By restricting the human relationship to the pre-individual to one that is mediated by technicity, Stiegler ignores the human's relationship to a wider range of onto-genetic possibilities that are irreducible to technicity (Combes 2013, 67–69). As Read puts it, the difference between Combes's and Stiegler's interpretation of Simondon lies between the former's more restricted understanding of transindividuation as a concept useful for disrupting existing assumptions about the relationship between the individual and the collective, and the latter's adoption of transindividuation as an essential component of a general philosophy of technicity (Read 2015, 213). Combes is indeed correct to note that by containing psychic and collective individuation within the limits of technicity, Stiegler does not pay fidelity to the word of Simondon's work. Rather than criticizing Stiegler on these grounds, it is more productive to recognize that he is attempting to read Simondon in an a-transcendental manner that prioritizes particular aspects of his thought.[8] These priorities can be summarized under what Jean-Hugues Barthélémy has referred to as Stiegler's "post-ontological" reading of Simondon, in which he attempts to "exit from ontology" (Barthélémy 2012, 67–69). To think post-ontologically is to investigate how psychic and collective individuation is conditioned by the a-transcendental. Individuation cannot be considered to be ontological, for it does not assume a fixed point of reference beyond the a-transcendental conditions of thinking. Simondon himself affirms this point when he claims that a theory of individuation, or ontogenesis, is "the starting point for philosophical thought . . . anterior to the theory of knowledge and to an ontology that would follow this theory" (Simondon 2020, 319). An ontology is a product of a particular process of individuation and therefore cannot properly account for individuation in general terms. Stiegler's version of this position is as follows: "Deeper even than ontologies, which are only the surface effects of transindividuation processes that have metastasized and that in so doing have erased the movement that produced them, there are individuation processes" (Stiegler 2014a, 194). This erasure refers to the sedimentation of quasi-causal accidents into an a-transcendental and metastable milieu that conditions further individuation. Stiegler's exit from ontology consists of this emphasis on the radically situated and accidental nature of thought within the philosophy of technicity. Philosophy can only access originary questions, like those of ontology, from within the locality of the process of individuation of which it is a product.

Here Stiegler sees the most important consequence of Simondon's work to lie in the claim that knowledge is conditioned by a particular metastable field of pre-individual potentials. Knowledge is not of individuation, it is a form of individuation: "we cannot *know individuation* in the ordinary sense of the term; we can only individuate, be individuated and individuate within ourselves" (Simondon 2020, 17). To know is to individuate an existing set of pre-individual conditions, and it is for precisely this reason that Stiegler sees stupidity or disindividuation as both the opposite of knowledge and its condition. However, in establishing this claim he breaks with Simondon by arguing that technicity is the condition of the inherited pre-individual funds that condition both knowledge and psychic and collective individuation. The technical is the translation of experience into a material, pre-individual field that makes a contingent, quasi-causal event necessary. I return to this conditioning of knowledge in the form of the a-transcendental after introducing how Stiegler develops the theory of individuation into the theory of general organology. Before this, two preliminary conclusions for the non-totalizing theory of the political can be drawn from Stiegler's reading of Simondon. First, politics must be understood as an open and non-totalizable process due to the inexhaustibility of pre-individual reality. But, second, responses to the pharmacological problems that occur within these processes of individuation develop into a new set of a priori and totalizing conditions for future individuation. Any political judgment, concept, or gesture engages in this dynamic relationship between preexisting conditions and their transformation that is constitutive of the non-inhuman as a process of individuation. As Read summarizes in his account of the significance of the concept of transindividuality: "Politics . . . is always taking place (even if disappointingly so) in the tensions and pressures that define every metastable articulation of individuations" (Read 2016, 289). Simondon provides Stiegler with a way to account for the conditionality of the political, reinterpreted as the pharmacological duality between quasi-causality as individuation and stupidity as disindividuation. The turn to general organology represents Stiegler's attempt to provide a method for analyzing the ongoing and non-totalizable composition of these two tendencies.

Principles of General Organology

Organology continues Stiegler's commitment to disavowing metaphysical and ontological accounts of the origin as it represents his attempt to come to terms with the historical conditions of the individuation of the non-inhuman. A late statement of intent regarding the concept makes this clear: "I argue that the question of knowing where, when and how man begins is of *no* interest: what is interesting is to know where, when and how there occurs in the history of life an epoch in which the organic must compose with the organological, *which thus becomes the condition of its individuation*" (Stiegler 2020d, 80). Despite Stiegler's critique of Simondon's understanding of the place of technicity with respect to psychic and collective individuation, he is the first of two key influences on the concept of organology, the second being Georges Canguilhem (Stiegler 2018a, 53).[9] Simondon's "mechanology" serves as an influence on organology insofar as it attempts to understand the intertwinement of the social and the technical (Simondon 2017, 66) and consider how technical activity alters the human environment (Simondon 2015). Despite Simondon's neglect of the *essential* nature of this connection (Stiegler 2016a, 131–32), mechanology nevertheless highlights the importance of the relationship between technics and social systems. Canguilhem's influence on the concept of organology is taken from a remark made in *The Normal and the Pathological* regarding the character of the health of the human: "Man, even physical man, is not limited to his organism. Having extended his organs by means of tools, man sees in his body only the means to all possible means of action. Thus, in order to discern what is normal or pathological for the body itself, one must look beyond the body" (Canguilhem 1991, 200–201).[10] If for Canguilhem the conditions of pathology include the use of tools, then for Stiegler the "normal" develops according to changes in the wider milieu of the human rather than the biological alone. Health is defined with reference to a technical milieu that is a "pharmacological context" because of its curative and poisonous tendencies, but also an "organological context" insofar as biological health and technical development are intertwined (Stiegler 2013f, 29). In Canguilhem and Simondon, Stiegler finds an emphasis on the intertwinement of the technical with, respectively, biological and social systems, which he develops into the concept of general organology.

Stiegler's own definition of organology combines these insights as follows: "General organology defines the rules for analyzing, thinking, and prescribing human facts at three parallel but indissociable levels: the psychosomatic, which is the endosomatic level, the artifactual, which is the exosomatic level, and the social, which is the organizational level" (Stiegler 2017a, 130). Here Stiegler reconceptualizes the biological as psychosomatic and endosomatic, or within the body, the technical as exosomatic, or outside of the body, and the social as organizational insofar as it coordinates the relationship between the endosomatic and the exosomatic. Stiegler adopts this terminology after his turn to the consideration of energy and entropy, which I address in chapter 7.[11] Here I take these terms to be interchangeable with the conceptual vocabulary in which Stiegler initially developed organology, as the tracing of how "the living being is itself included in the ensemble of transductive relationships that connect the different kinds of artificial and living organs (such as the brain) to the social organisations in which they evolve and transform" (Stiegler 2015b, 135–36). To give a complete account of how these relationships compose to form political problems, I first unpack how Stiegler defines these regimes of individuation.

Technical individuation is best understood in relation to Stiegler's conception of the technical dynamic. The dynamic of technical development is co-constitutive with, rather than constituted by, human agency. Technical individuation occurs through the re-functionalization and transformation of the pre-individual constraints established by preceding technical systems (Stiegler 1998, 35). Development and refinement of technical systems within these constraints engender the individuation of technical objects. This individuation can only occur within the specificities of particular social groups that characterize the pre-individual field that conditions technical individuation. The technical dynamic conditions the social while the social also influences the form that technical objects take: "none of the terms of the relation hold the secret of the other. This technical phenomenon is the relation of the human to its milieu" (Stiegler 1998, 49). Social individuation is constituted by the programmes, automatisms, and memories that orient a group's relationship to technical individuation and its broader environment, while technical individuation provides a pre-individual, determinate fund through which humanity codifies its experience: "The determinant technical tendency should be seen as the implementing of a calculation that, whether as a conscious modality or not, wants to determine the undetermined" (Stiegler 2009b, 77). By determining the undetermined, technics provides a pre-individual fund through which psychic individuals make sense of their experience, while technical development is itself conditioned by social individuation.

Stiegler gives a wide definition of this social appropriation and repetition of technical individuation. Social individuation refers to "families, clans or ethnicities, political institutions and societies, business and economic organizations, international organizations," encompassing "juridical, linguistic, religious, political, fiscal, [and] economic" realms (Stiegler 2010b, 34). These social organizations are shaped by technical tendencies, but they also support psychic individuation's repetition and individuation of a particular technical pre-individual milieu. Social individuation, then, is the development of "collective memory constituted by the *attentional forms of knowledge: knowhow, lifeskills, cognitive and theoretical knowledges*." These kinds of knowledge condition "forms that automate, ritualise, repeat and develop habits, in turn forming a *habitus* that constitutes the politeness and civility that is the essential basis of all relations" (Stiegler 2012d, 2–3). Social and technical individuation are transductively related because technical individuation conditions the forms that collective individuation can take, while collective individuation conditions habits that inform the individuation of technical objects.

Stiegler's use of the concepts of repetition and habit also informs his understanding of biological individuation insofar as they displace biological determinism in human behavior. Stiegler's criticism of such determinism with respect to the human is present from his earliest work.[12] Before the development of organology, he expresses this dissatisfaction in terms of a distinction between "heredity" and "heritage" to claim that a Darwinian perspective that focuses on genetic heredity alone cannot come to terms with the intertwinement of the genetic with the epiphylogenetic (Stiegler 1996, 107–8). After he develops the concept of organology, this reticence is expressed in the claim that "natural selection gives way to artificial selection," which "may derive from Darwin" but "must be redefined in relation to the organological context" (Stiegler 2018c, 41). Stiegler's claim here is not that the human escapes biological individuation, but that biological individuation occurs in a transductive relationship with technical and social forms of individuation. This "*localizes* biological constraints" with reference to "techno-logical . . . constraints and possibilities" (Stiegler 2020d, 74). Consequently, "there is no break in the strict sense between the animal and the human." Rather, this organological transductive relationship constitutes "a change in the regime of individuation" (Stiegler 2020d, 87). For the non-inhuman, the transductive relationship between an organism and its milieu is mediated by technical and social individuation.

The most common example Stiegler gives when making this claim is the human brain. From the organological perspective, the brain is a biological organ that develops by way of its internalization of social and technical individuation processes, rather than an isolated organ that has a strict, genetically determined path of development. Stiegler gestures toward research on neuronal plasticity to make this claim, particularly work that argues that the unfolding of the brain's genetic programme occurs through a relationship to epigenetic experience, and for the human, its technical supports (Stiegler 2010e, 74–75; 2018c, 88). He defines the brain as "*a relational organ that plastically internalizes social relational systems, systems that are themselves supported by . . . things, objects and artefacts*" (Stiegler 2013f, 66). Drawing on the work of Stanislas Dehaene (2009) and Maryanne Wolf (2008), he develops this claim with explicit reference to the epigenetic plasticity exhibited by the brain when it learns. Writing actualizes the genetic potential of the human by producing synaptic circuits through the repetition and interiorization of a particular technical practice, the technique of writing itself, and a particular social milieu, language, and established genres and forms of writing (Stiegler 2010c, 167; 2013a, 55; 2014a, 193–94; 2018c, 86–87). Within general organology, all human activities are formed by similar transductive relationships between biological, social, and technical individuation.

To establish the significance of this claim, I now briefly consider the relationship between Stiegler's and Catherine Malabou's uses of the concepts of plasticity and epigenesis. Malabou shares with Stiegler a commitment to reconsidering the transcendental as the product of history, and she uses contemporary neuroscience to explain the functioning of transcendental schema in terms of plasticity (2008) and epigenesis (2016). Malabou draws on the work of Jean-Pierre Changeux, whom Stiegler also refers to, to support the claim that the link between the brain and the transcendental should be conceptualized with reference to epigenesis. Changeux argues that the brain is not subject to strict genetic determination alone and that it instead develops according to "processes of another type, of an 'epigenetic nature,' that make possible a strong alliance of genes and experience in the construction of cerebral complexity" (Changeux 2007, 14 cited in Stiegler 2018b, 89). Malabou develops this position into the argument that the brain and social organizations "mutually give each other form" (Malabou 2008, 9), and therefore that the transcendental conditions of experience are both biological and social. Stiegler, by contrast, concludes that this co-constitution of the neurological, the transcendental, and the social requires the support of technicity. It is this essential role that Stiegler gives technicity within human epigenesis that distinguishes him from Malabou's understanding of plasticity and epigenetics (G. Moore 2017, 199–201).

Because of this difference, Stiegler accuses Malabou of neurocentrism, for he claims that from the organological perspective, Malabou's philosophy focuses on the brain to the neglect of technicity (Stiegler 2018c, 255–56; 2019d, 257). This critique is somewhat misled. As Ian James has noted, both Malabou and Stiegler derive their philosophical problems from "an absence of ontological ground" shared between both philosophy and science (James 2019b, 218), insofar as they are motivated by the consequences of the concepts of plasticity and epigenesis for non-totalizing conceptions of the human and of the transcendental. Where they differ is with respect to their focus on the sciences of the brain and their relationship to the environment in general, in the case of Malabou, or the brain in the context of a wider philosophy of technicity, in the case of Stiegler. With this in mind, Stiegler may be subjected to an inversion of his criticism of Malabou: that he focuses on the technical to the expense of extensive engagement with the science underpinning plasticity and epigenesis (James 2013). One can also note that Malabou refuses to treat the brain as an isolated organ and cannot, therefore, be considered to be neurocentrist (Hansen 2017, 187–89). If this is the case, then both Malabou and Stiegler could be considered as a-transcendental thinkers.

Such a possibility renders Stiegler's prioritization of technicity within his version of this post-ontological project in stark relief. The place of the brain within organology clarifies his conception of the a-transcendental insofar as it represents an attempt to short-circuit philosophical autonomy with respect to technical conditions. Any philosophical consideration of the problems faced by the human is situated within an organological context, and, from Stiegler's perspective, to suggest otherwise would be to posit a principle that somehow transcends this transductive relationship to technicity. Instead, organology focuses on the "defunctionalizations and refunctionalizations that determine the rhythm of the organological genealogy of the sensible and of what lies coiled up there—the intellect and the unity of its reasons, its motivations" (Stiegler 2017f, 17). Organology is thus seen by Stiegler as the condition of pharmacological analysis because of this integration of the technical object with its biological and social counterparts (Stiegler 2018c, 53–54; 2020d, 73). This leads to two questions central for understanding the dynamic relationship between organology, philosophy, and politics. First, what ensures that the relationship between organology and conceptual invention is dynamic and not static? Second, what is the specific relationship between organology and political concepts? The final section and conclusion of this chapter addresses each of these questions in turn.

Automatisms, Repetition, and the A-Transcendental

I have argued thus far that Stiegler's work represents an attempt to reconcile totalization with non-totalizing conceptions of politics. At this point of my account of organology, however, it is not entirely clear how these two terms are reconciled. On the one hand, the term refers to the intertwinement of three forms of individuation that, if taken as Simondon understands the concept of individuation, are connected by a transductive and indeterminate relationship to a pre-individual field. On the other hand, organological context seems to overdetermine the way that individuation occurs within a particular locality. I now turn to the concepts of automatism and repetition in order to imbue these localities with a recursive dynamism. Conceptual invention is not strictly determined by organological context but is facilitated by margins of indeterminacy—which Stiegler understands as the possibility for "dis-automation." By exploring this point, I show that the a-transcendental is not strictly determinist, and set the stage for a dynamic and recursive conception of the political.

Organology is a theory of both individuation and automatism. Within a process of individuation, automatisms, which exist in biological, psychic, and collective and technical forms, compose to form spontaneous and unreflective behaviors (Stiegler 2021b, 247). When Stiegler refers to general organology as a "genealogy of different regimes of individuation," he understands this in terms of the combination of automatisms and systems of repetition (Stiegler 2015a, 55). Repetition forms a particularly important part of Stiegler's theory here, for it is the repetition of social and collective knowledge, articulated and shared through technicity, that produces psychic individuation. Again, writing is a central example for Stiegler. The practice of repetition that constitutes the process of learning to read and write consists of "an internalization and externalization that require the acquisition of this competence as a *new automatism written into the cerebral organ through learning*" that allows individuals to "*access the consistences* that theoretical knowledge forms, and *thereby dis-automatize* automatic behaviours, whether biological, psychic or social" (Stiegler 2016a, 57). Here Stiegler integrates two apparently opposed terms, automation and dis-automation, with access to consistences. How can the totalization of automation be reconciled with the non-totalizable nature of consistences?

Stiegler returns to Deleuze here to think automation as the condition of dis-automation, in a manner that also draws closely on Simondon. As seen above, Simondon argues that every process of individuation requires a margin of indeterminacy to begin—a moment of unpredictable disindividuation occurs prior to all individuation. Because of this margin of indeterminacy, the repetition of automatisms is inexact. In *States of Shock*, Stiegler adopts this Deleuzian understanding of repetition, where he argues that "repetition" represents "a pharmacological field of possibility." He continues to state that "the individuation that is the history of the psychic apparatus—constituted through the sedimentation of experience—is here in some way a pharmacological linkage of repetitions, which are chains as well as unchainings" (Stiegler 2015a, 69–70). Here Stiegler interprets a passage from *Difference and Repetition* where Deleuze states that "if we die of repetition we are also saved and healed by it—healed, above all, by the other repetition. The whole mystical game of loss and salvation is therefore contained in repetition, along with the whole theatrical game of life and death and the whole positive game of illness and health" (Deleuze 1994, 6). Deleuze describes here what he takes to be the condition of a problem, the potential for difference within a particular form of repetition, which Stiegler understands "essentially as a pharmacological question" (Stiegler 2021b, 247). Repetition is the condition of individuation and dis-automation, the shaking off of existing habits and automatisms to respond to pharmacological problems. Equally, it can reinforce existing automatisms and perpetuate the stupidity and disindividuation that are, paradoxically, also the condition of individuation.

It is now possible to clarify how automatism and repetition contribute to the definition of the a-transcendental. Hui provides perhaps the most astute reading of this dimension of Stiegler's thought when he interprets repetition in terms of recursivity. Hui states that "Contingency for him is the quasi-cause, while recursivity often takes the name repetition" (Hui 2019, 201). Hui's translation of the language of quasi-causality and repetition into contingency and recursivity highlights the relationship between the indeterminacy that begins a process of individuation and the pre-individual conditions of future individuation. By incorporating a chance moment into its process of individuation, a psychic individual integrates it within the repetitive automatisms that form the pre-individual fund of its own individuation, which transductively influences the individuation of the collective that it constitutes along with other psychic individuals. It is in this way that an a-transcendental horizon is formed by the recursive integration of quasi-causes into the condition of future individuation. In Hui's words: "The exteriorization of memory in technical objects is also when the *posteriori* becomes *a priori*. This becoming is a transition from the empirical toward the a-transcendental—a-transcendental because it is neither purely transcendental nor empirical" (Hui 2019, 202).

Non-totalization is the condition of totalizing conceptual schemes because the quasi-cause is the root of individuation that engenders conceptual novelty, while totalization is simultaneously the condition of conceptual invention because it forms a pre-individual field of recursively generated a priori conditions that underpin psychic and collective individuation. Repetition plays two key roles here. First, it constitutes the transcendental, totalizing, and a priori conditions of thought by externalizing individual experience in technical forms, which are then reinternalized through further repetition by other individuals. For Stiegler, this repetition forms the condition of the experience of the world: "From the organological perspective . . . the schematism originally comes from technical exteriorization and the artefactualization of the world as the condition of the constitution of the world, that is, as condition of the projection in the world of concepts *constituting the given data of intuition*" (Stiegler 2020a, 42). Second, repetition enables the differentiation and transformation of these a priori conditions by enabling the incorporation of a posteriori modifications into the pre-individual field: "Repetition redoubles and 'appropriates' the effects of a technical tendency that is already realized, as already there, beforehand; through its redoubling, it frees new, unrealized, possibilities of the tendency" (Stiegler 2009b, 95). Conceptual invention, then, begins from a particular organological context but must by necessity transform it "*by expanding the experience of individuation beyond all calculation*" (Stiegler 2016a, 57).

Here the importance of the a-transcendental for combining totalization with a non-totalizing philosophical position is clear. Openness is conditioned by the closure engendered by the concepts that guide a particular process of psychic and collective individuation, but this closure is itself a product of the non-totalizable repetition of organological locality. In his last works, Stiegler developed the language of the exorganism to explore this conditionality. An exorganism, or an "exosomatic organism," is an organism that pursues its existence through the organological composition of biological, social, and technical individuation. Simple exorganisms consist of individuals—a particular psychic individual, for example—whereas complex exorganisms consist of "a collection of simple exorganisms sharing common exosomatic organs, such as a family, a workshop, a city, or a country" (Stiegler 2020a, 286). These complex exorganisms that regulate the operation of simple exorganisms are then subject to hierarchies and layers of complexity. For example, the conditions of a particular family regulate the life of its members while also being subject to the more complex exorganisms constituted by the state. These higher, superior complex exorganisms give meaning to and direct the relationship between lower complex exorganisms and simple exorganisms, directing and shaping locality while also being open to future individuation through these local repetitions (Stiegler 2020c, 269).

The nested nature of individuation takes on great importance here. Individuation of simple exorganisms is regulated by the a priori conditions of lower and superior complex exorganisms, but the individuation of these larger exorganisms is itself constituted by the multiplicity of transindividuation processes that they encompass. If "technical individuation, which is the process of exosomatization, must be observed as the exorganogenesis of artificial organs forming a system through complex exorganisms," then "we must posit that *it is never possible to start simply from the point of view of the simple exorganism*, and that thinking and healing exosomatic individuation always supposes *locating simple exorganisms in the multiple and heterogeneous movements and dynamics provoked and established by complex exorganisms*, these multiplicities and heterogeneities being *internalized by simple exorganisms*" (Stiegler 2018a, 81–82). While the language of the exorganism appears in the last phase of Stiegler's work and is adopted from the writings of Alfred Lotka and Nicholas Georgescu-Roegen (both of whom I return to in chapter 7), this integration of the various levels of exorganisms develops the concept of the idiotext that is present from some of Stiegler's earliest writings.[13] The "idiotext" is defined by Stiegler as "an open locality taken up within another, greater locality, or within what I describe as nested spirals as they co-produce a process of collective individuation by psychically individuating themselves" (Stiegler 2018c, 55). An idiom is the condition of a particular individuation subject to the *différance* that Stiegler understands as constituting the open nature of individuation in general, because of its participation in multiple scales at once, such as the family, the nation, or the global biosphere that conditions life.

These idioms and their exorganological conditions carry a heavy epistemological weight within the philosophy of technics, particularly with regard to the status of philosophical concepts. Concepts do not interpret the real so much as define it through active intervention and engagement with local, idiomatic conditions of individuation. Stiegler develops this claim by drawing on the work of Gaston Bachelard, whom he associates with the scaled constitution of knowledge across simple and complex exorganisms (Stiegler 2018a, 261). In *The New Scientific Spirit*, Bachelard argued that scientific developments of the early twentieth century, in particular those of quantum physics, revealed that the construction of scientific findings by scientific apparatuses undercuts the appeal to an observer-independent reality. Bachelard writes: "A truly scientific phenomenology is . . . essentially a phenomeno-technology. Its purpose is to amplify what is revealed beyond appearance. It takes its instruction from construction" (Bachelard 1984, 13). The real presented by science, for Bachelard, is produced by the phenomeno-techniques found in scientific methodology and instruments and is inextricable from the way they constitute knowledge. He claims that "to establish a scientific fact, it is necessary to implement a coherent technique. . . . Innate truths naturally have no place in science. Reason has to be shaped in the same way as experience" (Bachelard 1984, 171). Both the wave-particle duality, discussed above, and Niels Bohr's complementarity principle are central influences for Bachelard here, as in both cases the observed object is actively constituted by its measurement (Chimisso 2008, 388–90). The concept of the phenomeno-technique declares that scientific knowledge is not of a distinct object, but of an active relationship mediated by methods, techniques, and concepts that constitute both the observer and the observed.

Bachelard's claim here is that science pursues truth through a gradual construction of metastable techniques for rendering its objective perceivable. As Stiegler highlights, these techniques facilitate the repetition of a particular form of experience by formalizing its conditions. New knowledge, for

Bachelard, requires the disruption of existing techniques for constituting scientific knowledge. Like Simondon, he argued that transformation of these phenomenotechniques "requires a perturbation of the system" (Bardin 2015, 24). While this is observable in the context of quantum physics in which effects like complementarity upended assumptions about the independence of observation because of the interference of instruments within measurement, all scientific knowledge is conditioned by conceptual frameworks, mediated by the written word, that shape observation and that can be disrupted by new assumptions (Stiegler 2008a, 73–74). Textual idioms of science are as much phenomenotechniques as microscopes or large hadron colliders. Stiegler takes this point and applies it to knowledge in general. He sees himself as pursuing "what Derrida called a *history of the supplement*, but understood from the Bachelardian perspective of *phenomenotechnics*" (Stiegler 2016a, 234). By integrating his reading of *différance*, and therefore his understanding of Simondonian individuation, with Bachelard's conception of the phe-nomenotechnique, Stiegler claims that all conceptual knowledge formalizes the real by engaging with it within a transductive relation, constituted by moments of disindividuation. In Stiegler's words: "Reproducibility always contains an element of transformation regarding what it reproduces. If we were to imagine that *to describe* is to *reproduce*, the result would be that a description would *always* also be a transformation: there is no such thing as constantivity; there is always, in some respect, performativity" (Stiegler 2011c, 218). Organology, and the extension of general organology by complex exorganisms that link individual, simple exorganisms, is the study of how phenomenotechniques constitute both the observer and the observed across a history of changing transductive relations (Stiegler 2012d, 15; 2020a, 218). All concepts are situated within this interplay between the stability of local frames of knowledge and their disruption.

Stiegler's reconciliation of totalization with non-totalization can be seen quite clearly here in his use of Bachelard to facilitate this post-ontological understanding of knowledge. Concepts are constructed by, and represent a dynamic elaboration of, their conditions insofar as they are engendered by the disindividuation of established organological and exorganological automatisms, and they contribute to the ongoing production of these a priori structures by dis-automating them. We have traveled a long way from Simondon's original text; however, here Stiegler is very close to the spirit of his thought. Simondon argues that "ontogenesis is prior to any critique of knowledge. Ontogenesis precedes ontology and critique." Consequently, "it is impossible for the human subject to witness its own genesis" (Simondon

2020, 319). Similarly, for Stiegler knowledge occurs within a particular process of individuation and is constituted by its organological, exorganological, and idiomatic conditions. Ontology can only account for these conditions within the constraints of a pre-individual set of tensions and problems. No single ontology can generate explanations of the unpredictable and singular genesis of a new process of individuation in response to the pharmacological problem of disindividuation. Speaking of Bachelard's concept of the phenomenotechnique as that which facilitates the repetition of experience, Stiegler asks: "What links *scientific* experience, which is instrumental in the most general way, to *historical* experience—that is to say, to *politics* as the experience of the historical *passage* of time?" (Stiegler 2013c, 277). Stiegler's answer to this question is the technical object. Any single ontology is a phenomenotechnique that constructs knowledge of being from a particular, technically constituted locality rather than an exhaustive account of being.

In Stiegler's last work, he claimed that any epistemology that does not consider this role of locality within the constitution of knowledge would be "purely and simply vain" (Stiegler 2020c, 95). While I do not want to pursue the polemic implied by this allegation of vanity, if this refers to the conflation of one's local reflections for universal judgments, then this claim can be seen to constitute a third limit to political ontology in addition to the limits articulated in chapters 1 and 2. Despite their non-totalizing intentions, post-foundational political ontologies are constituted within the a priori limits of what counts as a political concept, themselves a product of the a posteriori development of a particular process of individuation, framed by a set of phenomenotechniques. They are constitutively incapable, like all concepts, of fully accounting for the construction of the real in other local contexts. Moreover, the autonomy represented by dis-automation that disrupts these contexts is irreducible to ontological explanation because it upends its conditions in an unpredictable and indeterminate manner. This dis-automation requires a set of totalizing circumstances that limit concepts, which nevertheless have openness as their very condition. In Simondon's words, a process of individuation is "a calling into question of the being, i.e. as an *element of an open problematic*, which is what the being's individuation resolves" (Simondon 2020, 364). Individuation is central to Stiegler's reconciliation of totalization and non-totalization insofar as it allows him to redefine the non-inhuman as part of the ongoing resolution of a problematic field, itself constituted by the transductive relationship between biological, social, and technical organs. It is in this sense that a-transcendental conditions both determine the nature of the non-inhuman while remaining open to dynamic and recursive alteration, putting them beyond exhaustion by the speculation of political ontology.

Conclusion: The Conditionality of the Political

What, then, constitutes a distinctively political concept within these dynamic and ongoing processes of transindividuation? This question is particularly pressing, as my reading of Simondon has led to the consolidation of Stiegler's understanding of the organological and idiomatic conditions of concepts with Bachelard's local and phenomenotechnical account of scientific knowledge. Most simply, Stiegler argues that "politics is above all the motivation and organization of a psychic and collective individuation process" (Stiegler 2011a, 17). This does not provide much in the way of definition, however, for in the above I suggested that individuation is situated within organological and exorganological categories and criteria that form its pre-individual conditions. All concepts, in some way, guide a process of psychic and collective individuation. Instead, we might add to this definition that politics motivates and guides a process of individuation by responding to the pharmacological problems unique to that locality. The concept of repetition introduced here extends the two pharmacological tendencies toward stupidity and the quasi-cause that were introduced in chapter 2. In its curative forms, repetition provides the opportunity to transform and contribute to an ongoing process of transindividuation through dis-automation. In its poisonous form, "repetition (which Derrida also called 'iteration') no longer produces either *différance* in Derrida's sense, or difference in Deleuze's sense" (Stiegler 2018c, 209). Politics here is the attempt to produce forms of repetition within the context of a particular pharmacological problematic by generating criteria that guide engagement with automatisms in a way that allows an open engagement with a totalizing set of pre-individual conditions. Hence, "The prescription of such criteria is called politics" (Stiegler 2020a, 38).

Stiegler's own political concerns addressed the eradication of this space for pharmacologically curative forms of repetition that he saw as the consequence of the spread of algorithmic calculation in the twenty-first century. I return to this political problematic and the judgments he articulates in response to it in chapters 4 and 7. For now, we can summarize that his concern with automation arose from his attempt to reconcile totalization and non-totalization within his organological and pharmacological conception of the political. A worldview constituted by the presuppositions that human activity can be subjected to calculation and that the determination of behavior can be extended as far as possible is pharmacologically poisonous insofar as it conceives of behavior in terms of a predictable form of repetition. Here humans are automatisms, as Stiegler himself claims, but not automatisms constituted by the ongoing recursive and indeterminate alteration of repetitive behavior. Algorithmic governance constitutes a form of automatism that narrows the space for non-totalizable forms of individuation from a set of pre-individual conditions. It is this form of totalization without openness that Stiegler sought to combat through a reconception of totalization as reconcilable with non-totalization.

Understood in this way, the political cannot be defined in a way that transcends the pharmacological tendencies of the particular process of individuation in which it is situated. Stiegler's post-ontological reading of Simondon allows him to conceive of human behavior as formed by a set of a priori pre-individual conditions that are recursively structured and altered by a posteriori engagement with those conditions. The explanatory power of all political concepts is curtailed by these limits, insofar as they totalize a particular set of organological conditions without exhausting the nature of politics. If "the political element is integrally organological" then "there is no 'natural element' of the political—'natural law' is a fiction" (Stiegler 2010e, 86). Simondon's work is central to Stiegler's establishment of this position because it allows him to conceive of political concepts as metastable resolutions of a particular set of pharmacological problems that encourage the ongoing and idiomatic transformation of a locality. Political ontology finds its third limit here, as it cannot account for the political in terms that transcend these conditions precisely because it is articulated from within a particular process of psychic and collective individuation. It may illuminate a particular political problem, but not the political as such. The problematic guiding the last three chapters of this book concerns the fidelity that Stiegler pays to these methodological constraints derived from Simondon and that he develops in the concept of organology. For now, the question open at this point, and to which I turn in chapter 4, is how non-inhumans become attached to and incorporate the idealities supported by these transindividuation processes into their psychic individuation. In the above, Stiegler takes it for granted somewhat that psychic individuals will do so. It is to a post-ontological theory of desire that he turns to respond to this challenge.

4

Libidinal Economy and Proletarianization

One consequence that has become clear in my account of Stiegler's critique of totalization is that he claims the human is a fiction. These fictions are not meaningless or inconsequential, for they allow us to act in the world and give meaning to it. Said more strongly, we actively desire these fictions. If Stiegler aims to replace transcendental understandings of the human with an a-transcendental philosophy, then he must account for the role that desire plays in facilitating the pursuit of these non-inhuman fictions. In this chapter I introduce the theory of libidinal economy that Stiegler uses to conceptualize our attachment to such images and argue that it should be understood in terms of the reconciliation of the critique of totalization with the need for totalizing fictions. This account of libidinal economy revolves around the pharmacological balance between openness and closure within the relationship between desire and technics, and the consequent possibility for the destruction of desire by totalization. As such, here I begin to more extensively consider the political stakes of totalization within Stiegler's work.

Libidinal economy is crucial to Stiegler's political interventions from the early 2000s onward (Hansen 2017, 171), as it underpins his critique of contemporary capitalism's relationship to desire (e.g., de Beistegui 2013; G. Moore 2018; Roberts 2013). However, it also takes on a fundamental role within the philosophy of technics (Bishop and Ross 2021, 129–30; Hörl 2014; Espinoza 2013; Hughes 2014; Voela and Rothschild 2019). One key idea underpins the role of desire in both of these elements of Stiegler's thought: the default of origin requires fictions that are desirable to make up for its lack of meaning. Stiegler attempts to account for the formation of desire within totalizing, historical, and organological conditions while maintaining that it is incalculable because of its relationship to the default. I argue that this claim constitutes a fourth limit to political ontology. The politics of desire cannot be explained in the totalizing terms of ontology because of its historical nature, and, unlike suggestions that an ontological conception of desire preexists or needs emancipating from totalizing constraints, it requires totalization to give meaning to individuation.

Desire's relationship to totalization presented an urgent problem for Stiegler under the conditions of twenty-first-century capitalism, in which desire, the infinite and the incalculable, are subordinated to, rather than co-constitutive with, their opposite, the finite, the calculable, and the totalizing. Here Stiegler concurs with those within the poststructuralist tradition who associate totalizing conceptions of desire with domination, such as Michel Foucault, Gilles Deleuze, and Félix Guattari. Unlike these thinkers, however, Stiegler does not oppose desire to the totalizing tendencies of authority that constrain its multiplicity because he claims that desire is produced by totalizing fictions. Desire is not constrained or dominated by capitalism so much as destroyed by its reliance on a pharmacologically poisonous form of totalization. Here the limit to ontological conceptions of desire lies in their inability to account for its political stakes, insofar as they conceive them in terms of liberation rather than the securing of pharmacologically curative forms of totalization. The fourth limit to political ontology is found in its reliance on a political ground or force that is constrained by totalization and that would precede technicity. However, I also ask whether the theory of desire that Stiegler develops to make this claim successfully balances totalization and openness. By answering this question in the negative, I suggest that Stiegler's account of libidinal economy rests on the association of a set of local problems with an apparently universal politics of desire.

To make this case, I begin with an overview of Stiegler's understanding of desire. Psychoanalysis is present in much of his work but is not articulated in a single, extended analysis (Voela and Rothschild 2019, 55). A key task for this chapter, therefore, is a reconstruction of Stiegler's fragmented discussions of desire. I first introduce his rejection of a-historical ontologies of desire, found primarily in his critique of Herbert Marcuse. The chapter then, second, introduces the components of Stiegler's theory of libidinal economy that are adapted from Sigmund Freud and Donald Winnicott: the distinction between drives and desire, sublimation and its relationship to the super-ego, primordial narcissism, and the transitional object. While Stiegler shares some of the concerns of Freud in his use of psychoanalytic concepts (Featherstone 2020), his development of the Freudian corpus is not characterized by fidelity, or indeed by extended readings of Freud's work. Across this chapter I reconstruct Stiegler's scattered discussions of psychoanalytic concepts around the central point that they are mediated by technicity. I then, third, introduce Stiegler's critique of the relationship between capitalism and desire. This rests on the argument that capitalism totalizes and destroys desire by channeling human behavior toward consumption in a calculable and predictable way. This claim signals the political stakes of Stiegler's differentiation of his understanding of desire as produced from an ontological and productive conception of desire. Finally, the chapter introduces and critically considers Stiegler's account of desire's relationship to knowledge as expressed within the concept of proletarianization. Proletarianization destroys desire by externalizing knowledge without the opportunity to re-interiorize and transform it, a tendency that Stiegler argues is exacerbated by the rise of automation and calculation within contemporary capitalism. Like fictional conceptions of the human, knowledge must be open and incalculable to be desirable.

Despite his intentions, I argue that Stiegler's account of proletarianization totalizes the space of politics without accounting for the need for this openness, as it neglects the conditions in which individuals experience the destruction of desire outside the exteriorization of knowledge within capitalist consumer culture. Desire can be destroyed by power, violence, and coercion, and not just the automation of the technical foundations of knowledge. As a political problem, proletarianization presupposes a universal subject of the politics of desire who is imperiled by the loss of cultural and symbolic knowledge, which does not account for the destruction of desire by other, violent means. Stiegler's understanding of proletarianization universalizes a particular aspect of experience under contemporary capitalism—the control of symbolic, cultural, and theoretical knowledge—and reifies it to the extent that it excludes the possibility of accounting for other ways in which desire is destroyed. By introducing this tension, this chapter foregrounds the problematic addressed in the final three chapters of this book. Do Stiegler's political judgments hold to the balance between totalization and non-totalization that his philosophy advocates?

Desire without Ontology

Stiegler's theory of libidinal economy rests on the claim that it is the question of the origin that leads to the emergence of desire. Without the desire to ask questions about the origin, there would be no human individuation.

This point is made clear in *Acting Out*: "The question of the origin is what constitutes the whole of human individuation, that is, the whole of *desire*: the whole of human being insofar as it is *essentially* desiring" (Stiegler 2009a, 7). Because desire is formed by questions about the origin, it is also constituted by the empirical history that facilitates access to it. This condition of default means that it should be presumed within accounts of desire that "*the 'structural' is elementarily 'historical' and as such 'accidental,'* and is neither guided nor contained by any ontology that would make it possible to define the constitutive elements of the process" (Stiegler 2011b, 161). Ontology cannot explain desire precisely because it is constituted by the condition of ontological incompleteness represented by the default of origin. This point can be seen clearly in Stiegler's reading of Herbert Marcuse's *Eros and Civilization*. Stiegler praises Marcuse for attempting to present a genealogical understanding of Freudian psychoanalysis (Stiegler 2014b, 2). In Marcuse's account, Freudianism is taken to task for its neglect of how the reality principle—which aligns human instincts with the needs of a particular group, society, or culture—is modified alongside the historical variation of needs (Marcuse 1955, 37). Marcuse demonstrates how Freudian theory "treats as natural a situation that is in fact historical, and therefore contingent" (Stiegler 2014b, 43). The reality principle is not an a-historical component of psychanalysis, but a historical relationship to wider social conditions.

Despite his historicism, Marcuse perceived the mid-twentieth century as a potential turning point in the history of desire. While historically desire has been subject to repressive variants of the reality principle that redirect sexual energy toward work and production, Marcuse argued that the productive capacities of capitalism provided an opportunity for the construction of an alternate reality principle based on the fulfilment of pleasure. He claimed that the "historical possibility of a gradual decontrolling of the instinctual development must be taken seriously . . . if civilization is to progress to a higher stage of freedom" (Marcuse 1955, 134). Stiegler claims that this gradual decontrolling of instincts presupposes that the pleasure principle "*precedes its domination* by the reality principle" (Stiegler 2014b, 45). Marcuse contradicts his own rejection of a-historicism, as he claims that pleasure precedes and is imposed on by the reality principle and can be distinguished from the historical permutations of desire's constraints. The critique of Freudian ontology resolves into the positing of an equally a-historical foundation for desire. Stiegler's criticism of Marcuse here rests on his organological method. As a component of the biological dimension of organology, pleasure is formed in tandem with the expectations and constraints placed on it by a particular process of collective individuation. Pleasure and reality principles co-compose one another (Stiegler 2014b, 56). In contrast, Marcuse claims that animal drives are "inhibited" by their transformation into human desire (Marcuse 1955, 11–12). A transductive libidinal economy that rejects ontology cannot conceive of pleasure as "inhibited," as this claim necessitates an a-historical gesture. By failing to recognize this, Marcuse does not go far enough in rejecting ontology within psychoanalysis, as his understanding of pleasure exists outside the a-transcendental relationship to technics.

Two consequences that exist in tension with each other arise from the claim that ontology cannot account for the technical condition of desire. If any conception of desire is historical, for Stiegler it must be situated within a totalizing technical context. However, desire is irreducible to its technical context because it is formed within responses to the question of the default of origin that exceeds any local ontology. Desire follows a quasi-causal logic: it emerges from the reality principle of a particular locality but "*exceeds all calculation*" insofar as it aims at consistences (Stiegler 2020a, 14). The consistences that desire pursues engender provisional totalization, or a "*télos*," which guides psychic and collective individuation (Stiegler 2009c, 35). As Robert Hughes summarizes, these objects of desire transform becoming into a future: "For Stiegler, it is helpful to distinguish the future (*l'avenir*) from the actual to-come (*le devenir*). What will actually come to be is, of course, something that one's fantasies of the future must 'negotiate' with, but philosophically one must not confound the fantasized future with this actual to-come" (Hughes 2014, 48). Here the recursive structure of individuation returns within desire. Desire provides answers to the question of the origin, but these answers will never come to pass in reality as we expect. They are perpetually transformed by attempts to realize consistences. As Hughes continues, desire "sustains an openness as a pure future, even while it poses itself in thought as the anticipation of narrative completion" (Hughes 2014, 49). The impossibility of fulfilling these desires means that the "ideal beings of ontology must be replaced by infinite motives" that inform individuation (Stiegler 2013f, 34). Openness and totalization intermingle in this account of desire, as positing either pure totalization or pure openness would fall into the trap of ontology. That is, an a-historical and totalizing account of the psyche represented by Freudianism or an ontological account of liberated pleasure represented by Marcuse. I now turn to Stiegler's own theory of libidinal economy to explore how it balances both totalization and non-totalization.

Elements of a Technical Libidinal Economy

My reconstruction of Stiegler's theory of libidinal economy focuses on three components that link totalization with openness: the distinction between instinct, drive, and desire; sublimation and its relation to the super-ego; and the transitional object. Stiegler uses these concepts to develop the claim that drives are sublimated into desire by technically supported and totalizing institutions that form a collective super-ego, and that this process is mediated by transitional objects and spaces. While they totalize desire, these institutions are also recursively transformed by it precisely because they rest on fictions that determine their nature quasi-causally. To desire an idea is to transform it, because to desire is to individuate. This claim is the crux of Stiegler's rejection of ontological approaches to desire, as desire is formed within, rather than simply transformative of, this recursive relationship.

The distinction between instinct, drive, and desire is the key building block of Stiegler's theory of libidinal economy. Desire "is not merely crude instinct but rather the *always already social* interaction of drives" (Stiegler 2011a, 48). Here desire is distinguished from biological instinct by two modifications: the transformation of instincts into drives, and the socialization of drives into desire. Stiegler uses these transformations to argue that desire is the product of organological relationships, creating distance between desire and ontology. The transformation of instincts into drives is the first step in this process. Drives and instincts are both biological automatisms that underpin behavior; however, Stiegler distinguishes between them by adopting Freud's argument that, while the relationship between instincts and their objects cannot be deliberately modified, the drive has no essential connection to its object (Freud 1953, 148). Stiegler expresses this separation between drive and object in terms of the organological composition of technicity and life. Drives are automatisms that have been diverted from biological aims by technical conditions and can therefore be oriented toward other goals (Stiegler 2020a, 208). The origins of this technical reading of psychoanalysis is found in *Civilization and Its Discontents*, where Freud refers to the repurposing of biological functions as the origin of human society: "the first acts of civilization were the use of tools," and "with every tool man is perfecting his own organs" (Freud 1961, 90). Stiegler develops this point most clearly in the second volume of *Symbolic Misery*, where he argues that libidinal economy is constituted by "a series of functional exteriorizations and correlative defunctionalizations" (Stiegler 2015b, 120). The difference between instinct and drive arises from this originary refunctionalization of the sexual drives induced by technicity.

While drives can vary their objects, desire represents a new relationship to this refunctionalization. Stiegler distinguishes between drives and desire as, respectively, concerned with the finite and the infinite, and defines "*desire as the power to infinitize*" (Stiegler 2018c, 57). Drives strive to satisfy their needs by consuming their objects in as immediate a way as possible. Immediacy is unreachable, however, for drives presuppose the differentiation of their objects by technicity. Desire prolongs and extends this gap indefinitely by taking consistences as its object. Here Stiegler draws on Freud's claim that the primary function of the mind is to redirect sexual energy toward non-sexual goals (Freud 1989, 45). Stiegler's take on this claim is as follows: "If desire was nothing but sexuality, it would be only drive: sexuality is based in the drives. Sexed animals also have a sexuality. But it is desire, constitutive of the process of psychic and collective individuation as such, that binds the drives, that is, that denatures them" (Stiegler 2006c). Desire does not exist outside these constitutive transformations: it exists in a state of default, is subject to the undecidability of *différance*, and is beyond ontological codification.

This account of the transformation of drives into desire rests on two modifications to the economic model of the Freudian psyche. The first is that drives become desires because of the intervention of the technical object within the formation of the psychic apparatus (Stiegler 2015b, 44). Psychoanalysis presupposes technicity because idealization requires technical supports. While Freud tentatively moved toward this point in *Civilization and Its Discontents*, for Stiegler he did not integrate technicity into psychoanalysis in a substantive way (Stiegler 1996; 2018c, 94; 2015b, 151). This post-Freudian model of the exchanges of energy that form the psyche requires the acknowledgement that technics "*enables a transformation of the drive into an object investment*" (Stiegler 2020a, 239). It is this investment that produces engagement with consistences. Stiegler's second modification to Freud's economic model of the psyche concerns sublimation's relation to the social. Desire is produced not just by the transformation of energy within the psychic apparatus but also within the relationship to collective individuation. For Stiegler, objects of consistence arise "from the sublimation of the sexual—a sublimation that can only be established as the *social* circuit of a desire that is thus, from the beginning and consubstantially, psychosocial" (Stiegler 2015b, 96).[1] He associates this sublimation with the super-ego, which binds sexual drives into a sociable form: "desire is produced by that apparatus that transforms the drives into investments in objects, via binding systems that are at once super-egoic and sublimatory" (Stiegler 2011b, 156). For the Freud of *The Ego and the Id*, the super-ego takes "the form of a categorical imperative" that disciplines the energies of the psyche (Freud 1989, 31). The ego adjusts the drives to the demands of the reality principle, whereas the super-ego provides a set of ideal expectations for the ego to fulfil. If the super-ego is constituted by these idealities in Stiegler's reading of Freud, then "sublimation . . . lies at the very origin of the super-ego" because the ideal expectations of the super-ego take the form of collective consistences, which find their origin in the sublimation of drives in the form of desire (Stiegler 2014b, 15).

The logic of the default of origin is at work here. The super-ego presupposes sublimated drives, and sublimation requires direction from the super-ego. This aporia is used by Stiegler to situate the origin of the psyche within collective individuation: there can be no biological or ontological explanation of desire because it is produced by the social shaping of the super-ego. Objects idealized by the psyche are primarily social objects. Parents are idealized by infants, insofar as their presence is not perpetual, and this primary idealization constitutes the capacity to form ideal objects in general (Stiegler 2010e, 4; 2013b, 54). If idealizations of parents, and therefore the formation of the child's super-ego, occur within a technical system that supports the ideal objects of consistences, then the super-ego with which the child identifies in its earliest moments is always-already shaped by its context (Stiegler 2019d, 33). Hence, the production of the parent as ideal object reveals that "the *psyche* is an originarily social reality" (Stiegler 2011a, 48). Desire cannot be understood outside the process of transindividuation in which it is formed, or in which sublimation and the functioning of the super-ego occur, for it has no direct access to its origin.

Libidinal economy must give an account of this formation of desire within psychic and collective individuation, the results of which guide how individuals attach themselves to the idealizations of particular transindividuation processes. If this account of desire is part of a critique of totalization, several critical questions must be asked here. Is the super-ego not a totalizing concept? How can desire be associated with non-totalization if it is produced from a totalizing set of conditions? Openness can be brought back into this account by introducing the role of primordial narcissism within Stiegler's account of the super-ego. This seems to raise another problem, however. How can narcissism be reconciled with a collective model of the super-ego? This issue can be dissolved along with the totalizing image of the super-ego by recognizing that Stiegler's use of narcissism does not refer to self-absorption, but to the diachronic adoption of collective norms in individual form. Primordial narcissism refers to the singular interiorization of a collective horizon of individuation (Stiegler 2010e, 59). Narcissism distinguishes the individual from the idealizations of the *We* as it facilitates the transformation of collective consistences with which the individual identifies. The capacity to desire "*depends on primordial narcissism, and . . . this in turn depends on primordial diachrony*" (Stiegler 2009a, 64). Narcissism requires the individual reflect on itself insofar as it is distinct from any collective system of reference. This diachrony is necessary because "*the object of desire is always* a singularity" (Stiegler 2011a, 23). Totalizing, synchronic fictions that individuals identify with are transformed by diachronic processes of identification that produce consistences as singularities.

This diachrony is not opposed to synchrony. Primordial narcissism strengthens collective individuation by projecting the self onto the process of collective individuation, and by facilitating the recognition of oneself within the *We* (Stiegler 2009a, 40). Moreover, Stiegler argues that the *We* is also characterized by its own narcissistic requirement of "symbols, that is, auto-erotic fetishes, in which it can be reflected" (Stiegler 2009a, 48). Collective individuation rests on the narratives it weaves and the artefacts that reflect its stories and facilitate the identification of individuals with those fictions. The binding of individuals to a non-inhuman future occurs through this process of composition: "This desire to rejoin an original fusional milieu is *founded* in my primordial narcissism, that is, in the *intimate knowledge* that I am singular, *that I am not* the other. I *am* nothing but de-synchronized in relation to the other-in diachrony, the condition of harmony, just as in music, where one needs . . . several instruments or voices, or . . . several intervals forming a mode" (Stiegler 2009a, 64). Desire is formed by the binding of the drives by the regulations of the super-ego, which are, in the first instance, collective. However, one can only identify with these regulations if they are internalized in a diachronic and singular manner. Totalization forms desire but only on the condition that it can be transformed.

Technical objects mediate this relationship between the narcissisms of the *I* and the *We* insofar as they form a space that enables the transductive relationship between them. Stiegler adopts the concept of the transitional object from Winnicott to conceptualize this relationship. For Winnicott, transitional objects refer to an "intermediate area of experiencing" that facilitates psychological development in infants (Winnicott 2005, 3). Infants project the illusion onto these transitional objects, such as blankets or teddy bears, that they are part of themselves and that the world responds directly to their desires, which bridges the gap between their nascent psyche and externality. In time the transitional object itself is disenchanted, but the transitional space does not disappear. These spaces multiply and "spread out over the whole intermediate territory between 'inner psychic reality' and 'the external world as perceived by two persons in common.' that is to say, over the whole cultural field" (Winnicott 2005, 7). Transitional objects mediate the development of the infant, and then come to constitute our relationship with the external world. In *What Makes Life Worth Living*, Stiegler links the illusion that infants project onto the transitional object with consistences. The transitional "space opens up a relation to consistences, that is, to what does not exist but consists: a relation to what 'makes life worth living'" (Stiegler 2013f, 68). Primordial narcissism requires transitional objects that support these consistences, as they are "the means of falsification of the self as circuit, that is, of the self as a relation for which the transitional object is the mediating factor" (Stiegler 2013f, 71). As a transitional object, the technical object facilitates the identification with the shared consistences of a collective process of individuation and enables desire to be formed.

As is constant across Stiegler's philosophy of technics, the transitional object is characterized by two pharmacological tendencies. A healthy relationship to the transitional object can engender autonomy, understood by Stiegler as the adoption, internalization, and transformation of the ideal objects that it supports (Stiegler 2013c, 3). In contrast, poisonous relationships to transitional objects lead to unhealthy psychological states, an inability to detach oneself from transitional objects, and a failure to infinitize the ideal objects that the transitional space supports. These psychological states are associated with the drives, which cannot maintain a relationship of consistence with their objects. Here Stiegler associates desire and drives with the curative and poisonous dimensions of the *pharmakon*: "Technics, which thus pharmacologically constitutes the default insofar as it forms the horizon of desire, simultaneously opens two antagonistic yet inseparable paths: that of the drives, and that of sublimation" (Stiegler 2013c, 24). Drives are not only associated with the poisonous tendencies of the *pharmakon*; they are explicitly distinguished from sublimated desire.

The libidinal economies within which these two pharmacological tendencies compose are political insofar as Stiegler sees them as the staging ground for the articulation of the values that give meaning to individuation. In his words: "It is the libidinal economy . . . that constitutes the criteriologies characteristic of the ages, eras and epochs of exosomatization. As an economy of the drives, it produces collective protentions with respect to the future of what amounts, not just to a human species, but to a non-inhuman kind" (Stiegler 2019d, 275). These perspectives on the future are produced by the attachment to, and individuation of, consistences within the processes of primordial narcissism and sublimation. Desire's recursive identification with consistences mirrors the production of the concepts that guide a process of individuation. However, these contexts are also characterized by tendencies toward drive-based behaviors that do not maintain relationships of desire with their objects. These pharmacologically poisonous relationships to technical objects prevent the articulation of consistences that might guide the future of a process of collective individuation in an open and non-totalizing manner. I return to Stiegler's account of this problem in more depth below in his account of capitalism's relationship to desire; however, for now I summarize how his understanding of desire leads us to two points that concern the relationship between totalization and openness. First, his historical theory of libidinal economy presents desire as a non-inhuman capacity rather than a human one. It is for this reason that Stiegler integrates the principle of non-totalization into his theory of desire while also attempting to account for our need to attach ourselves to totalizing consistences. Desire combines the determinacy of a particular tradition and sublimation process with the indeterminacy of the individuation of the ideal objects that characterize that locality. Second, this balance between openness and closure is fragile. At times, the social integration that desire promises fails to materialize because of the pharmacological status of the objects that mediate its production. Drives can be unbound with destructive consequences: "*the regression in which . . . the unbinding of the drives consists is always not only possible but imminent* for the non-inhuman being" (Stiegler 2016a, 46). This possibility of the failure of the binding of the drives entails that the political significance of desire cannot be articulated in ontological, or purely totalizing, terms. For Stiegler, it is engagement with totalizing institutions that produces both desire and the transformation of those institutions. In contrast, some social organizations enforce a totalizing conception of human motivations without the opportunity for transformation that desire represents. This is the accusation that Stiegler levels at contemporary capitalism.

Capitalism and the Destruction of Desire

This critique rests on Stiegler's claim that capitalism functions by soliciting drive-based behavior and by subjecting it to totalizing calculation to ensure the creation of profit. A libidinal economy cannot function without a relationship to the undetermined. Capitalism's incessant need to promote growth and capture profit presupposes the eradication of the indeterminate, as the incalculable does not guarantee profitable activity. Here Stiegler holds to Marx's argument regarding the tendency of the rate of profit to fall (Beardsworth 2010, 187), but he also claims that the critique of political economy must be reconstituted with reference to Freudian libidinal economy and the philosophy of technics (Stiegler 2010b; 2020a, 27).[2] Stiegler argues that in the twentieth century, capitalism counteracted the tendency of the rate of profit to fall by its appeal to the desires of consumers. However, because consumption is concerned with the finite, such an appeal can only be made to the drives, which has the unintended effect of undermining and destroying the processes that form the desires on which all social systems rest. Thus, in response to the falling rate of profit, "marketing was forced to *directly* solicit and exploit the drives—being incapable of capturing desires that *no longer exist* because, *all their objects* having been turned into *ready-made commodities*, they *no longer consist*" (Stiegler 2016a, 34). The logic of calculable returns replaces the indeterminacy of the identification that forms desire.

Stiegler claims that this process has two components. The first is a pathological relationship between capitalism and belief. For Stiegler, belief rests on the structural incompleteness of its objects. One cannot believe in something certain, for this would no longer be belief. While he does not condemn calculation in itself, Stiegler nevertheless argues that within capitalism, belief is reduced to trust understood as calculation. Trust refers to the elimination of uncertainty in contrast to a belief in something despite uncertainty, a relationship that "destroys all *possibility of believing*: all possibility of believing in the indetermination of the future" (Stiegler 2011a, 45). Attachment to consistences becomes impossible in such a situation because consistences worth desiring are incalculable: "Precisely because reason is a *motive*, which is to say, an object of desire, and not just a consequence of the present, these anticipations cannot consist simply of calculations. To put it differently, anticipation is anticipation of the improbable, of a singularity, the unanticipatable, or again: the incalculable" (Stiegler 2015b, 51). Desire can only be formed if its objects are incalculable, yet capitalism destroys belief by trying to secure returns on its investments through extending calculation as far as possible.

The second component of capitalism's regression of desire into drives is the production of calculable behavior by intervening within the identification processes that form the psyche. Stiegler argues that desire is formed across intergenerational processes of primary identification that are "the condition of access to the superego" (Stiegler 2010e, 4). However, capitalism requires the diversion of attention and identification away from intergenerational processes and toward consumption, which replaces parental and social relationships with the objects of the culture industry: television, films, and social media.[3] These objects substitute the "transgenerational superego . . . with an *attentional control*—that in fact, unfortunately, creates only channel surfing and loss of all authority, of any generalized individuation on the psychic or social level" (Stiegler 2010e, 9). Investment in the objects of belief that both primary and secondary identification require is replaced by the redirection of attention toward calculated and homogenized cultural products in which identification occurs through short circuits of individuation. A short circuit is distinguished from a long circuit of individuation insofar as the latter enables primordial narcissism and facilitates the sublimation of collective consistences, whereas the former exploits desire by rendering it predictable in the form of the drives. If "long circuits connect or bind the drives that are disconnected or unbound by short-circuits," then capitalism systemically short-circuits desire by soliciting subsistence-based behavior that requires immediate gratification (Stiegler 2013f, 25). This logic underpins Stiegler's claim that the "harnessing of libidinal energy leads to its destruction," as "it submits to calculation that which, as object of desire, is only constituted through becoming infinitized, that is, through surpassing all calculation" (Stiegler 2010b, 82). Drives are unbound by this totalizing integration of calculation into all aspects of life.

Stiegler sees this account of capitalism's impact on desire as an extension of Deleuze's control society thesis. For Deleuze, governance through control replaces Foucault's disciplinary hypothesis. Individuals are no longer disciplined into particular behaviors or patterns through confinement within discrete spaces, such as the hospital, the school, or the prison. Under the logic of control, individual behavior is constantly adjusted and modulated by market forces that operate analogically across a range of different spaces (Deleuze 1995, 178–79). The discrete totalization of the individual within the confined spaces of discipline is superseded by constant modulation of the constitutive components of individuality. As Iain Mackenzie and Robert Porter put it, "dividuation" treats individuals as bundles of elements, interests, and drives that can be appealed to by multiple institutions at once, "tending towards total absorption with the technological mechanisms of control" (MacKenzie and Porter 2021, 238). In his adoption of the control society thesis, Stiegler emphasizes the role of marketing as that which reduces individuals to dividuals by soliciting drives in a way that does not allow them to be bound as desire within a single process of individuation. Marketing demands that social structures and individual lives should be constantly adjusted to allow for the maximization of profit, which leads to "*the 'flexibilization' of all social structures . . . in which all existence and all consistence are reduced to the imperative to produce and circulate subsistences*" (Stiegler 2013b, 26–27). In societies of control, identification is subsumed within marketization, which destroys desire by preventing the infinitizing of ideal objects that are irreducible to constant modulation.

The methods by which capitalism seeks to exploit drives by subjecting them to the modulating powers of control have developed since Deleuze's initial considerations of control societies in 1990. In Stiegler's earliest mentions of control societies, he is largely concerned with the ability of audiovisual technologies to capture attention and destroy primordial narcissism (e.g., Stiegler 2010e, 9; 2013b, 7; 2014e, 83–84; 2015b, 9). In later works, particularly in *Automatic Society*, he argues that this system of audiovisual control has been superseded by a form of algorithmic governance. Algorithmic control functionally integrates data from consumers with the capacity to compute how to best construct personalized profiles on which future appeals to individuals can be based. This faux-personalization rests on "*formalizable and calculable* correlations" rather than the individuation of ideal objects (Stiegler 2016a, 110). The goal of such a system is the production of behavioral automatisms and forms of repetition that are predictable and profitable. Here the importance of Stiegler's adoption of Freud's distinction between drive and desire for his critique of capitalism is clear. Control seeks to "function on autopilot" by exploiting drive-based automatisms that guide subsistence, whereas desire dis-automates such automatisms and is irreducible to the correlations of algorithmic causality (Stiegler 2016a, 114). A totalizing system that does not allow space for indeterminacy can only appeal to the drives.

Antoinette Rouvroy and Thomas Berns's essay on algorithmic governmentality is a key reference point for Stiegler's argument regarding the nature of control. Rouvroy and Berns argue that within algorithmic governmentality: "The aim is no longer to exclude anything that does not fit the average but to avoid the unpredictable" (Rouvroy and Berns 2013, 9). Algorithmic governmentality does not enforce particular norms, as in the case of disciplinary societies, but requires the harvesting of data and the tailoring of products to personal profiles so that they can capture the full spectrum of automatic, drive-based behavior. Stiegler perceived this channeling of individuals into automatic behaviors as an all-encompassing and totalizing process. The integration of technological objects across the globe has created a new form of "associated technogeographic environment" in which libidinal economy is exploited in much the same way as other natural resources (Stiegler 2018a, 197). It is worth emphasizing that Stiegler does not object to digital technologies as such (Rouvroy and Stiegler 2016, 18). Instead, he objects to the use of algorithms, machine learning, and nascent forms of artificial intelligence to eliminate the unpredictable and the quasi-causal by the appeal to the automatisms found in the drives. Drives may be reducible to automated calculation, but desire is only sustained by a relationship with the incalculable.

Stiegler's critique of capitalism's relationship to desire demonstrates the political consequences of pharmacologically poisonous forms of totalization. Desire can only function if the totalizing fictions it attaches itself to are open to critique, transformation, and individuation. Capitalism structurally eliminates space for the indeterminate and therefore reduces desire to drives. Here lies the payoff of Stiegler's rejection of ontological conceptions of desire. Ontological accounts of the politics of desire cannot come to terms with the need to cultivate and care for desire within long circuits of individuation that necessitate a vision of the future produced by totalization. Stiegler's critique of Marcuse is underpinned by this point, but it also lies behind his critique of poststructuralist theories of productive forms of desire. Like poststructuralists, Stiegler is critical of totalizing understandings of desire that constrain its possibilities, and he continues Deleuze and Guattari's historical intervention within the philosophy of desire. For Erich Hörl, in *Anti-Oedipus*, Deleuze and Guattari sought "to no longer consider desire as a fundamentally spontaneous and natural determination, nor as a symbolic one that would go hand in hand with the lack of the object (as the hypothesis of lack would have it), but as a [sic] something that is part of a heterogeneous ensemble of people, things, institutions, machines, and animals within which desire circulates and steadily produces" (Hörl 2014, 3). This argument was, in essence, a critique of domination within both Lacanian psychoanalysis and twentieth-century capitalism (Widder 2012, 94). Such a claim historicized desire. It can no longer be totalizing because it is shaped by history and is productive of history itself. Hörl highlights how technical developments, like cybernetics, influenced the desiring machines that Deleuze and Guattari saw as underpinning both the production of the social and the processes described within Deleuze's control society thesis (Hörl

2014, 5–6). However, he also argues that Stiegler responds to a lacuna in their accounts: a proper articulation of the constitutive role that technical development plays in the history of desire.

Hörl understates Stiegler's position here somewhat. Stiegler does indeed historicize desire by seeing it as a product of the relationship to technical objects. However, he also claims that while poststructuralists such as Deleuze and Guattari recognized the importance of Freud, they failed to see the significance of his distinction between drive and desire (Stiegler 2013e, 495). Even though Freud himself neglected technicity, Stiegler argues that he made it possible to conceive of desire as formed by the binding of the drives within a particular technical context. Desire is distinguished from the drives by its projection of a totalizing image of what matters in a particular locality; it creates an image of the future that is distinct from mere becoming by recursively engaging with a particular libidinal economy. While the theory of desire articulated by Deleuze and Guattari contains critiques of a-historical accounts of the psyche similar to Stiegler's, they presume that desire preexists its channeling by totalizing social organizations. One illustrative version of this position is Deleuze and Guattari's infamous claim in *Anti-Oedipus* that

> the social field is immediately invested by desire, that it is the historically determined product of desire, and that libido has no need of any mediation or sublimation, any psychic operation, any transformation, in order to invade and invest the productive forces and the relations of production. *There is only desire and the social, and nothing else* (Deleuze and Guattari 1983, 29).

Stiegler argues that here Deleuze and Guattari fail to perceive the distinction between drive and desire, and to recognize that desire is itself a product of totalizing social organizations that facilitate the binding of the drives (Stiegler 2015a, 139; 2015c, 147).

This brief comparison of Stiegler's theory of desire with the version given by Deleuze and Guattari highlights the political consequences of his claim that poststructuralism's failure to think technics leads to an inability to distinguish between drive and desire. A politics based on an ontological and productive conception of desire cannot account for its destruction or its reconstruction by totalizing fictions that project a particular image of the future that unites a process of collective individuation. For Stiegler, this productive conception of desire informs what he sees as a disastrous political commitment to the opposition between desire and authority, represented most clearly by the protests of May 1968, which he understands as a reaction against traditional forms of morality (Stiegler 2013b, 26). He locates the origin of this position in Marcuse (Stiegler 2013b, 26); however, he also claims that the poststructuralists adopt a similar stance by failing to criticize Marcuse's postulation of an uninhibited pleasure principle (Stiegler 2013e, 496). By posing an image of desire liberated from constraints such as sublimation, poststructuralism commits two errors. The first is conceiving of desire in ontological, and therefore a-historical, terms. Because they collapse the distinction between drive and desire, Deleuze and Guattari are guilty of articulating an "a-criticism" that is not capable of distinguishing between becoming and the future or of reckoning with the need to consider how desire is produced in a way that is irreducible to ontology (Stiegler 2018a, 119). As Mark Kelly has put it in his reading of Deleuze, this constitutes a "positive account of reality in order to free constrained creative forces" (M. G. E. Kelly 2018, 76). It is this ontological account of totalization as a constraint on creative desire that Stiegler argues characterizes the misinterpretation of the distinction between desire and drive within poststructuralism.

The second error can be perceived only with historical hindsight. A liberated conceptualization of desire has been, according to Stiegler, incorporated into capitalist production. Aversion to bourgeois morality represented by the work of Marcuse, poststructuralists, and the critique of authority associated with 1968 is now a central component of capitalist accumulation. To solicit drives and stimulate consumption, traditional sites of intergenerational care, social solidarity, and moral authority are disrupted and replaced by consumer services and products that encourage disinhibition (Stiegler 2019d, 237–40). Ultimately 1968 was "extremely useful to capitalism," as it enabled "the destruction of barriers, of the superego, of idealisation," all terms that are subject to critique by Marcuse, Deleuze, and Guattari (Stiegler 2012a, 176).[4] Stiegler's analysis of these figures is truncated, and even in texts dedicated to pursuing these claims, like *States of Shock* and *Pharmacologie du front national*, they are made in short, polemic arguments. Nevertheless, when situated within Stiegler's broader understanding of desire, it is clear that his concern stems from the goal of conceptualizing the threat the *pharmakon* poses to the recursive transformation of collective individuation through desire. Within this project he reconciles totalization and non-totalization within the politics of desire in a way that refuses the simplicity of a non-totalizing and productive conception of desire that would inform politics, as part of an argument that necessitates the distinction between desire and drive, which he claims is absent from poststructuralism (Stiegler 2013c, 219–20). As Daniel Ross summarizes, the effects of this politics of desire for Stiegler is a misleading commitment to a conception of totalization, or " 'normativity,' " as something to be " 'opposed' and 'resisted' " (Ross 2021b, 63). Stiegler's political understanding of desire emphasizes the need to critically assess the pharmacological nature of its relationship to totalization rather than presupposing an ontological, productive desiring force that is opposed to totality. To understand the payoff of this gesture, I now explore how Stiegler leverages it in his critique of proletarianization, which enables us to perceive the shortcomings of his attempt to produce an a-transcendental politics of desire.

Proletarianization and the Destruction of Knowledge

I have shown above that for Stiegler, capitalism threatens the balance between totalization and openness within the formation of desire by systematically eliminating its incalculable dimension. The most pressing consequence of this totalizing tendency within capitalism is the elimination of knowledge. All knowledge is constituted by desire because it takes the form of consistences and, therefore, is threatened by the elimination of unpredictability under capitalism. To make this claim regarding the nature of knowledge and desire, Stiegler often refers to Socrates's recollection in the *Symposium* of the arguments of Diotima regarding the nature of love (Stiegler 2011b, 156; 2015b, 134–35; 2017c, 63). He takes inspiration from the suggestion that the pursuit of knowledge is in all its forms derivative of desire for, or love of, the good (Plato 1997d, 487–88, 204e–5). In Stiegler's words: "Idealization stems from desire, which is what Diotima claimed in Plato's *Symposium*: what characterizes desire is the capacity to invest in an object by infinitizing it, that is, by making it *incomparable to everything that exists*— and by projecting it onto the *plane of consistence*" (Stiegler 2020a, 210). Knowledge is not simply the possession of "facts." It is an investment in a field of practice that one individuates and can contribute to in the form of a singular projection about why and how it matters, thereby distinguishing an open future from mere becoming. Knowledge of literature, for example, will rest on a differential understanding of what authors are worth reading or what themes are important in their books. There is no determinate relationship between a particular book and its interpretation, and therefore knowledge of the text requires engagement with the consistences it supports in an incalculable manner. It is this infinite, or quasi-causal, projection that is threatened by the totalizing tendencies of capitalism.

Stiegler conceptualizes the loss of this form of knowledge through proletarianization. This term is closely related to the politics of libidinal economy. Indeed, Stiegler argues that the poststructuralist misunderstanding regarding desire is accompanied by a second error regarding the nature of proletarianization (Stiegler 2015a, 139). By conceiving of the proletariat as a distinct class—and thus as part of an oppositional and totalizing political position—they cannot account for proletarianization as a process that destroys desire and knowledge. Proletarianization is united with desire in Stiegler's critique because it highlights what poststructuralists fail to recognize: that desire is produced within a libidinal economy and can be destroyed along with the forms of knowledge that it facilitates. It is clear here that Stiegler does not define proletarianization in a traditional way. He argues that "the proletariat is constituted not by the working class or labour in general" but by the process in which knowledge is exteriorized and lost by the individual (Stiegler 2015a, 138), which induces both "a loss of knowledge" and "a loss of the capacity to individuate oneself" (Stiegler 2011a, 104). Hence, proletarianization is the extension of the short-circuiting of identification and sublimation by the appeal to the drives within capitalist production, which induces repetition without dis-automation.

Stiegler draws on three sources to define proletarianization in this way. The first is a passage in the *Grundrisse*, where Marx argues that industrialization leads to forms of production that render "workers themselves . . . as its conscious linkages" rather than active laborers (Marx 1973, 692). The second is Simondon's understanding of the Industrial Revolution as a moment where the human is alienated from technical objects by "the replacement of the individual human tool bearer by the machine individual" (Simondon 2017, xvi). Both of these accounts try to come to terms with the discretization "of the *gestures* of producers with the aim of making possible their *automatic reproduction*" (Stiegler 2010b, 33). Skilled labor is replaced by the operation of machines, within which production is reduced to calculated repetition without quasi-causal differentiation. If the knowledge of the worker can be externalized and replaced by a machine, then it follows that other kinds of knowledge can be subjected to the same process. Stiegler's third source for conceptualizing this dimension of proletarianization is Plato. If writing represents the possibility for pharmacological dependency on external supports of knowledge, as seen in Stiegler's reading of the *Phaedrus*, then Plato should be considered as the "first thinker of proletarianization" (Stiegler 2006a;

2010b, 28–36). Stiegler disassociates proletarianization from a particular set of historical conditions or an eschatological horizon of political action, and instead defines it as a movement toward the externalization and eradication of knowledge facilitated by pharmacologically poisonous forms of repetition.

The eradication of working knowledge by the mechanization of labor is the first of three forms of proletarianization that account for its extension beyond production. The "*disindividuated* worker" is "a labourer whose knowledge has passed into the machine in such a way that it is no longer the worker who is individuated through bearing tools and putting them into practice" (Stiegler 2010b, 37). This loss of *savoir-faire*, or knowledge of how to do, is supplemented by the loss of *savoir-vivre*, or knowledge of how to live. By employing "technologies of *control*, and not *of individuation*, service capitalism generalizes a process of proletarianization in which the producers have lost their *savoir-faire* to the same extent that consumers have lost their *savoir-vivre*" (Stiegler 2014f, 32). Knowledge of how to live consists of the capacity to participate in and render incalculable collective transindividuation processes of all kinds—including the family and civil society more broadly. The loss of these public and private forms of knowledge accompanies a third form of proletarianization, corresponding to what Stiegler calls theoretical knowledge.[5] This becomes particularly important within his claim that algorithmic governance displaces not just knowledge of living but also knowledge regarding thinking. "Critical knowledge" is eliminated by algorithms, artificial intelligence, and machine learning devices that outstrip human capacities and render the "critical labour" of judgment impossible (Stiegler 2016a, 29). Within this form of governance, which overlaps with control, "intensive computing and 'deep learning' lead to the proletarianization of intellectual and scientific work, and, more generally, to the proletarianization of conception" (Stiegler 2019d, 243). Proletarianization of *savoir-faire* and *savoir-vivre* is supplemented by the externalization of judgment itself.

This conception of proletarianization extends Stiegler's understanding of the politics of stupidity, as the three forms of knowledge that it destroys are required to produce singularities. Systemic stupidity is the generalized inability to respond to the problems characteristic of a particular process of individuation with quasi-causal judgments. Desire is destroyed in this process because it is formed by the capacity to individuate knowledge singularly and unpredictably: "Systemic stupidity is engendered by *generalized proletarianization*, from which there is no escape for *any* actor within the consumerist industrial system, proletarianization resulting precisely from a pharmacological development, where the *pharmakon* short-circuits those whom it inscribes in the circuit of production, consumption and speculation, and does so by destroying *investment, that is, the desiring projection of imagination*" (Stiegler 2013f, 22). The political role of proletarianization is to account for this pharmacological disruption of desire by capitalism and the liquidation of the capacity for judgment by automated decision-making processes. It is clear here why Stiegler feels that the productive understanding of desire prominent within poststructuralism cannot come to terms with this political conjuncture. The opposition between totalization and desire cannot account for how desire *itself* is produced, and therefore how both capitalism and proletarianization undermine the capacity to judge on images of the human that underpin projections of a future worth attaching ourselves to. As Gerald Moore summarizes, "Stiegler's concern is that his philosophical precursors lend themselves to this process, by glorifying the collapse, rather than the construction, of the human" (G. Moore 2013, 33). Rather than dissolve the human within a productive field of desire, Stiegler salvages it as the non-inhuman, a concept that is totalizing, to give meaning to the default, but also open, so desire can function.

Here I wish to question the extent to which Stiegler balances openness and totalization, however. Proletarianization is not intended to act as a perennial political problem. The capacity to desire is formed through a recursive relationship with its conditions (Crowley 2019, 146), and therefore desire alters the institutions that constitute it without standing above or below it in a state of metaphysical or ontological transcendence. Despite this, within Stiegler's critique of capitalism, proletarianization is presented as an inexorable and inescapable problem that focuses on knowledge to the expense of other ways of understanding the politics of desire. Capitalism is "*based on proletarianization as it generates absolute non-knowledge and as such no one escapes it*" (Stiegler 2018a, 340). Stiegler often argues that the universality of proletarianization is represented by Alan Greenspan's account of the 2008 financial crisis in front of the US Congress, which rested on the claim that it was the lack of traders' knowledge of automated financial systems that was to blame for the crash (Stiegler 2016a, 4–5; 2010b, 47). Greenspan "defended himself by arguing that economic knowledge had been transferred to machines and automatons" and "hereby sketched the figure of a new kind of proletarian" (Stiegler 2018c, 181). The proletarian is not representative of a particular class relation but a universal figure of subjectivity within computational capitalism that encompasses all degrees of the class spectrum.

There is much that could be said here regarding the politics of the financial crisis; however, I limit my analysis to the consequences of proletarianization for the philosophical components of Stiegler's critique of capitalism.[6] The simplest of these consequences is that the local and organological mode of analysis is replaced with a general one: "all of us" are implicated in this encounter with calculation and computation (Stiegler 2020b, 67). This claim totalizes insofar as it applies to all humans without exception. This position suggests a reversal of Stiegler's apparent correction of the relationship between desire and history in the work of Deleuze and Guattari. If desire is a-transcendental because of its relationship to technicity, then can we speak of the "destruction" of desire, or even the psychoanalytic concepts of instinct, drive, sublimation, or super-ego, in a way that applies to "all of us" in the same way? Stiegler claims that the interaction of these components of the psyche is conditioned by local, organological conditions but also that all are equally impacted by proletarianization's relationship to desire. The issue here, as Miguel de Beistegui has suggested, is that "one might wonder whether the very appeal to desire in the terms originally defined by Freud isn't itself determined, if not overdetermined, by a certain energetics and a certain political economy" (de Beistegui 2013, 189). Here de Beistegui highlights how the Freudian corpus was formed within a particular political context that might work against Stiegler's historical understanding of libidinal economy. Some of the theoretical consequences of this model's assumptions are addressed in more depth in chapter 7; however, de Beistegui poses an important question for the reconciliation of totalization and non-totalization within Stiegler's theory of desire. Can Stiegler's development of the Freudian conception of libidinal economy within his theory of proletarianization account for the ways that political judgment may respond to the diversity of pharmacological problems?

Of particular importance here is the problem of whether Stiegler's understanding of general proletarianization imposes on the diversity of ways in which desire might become political. One might argue that, despite Stiegler's tendency toward hyperbole, the concept of proletarianization simply needs to be modified to account for the ways that capitalism is experienced by different groups. This would entail overcoming the critique that proletarianization is a concept lacking in a clear class analysis (Hutnyk 2012). However, this concession undermines the very basis of Stiegler's critique: calculation poses a problem precisely because of its all-encompassing and totalizing nature. It is the totalizing nature of this problematic that conflicts with the a-transcendental aims of Stiegler's theory of libidinal economy. General proletarianization concerns the destruction of knowledge by the cultural control of productive, symbolic, and conceptual apparatuses by capitalism. As Jason Read has argued, Stiegler's development of proletarianization in this way "simultaneously limits and expands the definition of the concept" (Read 2016, 179). It extends proletarianization by defining it as a problem experienced by all humans, while simultaneously confining this problem to the relationship between consumption and knowledge. To what extent does this account neglect the role of variables like power and violence within capitalism's destruction of desire, thereby presenting a particular experience of capitalism as universal? I conclude by answering this question through a brief comparison of Stiegler's account of the destruction of desire with Frantz Fanon's account of the relationship between colonialism and psychological disruption.

Fanon does not use Stiegler's language in his account of the disruption of "psychological mechanisms" by colonialism (Fanon 2008, 72). However, he describes the effects of this disturbance in terms analogous to the concept of disindividuation: "I begin to suffer from not being a white man to the degree that the white man imposes discrimination on me, makes me a colonized native, robs me of all worth, all individuality, tells me that I am a parasite on the world, that I must bring myself as quickly as possible into step with the white world" (Fanon 2008, 73). Colonization disrupts existing cultural codes and prevents the reestablishment of individuation in response to a disindividuating force. For Fanon, however, this disindividuation occurs because of the subversion of cultural norms by power, violence, and coercion rather than the control of symbolic and cultural forms of knowledge alone. Glenn Coulthard's development of Fanon's work highlights this point. In his account of the dispossession of the land rights of Indigenous populations in Canada, he argues that the transfer of these rights to the state is the primary manner in which these populations have experienced the negative impact of capitalism. Land transfers facilitate the extraction of value from territory previously held by Indigenous populations (Coulthard 2014, 56–66). Here the violence of spatial dispossession supported by state coercion plays a bigger role in Indigenous politics than the disruption of knowledge or judgment by computational capitalism. Indigenous cultural knowledge is disrupted by an assault on culture that derives in the first place from dispossession of land because of "the position that land occupies as an ontological framework for understanding *relationships*" (Coulthard 2014, 60). As Audra Simpson has argued, those who reflect solely on "cultural loss" within Indigenous politics do so "only because the critical context of land loss and sovereign diminution is not centered in their assessment of the membership problem" (Simpson 2014, 48). Both Coulthard and Simpson trace the contours of a particular pharmacological problematic that is distinct from that represented by computational capitalism, consumerism, and their relationship to libidinal economy, but is nevertheless concerned with knowledge and desire.

I cannot do justice to the literature on the political significance of land dispossession within Indigenous political theory here. However, I would argue that even this cursory summary of one of its concerns disrupts Stiegler's assumptions about the universality of proletarianization.[7] The relationship to the land forms the bedrock of a particular kind of knowledge, but it is violent dispossession that precedes the disruption of this knowledge rather than consumerist control of dominant institutions of cultural production. Here the central political issue for Indigenous populations lies primarily in struggles around dispossession from which the politics of knowledge then follows. Within the locality represented by the relationship between Indigenous peoples and colonialism, dispossession is primary with respect to proletarianization as Stiegler defines it. Knowledge is disrupted by colonialism and its aftereffects, which are related to, but distinct from, the profit motive as expressed within computational capitalism. Moreover, this dispossession requires the establishment and maintenance of an understanding of the human particular to this local pharmacological problematic. Land dispossession demands a system of recognition and *"field of power through which colonial relations are produced and maintained"* (Coulthard 2014, 17). Here Coulthard draws on Fanon's claim that the recognition or value attributed to the human arises from the processes that maintain social relations and institutions. Colonialism and ongoing colonial relations within states represent one such institution, maintained primarily by violence and coercion, whether this takes the form of literal violence or the violence of dispossession. In both cases, violence and domination are a precondition of the destruction of cultural knowledge, heritage, and the forms of desire that arise from them.

This brief discussion of Indigenous land politics work serves as a contrast that demonstrates that Stiegler draws his attention away from dispossession and toward a supposedly universal theory of proletarianization that is limited to questions of knowledge understood in a narrow cultural and symbolic sense. Proletarianization represents an ostensibly universal political problem insofar as it has now become a planetary issue that impacts all of humanity. However, the universality of proletarianization neglects other ways in which desire is destroyed. Coercion and violence, represented by colonialism and the perpetuation of colonial social relations through the dispossession of land, are nonexistent in Stiegler's account despite the importance and priority that these political problems might take within some localities. This point is particularly troubling within the perspective of his work because of the emphasis it places on the political importance of the local, as seen in chapter 3. Benoît Dillet's critique of proletarianization rests on a similar skepticism toward the generality of Stiegler's general use of the term, insofar as it "muddles the concept itself" (Dillet 2017, 90). In pursuing a claim similar to Dillet's, here I share with other commentators on Stiegler's work a concern for how aspects of his arguments universalize particular forms of experience and a particular narrative regarding the politics of the historical development of capitalism (Hansen 2004, 600; 2009, 301; Pettman 2011, 255). My point here is more substantive, however. Not only is the concept of proletarianization addressed to humanity as a whole, but it actively presents a particular political problematic—that of the consumer deprived of their knowledge, desire, and judgment—as the primary issue facing humanity.[8]

This is not to deny the pressing nature of issues such as the use and regulation of artificial intelligence or how to think about developing a culture that is participatory rather than consumerist. Nor do I wish to suggest that Stiegler is not concerned with the concept of power at all. My concern is that his focus on the "psychopower" (Stiegler 2010e, 36–40; 2011b, 158–59; 2013f, 87–88) that culminates in the concept of algorithmic governmentality and the narrowing of cultural and symbolic horizons treats a particular political problematic, the psychic health of Western citizens qua consumers, as universal insofar as proletarianization is taken as a general issue that impacts all humans. Such a perspective represents a totalizing judgment that is not open to suspension by claims that focus on how the exercise of power, dispossession, or economic inequalities might lie at the root of the problem of desire in other localities. In other words, while cultural control is indeed an important problem, it has not supplanted other forms of power in the way that Stiegler suggests. It is in this way that the political frame of general proletarianization acts as a totalizing judgment on the politics of desire that leaves little room for its suspension.

Conclusion: The Closure of Non-Totalization

In this chapter I began from an account of Stiegler's theory of libidinal economy, which led us to a fourth limit to political ontology when it takes the form of an ontological conception of desire opposed to the totalizing stratification of the social. Within Stiegler's conceptualization of libidinal economy, desire is formed by the balance between totalizing alignment with the consistences of a particular process of collective individuation and the space to diachronically incorporate those ideas into one's psychic individuation. This leads him to reject ontological understandings of desire, as he claims that desire is produced *within* a particular process of individuation. It is on these grounds that Stiegler criticizes Marcuse's claims regarding the liberation of the drives and the poststructuralist position that desire is productive of social systems, because desire does not exist outside a particular a-transcendental horizon in which it is produced. The shortcoming of these approaches to libidinal economy lies in their inability to account for the way that capitalism destroys both desire and the ability to critically assess and attach ourselves to consistences that would define a non-inhuman future, thereby distinguishing desire from the becoming of the drives.

However, while I have argued that this theory of libidinal economy is intended to further the balance between totalization and non-totalization within Stiegler's work, the case has also been made that he is less successful in balancing totalization and openness within the concept of proletarianization. Proletarianization is immediately concerned with the disindividuation of knowledge and the power to control cultural and symbolic forms and less concerned with how more directly coercive forms of power and violence also prevent individuation. What at first appears to be a minimal theory of desire directs us toward specific political concerns generated from within a particular process of individuation—that of post-industrial and consumerist Western democracies. The concern with proletarianization by the control of culture is not a primary issue for all, and desire may be destroyed by other means in other a-transcendental contexts. Stiegler does not succeed, therefore, in meeting the challenge he sets for himself: the development of a politics of desire that is fully non-inhuman and a-transcendental. This represents the problem that the second half of this book addresses. To what extent does Stiegler manage to balance the demands of openness and totalization within his political judgments? To facilitate the exploration of this problem, in the next chapter I introduce Stiegler's understanding of judgment in more detail.

5

Stiegler's Theory of Political Judgment

So far I have provided an overview of Stiegler's reconciliation of totalization and non-totalization within the core concepts of his philosophy of technics and developed the consequences of these concepts for theories of the political in the form of four limits to political ontology. These limits can be summarized as follows. Post-foundational theorists of the political totalize without recognizing that they are doing so, as all political concepts must fictionalize a response to the default of origin; pharmacological problems condition politics in a way that is irreducible to a single ontology; concepts of the political are recursively generated from a set of pre-individual conditions that are prior to and frame ontological conceptualization; and, finally, ontological conceptualizations of productive desire neglect the historically constituted nature of desire that eludes ontology. These four limits can be expressed in a single overarching theme that runs across them: ontological approaches within continental political theory attempt to provide a definition of the political that escapes totalization, but neglect both the need to critically assess the totalizing nature of their local judgments and the necessity of providing totalizing judgments that respond to the problems posed by the *pharmakon*. Stiegler attempts to respond to this problematic by way of a renewed commitment to totalizing judgments on the nature of the non-inhuman. These judgments must establish a future from the mere facts of a particular a-transcendental context while maintaining an openness to the non-totalizing diversity of human existence.

This commitment to political judgment provides a clear indication of the gap between Stiegler's work and theories of political ontology in continental political theory. Where many retreat from judgment into ontology because of the totalizing connotations of the former (Zerilli 2016), Stiegler is committed to political judgment because of the pressing need to give meaning to the non-inhuman in response to a particular set of pharmacological problems. In particular, he was exercised by the tendency toward totalization without openness represented by capitalism's channeling and destruction of desire through increasingly sophisticated algorithmic marketing techniques, the generalized proletarianization induced by the spread of these techniques into ever-widening areas of life, and the tendency toward the replacement of rationality with artificial intelligence. In the face of these issues, judgments on totalizing images of the non-inhuman are necessary for giving meaning to the political problems posed within diverse, pharmacological localities without reducing them to the forms of totalization endemic under capitalism. *Pharmaka* pose a "need to decide" that raises "the very question of *making a difference*, within ontological *in*difference" (Stiegler 2011c, 6). This need to actively judge upon the nature of the political shows that, rather than articulating a single vision of politics, the philosophy of technics unites totalization and non-totalization in a way that renders the political as conditional and plural. This chapter consolidates my account of the reconciliation of totalization and non-totalization in Stiegler's work with an overview of the theory of political judgment that he situates between himself and his predecessors within continental political theory. It is this conception of judgment that constitutes the limit to ontological conceptions of the political.

My primary aim in this chapter is to reconstruct the unifying role that the concept of judgment plays in Stiegler's thought. Judgment is central to the architectonics of the philosophy of technics as it forms intermittent moments of active engagement with the recursive structure of individuation. By judging, one contributes to the pre-individual conditions of individuation while simultaneously transforming them. If, as shown in chapter 4, desire represents the capacity to singularize a synchronic set of consistences, then "judgement is what brings desire its reward" by enacting this diachronic transformation (Stiegler 2015b, 107). While many have highlighted the importance of judgment and decision in Stiegler's work (e.g., Abbinnett 2018, 8; Kouppanou 2015; Ross 2013; Vesco 2015, 86), neither the nature of his theory of judgment nor its methodological consequences have been articulated at length.[1] Here I argue that Stiegler's theory of judgment suggests that conceptions of the political always produce non-political spaces or ideas that arise from the totalization required by political judgment. This divide is produced by the a-transcendental conditions of political judgments. Differences between the political and the non-political are a product of the characteristics of particular processes of individuation and should be considered to be radically plural because of the non-totalizable conditions of political judgment. This argument also suggests that this conditionality applies to the activity of political theory. Political theorists judge on the nature and limits of politics, even when they intend to define those limits in a non-totalizing and post-foundational way. Consequently, I argue that no ontology can account for the plurality of ways in which political judgment responds to pharmacological problems because political judgment actively forms the political. This insight underpins my immanent critique of Stiegler's own political judgments in the following chapters, where I explore if Stiegler's political judgments maintain this tension between judgment and non-totalization or whether they lapse into totalizing decisions on the nature of the political.

This chapter gives an overview of this totalizing yet open understanding of political judgment. First, I draw on the work of Linda Zerilli to conceptualize the reticence toward political judgment within continental political theory. I show that this takes the form of resistance to totalizing criteria that define what counts as acceptable political judgment, to which Zerilli contrasts a conception of political judgment that need not be opposed to non-totalizable and affective components of political experience. Second, I give an overview of Stiegler's a-transcendental understanding of political judgment that combines totalization with non-totalization in a way that aligns with Zerilli's response to the continental rejection of judgment. I then show, third, that this understanding of political judgment implies a plurality of distinctions between political and non-political realms. By drawing on the work of Roberto Esposito, Laurent Dubreuil, and Inna Viriasova to extend Stiegler's understanding of political judgment, I argue that political decisions distinguish between the political and the non-political by totalizing the space of politics. Fourth, I draw on the ontological turn in anthropology to articulate the plural character of these distinctions between the political and the non-political because of the variety of ontological positions that underpin them. These discussions build toward the conclusion that judgment is necessary for establishing the meaning of the non-inhuman and that the distinction between the political and the non-political is a product of such judgments. Totalization is integral to political theory even when it is actively resisted by attempts to articulate non-totalizing ontological positions. Stiegler's work asks us to consider whether such totalizing judgments make space for the non-totalizing transformation of existing political concepts.

Continental Political Theory and the
Nature of Political Judgment

At face value, it would seem misplaced to associate Stiegler's work with political judgment given his position within a continental tradition that is skeptical of this term. This skepticism is motivated by a rejection of the reduction of politics to transcendental, and thus universal, categories. For Gilles Deleuze, "the essential effect of judgment" is that "existence is cut into lots, the affects are distributed into lots, and then related to higher forms" (Deleuze 1997, 129). Judgment reduces the world of politics to predetermined categories. Similarly, for Rodolphe Gasché, Jacques Derrida was also hesitant toward judgment insofar as "it presupposes the active doing of a sovereign subject" (Gasché 2016, 90). Deleuze and Derrida express a reluctance to accept the necessity of judgment because this requires both a predetermined set of categories that define the nature of politics and a transcendental subject that possesses the capacity to judge. This is politically catastrophic for both, as it "coincides with an instrumentalist urge to dictate the conditions of possibility for value that are subsequently deployed to direct political action" (Panagia 2009, 23).

These conditions of possibility for value, as Davide Panagia puts it, are seen by continental political theorists more widely to contrast with concrete criteria that predetermine in advance what counts as a political judgment. Zerilli argues that this leads to a divide between Neo-Kantian theorists of public reason and continental critics of rationalism who argue that judgment negates the affective conditions of politics.[2] Where the former conceptualize the conditions for turning opinion into judgments suitable for the exercise of public reason, the latter is wary of standards of corrigibility that reduce the variety of affective life to abstract universals. According to Zerilli, both sides of this divide affirm an understanding of judgment that "remains in the grip of the intellectualist conception of knowledge, according to which judgments, to be rational, require that the judging subject disengage its affective propensities and exercise a fully cognitive grasp of concepts" (Zerilli 2016, 6). Conceived in this way, politics must either be tethered to abstract, universal forms of judgment, or untethered and left to drift on plural, yet stormy, seas of political affect. This leaves us unable to think of both acceptable criteria of public reason and the affective conditions of politics within a single theory of political judgment.

Zerilli finds a solution to this impasse in Hannah Arendt's reading of Kant's understanding of aesthetic judgment. Arendt's reading of Kant's third critique provides a model of legitimacy that avoids objectivism, in which judging something as beautiful does not subsume a particular within a universal as one determines the beauty of *that* thing (Arendt 1990, 13–14). By contrast, determinate judgments proceed by way of categories demonstrable beyond subjective apprehension. Aesthetic judgments are valid as a matter of individual feeling that could nevertheless be affirmed by all on the basis of this shared capacity for aesthetic appreciation. For Arendt, political judgments share with aesthetic judgments this possible universalization through argumentation that does not necessarily fit the rules of predetermined criteria (Arendt 1990, 40–41). In Zerilli's words, "both forms of judgment . . . make an appeal to universality while eschewing truth criteria and the subsumption under rules that characterize cognitive and logical judgments" (Zerilli 2005b, 158–59). Understood in this way, political judgment does not affirm its validity through determinate criteria but through the possible accordance of one's perspective with others.

Critics of Arendt claim that this evacuates truth and argumentation from politics.[3] For Zerilli, this criticism misses that political judgment is not concerned with facts and proofs—though it may mobilize them in its argumentation—but instead "involves the creation of coherence and meaning that does not efface contingency and thus freedom" (Zerilli 2005a, 163). A political judgment does not reduce politics to axiomatic demonstrability but instead exhibits freedom by attributing political meaning to a particular state of affairs. In Zerilli's account of Arendt, political judgments derive their validity from the conditions of intelligibility that they engage with. Political judgment mobilizes "patterns of support" considered to be foundational for articulating valid judgments in a particular context (Zerilli 2016, 18). Patterns of support consist of the everyday manner in which we are convinced by judgments, which may include logical or cognitive standards of evaluation, but also encompass the affective conditions of politics that continental political theory draws on to criticize the rationalism of public reason. This understanding of judgment eludes distinctions between the conceptual/non-conceptual and the cognitive/non-cognitive precisely because a convincing judgment need not be produced through the standards of public reason.

Such an understanding of judgment has consequences that pull in two directions. On the one hand, norms regulate political judgments according to established patterns of support. On the other hand, these norms cannot be separated from the judgments that support them and put them into practice. To fail to follow up the first of these propositions with the second would fall into a neo-Kantian rationalism where norms and rules are separated from, and brought to bear upon, political utterances (Zerilli 2016, 24–26). Patterns of support, in contrast, do not exist outside a manifold of judgments from which they could be isolated; it cannot be predetermined what will count as a political judgment in all cases. Use of political language is guided by patterns of support that open judgment onto a vertigo of potential unintelligibility because it is our own utterances that produce these rules and may deploy or transform them in unexpected ways. A political judgment is not designated as such through its corrigibility with particular, preexisting standards—no matter how historical or contextual they are deemed to be. Judgment involves "someone speaking a particular sentence in a particular context and to particular others that creates meaning," and the political nature of such activity can only be determined with reference to its conditions (Zerilli 2016, 149–50). Passages from subjective judgment to the totalizing nature of patterns of support are inseparable from the criteria of validity that guide them.

The consequence of Zerilli's understanding of judgment is that it need not be considered as a form of violence or abstraction that is brought to bear upon particularity, as political judgment draws on and mobilizes the particular, the local, and the everyday in both conceptual and cognitive or non-conceptual and non-cognitive activities. For Zerilli: "What we count as 'political' arises in, is internal to, the very process of judging itself. Understood in this way, judging is an activity that constitutes the space in which the objects of judgment can appear" (Zerilli 2016, 267). While political judgment is typically taken to concern the correct course of action for a particular group or state (Beiner 1983, 128; Steinberger 2018, 2), it is also conditioned by a set of concerns irreducible to the dictates of public reason that shape the very nature of judgment, in a manner that might be called transindividual (Skeaff 2018). Concern within continental political theory for the totalizing nature of judgment is misplaced because of the role that affective and everyday life plays in constituting the patterns of support that underpin political decision making.

Stiegler's Theory of Judgment

Stiegler shares Zerilli's concern that continental political theorists unjustly neglect judgment. He argues that poststructuralism in particular reneged on the political urgency of the decision in the context of the problems posed by capitalism (Stiegler 2015a, 75–76) and, in Benoît Dillet's words, "called for resistance without proposing alternatives" (Dillet 2017, 92). That is, poststructuralists resisted capitalism without providing judgments that might respond to poisonous forms of totalization. Stiegler takes up this task of articulating an understanding of judgment that combines the necessity of a totalizing set of conditions with the transformative nature of the decision. In doing so, he echoes Zerilli's commitment to an understanding of judgment that is both rooted in totalizing conditions and exceeds, transforms, or gives direction to those conditions in a non-totalizing manner. By way of an account of the nature of judgment in Stiegler's work, I show how it unifies his philosophy and underpins my critique of ontological conceptions of the political.

Stiegler's understanding of judgment follows the lines of his argument regarding the co-implication of the transcendental and the empirical. This can be seen most clearly when he discusses Kant in volume three of *Technics and Time* to claim that

> A priori synthetic judgment would be supported by an "a priori" prosthetic synthesis—"a priori" still in quotation marks because in examining the terms more closely we see that there is an apriority of the synthetic judgment of consciousness as the *after-effect* of, and a posteriori to, prosthetic synthesis . . . but that by the same token inherits the apriority of the very synthesis of judgment that it has made possible—an after-effect that is in some way fictional, performative, and grounding—and that, being one of the conditions for the very possibility of experience-as-recognitive, is "transcendental" in existing only in and through conditions of the a-posteriority of the history of technical inventions.
> This is the "a-transcendental." (Stiegler 2011c, 141)

This is a lengthy and dense passage. However, it contains two important consequences for judgment within Stiegler's philosophy. First, judgment is conditioned by technics and is an "*after-effect*" of the a-transcendental rather than the exercise of a transcendental faculty. The individual capacity to judge is formed within a particular set of pre-individual and organological conditions. Here Stiegler's claim about the organological relationships established by writing acts as a useful example. New forms of judgment made possible by literacy are inextricable from the transductive relationship between the brain, the technique of writing, and the social system that supports it. After the invention of writing, the a priori is modified by these new organological conditions. Second, this prosthetic a priori is the result of the externalization of individual experience in technical form. The directive a priori field "inherits" "the very synthesis of judgment that it has made possible." Judgment is conditioned by the prosthetic, technical a priori, but this is itself a product of previous judgments and embodies the recursive relationship between technicity and individuation.

It is worth pausing here to note that Stiegler uses the terms decision and judgment interchangeably throughout his work, which can be seen through his adoption of understandings of judgment found in Aristotle and Hippocrates.[4] Stiegler understands reason as a "becoming-symbolic," within which "expression" would refer to "discernment, *krinein*, judgment, making-a-difference" (Stiegler 2011a, 133). This construction of difference requires the active totalization of a decision. In a note that supplements this list of terms in the first volume of *Disbelief and Discredit*, Stiegler refers to a passage of Aristotle's *On The Soul* where the distinction between different senses, such as bitter and white as opposed to white and black, occurs within a single discerning faculty that ensures that they can be differentiated despite being perceived by different sense faculties (Aristotle 1986, 150–51). Stiegler understands *krinon* in this context "as 'discernment,'" for he claims that "what Aristotle says here is that a sense can only feel through comparisons, while making differences" (Stiegler 2011a, 181, n.7). Judgment is a form of critique that engages in this act of discernment: "Judging is always *critiquing* in this sense: in Aristotle's language, judgment is to *krinon*, from the verb *krinein*, which means 'to sift' and 'to discern' " (Stiegler 2015b, 108). In his reading of Aristotle, Stiegler stays largely within the lexicon of judgment; however, a semantic slippage between judgment and decision can be found in his discussion of Hippocrates. He highlights that the Aristotelian *krinon* derives from "*krinein*, a verb sharing the same root as *krisis*, decision" (Stiegler 2016d, 480). Here decision and judgment respond to a moment of crisis, suspension, and challenge. When Stiegler refers to Hippocrates's use of *krisis*, it is precisely to define judgment in this way, as "the moment when the outcome of an illness is decided." Such a decision, he continues, is a response "to a question arising from a challenge" (Stiegler 2013f, 126).

In *Automatic Society*, the stakes of this challenge are precisely the power to judge in response to the "illness" of pharmacological problems: "*Krisis* refers in Hippocrates to a decisive bifurcation or turning point in the course of an illness and is the origin of all critique, of all decision exercised by *to krinon* as the power to judge on the basis of criteria" (Stiegler 2016a, 28). Both decisions and judgments produce projections that bifurcate, dis-automate, and individuate their conditions to constitute criteria, or future patterns of support, for judgment.

Here it is clear that for Stiegler, judgments and decisions play a unifying and totalizing function in response to pharmacological problems that is inventive and productive, and thus open to non-totalization insofar as they rearticulate a given state of fact. Judgment is "open to the possibilities of what is-not-yet" but "must nonetheless emerge from the unity of what-has-been" (Stiegler 2011c, 57). Judgment plays a crucial role in rearticulating the pre-individual fund that underpins psychic and collective individuation through a projection into the future that constitutes "what-is-not-yet" from "what-has-been" in the form of a priori conditions that are the product of a posteriori judgment. With this basic definition of the terms decision and judgment established, I now expand upon two key characteristics of Stiegler's understanding of judgment. First, why aesthetic judgment provides a model for the singularity and undecidability of the decisions that transform a collective fund of prejudgments and, second, why this model of aesthetic judgment is adequate for thinking political judgment. Both of these characteristics of Stiegler's work can be followed throughout his references to Kant's understanding of aesthetic judgment, from writings that predate *Technics and Time* (Stiegler 2018b, 60) to later work in *The Age of Disruption* (Stiegler 2019d, 181–82). The importance of this attention to Kantian aesthetic judgment can be seen by tracing his explicitly aesthetic considerations of judgment toward a more general understanding of political decisions.

To link aesthetic judgment to singularity, Stiegler gives a definition of aesthetic judgment that is close to Zerilli's adoption of Arendt's reading of Kant. It is "a judgment that cannot be proven, and that therefore could never be apodictic," yet "I necessarily think that everyone *should* find it beautiful" ("it" referring here to the work of art subject to scrutiny) (Stiegler 2017f, 7). Stiegler emphasizes that such judgment occurs within a shared set of aesthetic criteria, or tastes, that condition it, and that are supported by techniques of artistic practice and learning: "reflective judgment is not only shared but also constructed . . . it comes about through various artifices." This constitutes what Stiegler refers to as the "*artifactual formation of judgment*" (Stiegler 2017f, 8). These judgments are "inscribed in the *organo-logical becoming* constituting the fabric and the tissue (*histos*) of the history of art (*tekhnē*)" (Stiegler 2017b, 24). Reflective, aesthetic judgment requires organological conditions that provide the starting point for the singularity of judgment, which then embeds itself within the history of aesthetic claims. Judgment is both constituted by and constitutive of the existing state of the aesthetic field. Understood in this way, aesthetic judgment takes on the structure of psychic and collective individuation more generally. Psychic individuation, as described in chapter 3, responds to a contingent moment of disindividuation that can lead to the quasi-causal transformation of the collective, pre-individual fund from which it takes its form. Disindividua-tion is a condition of new forms of individuation, and aesthetic judgment requires similar "conditions of crisis . . . because *judgment in general* (*krinon*) is *essentially a crisis* (*krisis*)" (Stiegler 2017b, 29–30).[5] These crisis conditions can be understood as broadly as the moments of disindividuation that are required for individuation. Judgment responds to disindividuation by artic-ulating conditions for a new process of individuation—here a position on a particular artwork that might inform future aesthetic engagement.

Understood in this way, aesthetic judgment exemplifies the recursive relationship between psychic and collective individuation and technicity. For Stiegler, "Art, as *techne*, is the quintessential plane of existence," as it produces singularities from "practices and care, cures, curates and tools of worship" that "are the tools of what I called a general organology" (Stiegler 2008b, 38).[6] The artefactual support of aesthetic judgment is an instance of the more general relationship between the technical conditions of decision and consistences that give existence meaning. Art requires judgment to be non-totalizing for aesthetic innovation to exist, but this innovation occurs within a tradition of totalizing aesthetic judgments. To engender and guide individuation, judgment must be both totalizing and open. This point can be seen clearly in a description of the link between transformation under-stood as dis-automation and the shift from vital to psychic and collective individuation induced by the organological condition: "The passage from *psycho-biological automatic selection* to its *dis-automatization* as *decision* is possible only when *organic* organs combine with, and form a *system* with, the organological organs . . . opening up an *interpretive play* (a *différance*) through which criteria of selection become criteria of decision, that is, of *psychosocial individuation*, and not just vital individuation" (Stiegler 2017a, 139). As criteria of selection and decision, aesthetic judgments are instances of the conditionality and recursivity of all decisions and judgments within psychosocial individuation.

To return to the specific form of political judgments, Stiegler argues in a manner similar to Zerilli that aesthetic judgments share with political judgments the need to convince others of the validity of one's decision. Where art "is *originally engaged* in the question of the *sensibility of the other*," Stiegler claims that "politics is essentially that of the relation to the other in a feeling-together or *sym-pathy*. The problem of politics is one of knowing how to be together" (Stiegler 2014e, 1–2). Political and aesthetic judgments both represent the capacity for singularity to transform a collective mode of existence. Judgments on fictions that guide collective individuation act in this way: "What is politics, in fact, if not the question imposing itself on human beings insofar as they live together, and insofar as living together, *they must make decisions, that is, create fictions*? Because *taking* decisions cannot be other than *creating* fictions, *transforming* the world—and making it in *conditions* of *tekhnē*." Here political judgment articulates fictions that form the a priori conditions of future individuation. However, as individuation is a recursive, ongoing, and incomplete process, these decisions are subject to criticism, reinterpretation, and transformation by future judgments. Stiegler goes on to claim that we will never fully agree on our political judgments "because these decisions rest on fictions, insofar as they *only are* in being taken, and find their origin and their necessity in the (de)fault of origin, that is, in the felicitous incompletion of the psychic and collective individuation process" (Stiegler 2011a, 148). Political judgments create fictions by drawing on a local pre-individual fund of prejudgments to inform future individuation, but precisely because of their status as fictions they are open to challenge and transformation. In a tone similar to Zerilli's refusal to separate a political judgment from its conditions of utterance, Stiegler suggests that political decisions "*only are* in being taken." They are both conditioned by and conditioning of psychic and collective individuation within a local a-transcendental context.

Political judgment is defined by this interplay between conditions and their transformation, which Stiegler also refers to as dis-automation. When one engages with politics, one must "deliberate and decide, by *inscribing* oneself in new circuits of transindividuation," which means "*pursuing* them through *bifurcations* that dis-automize them" (Stiegler 2016a, 84). Bifurcation and dis-automation represent the possibility for judgment to articulate the undecidability of the default of origin by projecting the consequences of a decision in the form of a fiction that reorients a process of psychic and collective individuation. Judgment is defined, then, as "a *quasi-causal power (in the Deleuzian sense) to bifurcate, that is, to produce, in the jumble of facts, a necessary order forming a law*" (Stiegler 2018c, 56). Stiegler sees this production of a law that makes sense of organological conditions as an essential component of judgment. These laws posited by political judgment respond to and take care of pharmacological problems by posing an image of the future in response to a pharmacologically induced critical moment. Such a moment of disindividuation "opens a *krisis*, a decision, which means that the process of transindividuation is a critical process . . . which I thus relate back to the question of pathogenetic epokhality typical of the pharmacological-being that we are in becoming" (Stiegler 2013f, 126). Political judgment is not simply conditioned by an existing field of prejudgments. It is also engendered by the contours of the pharmacological problems to which it must respond.

The twofold importance of political judgment for Stiegler can now be made clear. First, and most simply, it is required to respond to pharmacological problems. The necessity of judgment is articulated in the face of what Stiegler sees as the destruction of the conditions of decision in control societies, where the "faculties of theorization and deliberation are short-circuited by the *current operator of proletarianization*" (Stiegler 2019b, 36). Put more extensively, the control characteristic of algorithmic governmentality "*involves a delegation of the analytical function of the understanding to an automatic retentional system* that leads to a *hypertrophy of the understanding* and to a *regression of reason* in the Kantian sense—as the faculty of deciding, operating through a synthesis that is also called judgment" (Stiegler 2020b, 73). The response to this hypertrophy constitutes the second role that political judgment plays within the philosophy of technics. Judgment unifies disparate processes of individuation within a particular organological context in a way that contributes to the ongoing production of an a priori set of conditions for future decisions. Such decisions are "possible only because *knowledge has always been organologically constituted*" (Stiegler 2016a, 175). Stiegler's concern for political judgment arises from his critique of the undermining of the capacity to contribute to the production and arrangement of the conditions of decision within control societies.

As a political task, this defense of judgment cannot fall back on transcendental foundations. The a priori conditions of judgment are themselves constituted within a particular process of individuation and are thus tied up with a particular image of the non-inhuman that unifies that locality. Rather than a faculty that is articulated at will, judgment is constituted by an intermittent tendency toward non-inhuman activity: "The duty of reason and of every reasonable being—and every non-inhuman being is *reason-able, that is, affected and pained by injustice, falsehood and ugliness*—is to *always struggle to be worthy of the non-inhuman* that we must try to be" (Stiegler 2016a, 46). Reason is the process that, through judgment, projects a particular image of the non-inhuman to which a process of individuation strives toward. In chapter 3, I demonstrated how Stiegler uses Gilbert Simondon's understanding of transindividuality to explain the genesis of concepts from within a particular process of individuation. To adapt Simondon's phrase, we do not come to know individuation in a detached way, but instead we come to know it through participation. The desire of particular non-inhuman fictions in response to the irresolvable aporia of the default of origin gives meaning to particular organological and pharmacological conditions and facilitates participation in this transindividual relationship. Political decisions condition and inform processes of psychic and collective individuation by unifying them with reference to an ideal that cannot be reached because it is transformed by judgment that is both intermittent, as it is characterized by the pharmacological tendencies of technicity, and a-transcendental, as it is the product of a posteriori conditions established by previous judgments.

Here Stiegler's theory of judgment unifies the limits to ontology that I have articulated across the previous four chapters. Ontological reasoning takes the form of one such judgment on the nature and character of the political that is conditioned by a set of a priori conditions and that participates in the recursive generation of a posteriori conditions for later judgments. Stiegler's contention, presented briefly in chapter 1, that the Heideggerian ontological difference neglects the technical condition of conceptual judgment can be stated more forcefully here. Because Heidegger disregards the technical condition of access to questions of the origin, including ontological claims, he fails to see the impossibility of articulating such answers in a way that would not be conditioned by the already-there. This absence of technicity within Heidegger's work means that "the *ontological difference* is not, for Heidegger, the presentation of the question of the *difference we must make* in the history of an *original disposition to adopt retentional systems.*" Because the technical condition demands that we give meaning to the non-inhuman condition, rather than deriving that meaning from the revealing of the ontological difference, "Heidegger . . . is unable to pose the *political question of interpretation*, the question of interpretation as the question of a politics of adoption and of the constitution of criteria of orientation" (Stiegler 2020a, 147). Ontological accounts of the origin are articulated within the a priori conditions established by technicity and are themselves a product of a judgment that is political in some way. To pose the question of difference without thinking about how it is constituted through technical artifice is to totalize without recognizing the diversity of ways of conceptualizing that difference.

When thinking about the nature of politics in the context of this understanding of the decision, for Stiegler, "The political question is always this: what are society's criteria for retention?" If political judgment shares with aesthetic judgment the production of a particularity, singularity, or bifurcation from a set of organological conditions, then it must be acknowledged that within those conditions "there is a particular economy of selection that is the possibility of universalisation" (Stiegler 2017c, 100). Political judgments totalize a particular process of individuation, but only by positing a unification that is perpetually to come. Here Stiegler allows me to claim that political decisions cannot be explained in advance by the ontological reduction of politics to a single understanding of being, as such a judgment would itself be conditioned by an a-transcendental horizon of prejudgments. This claim applies as much to post-Heideggerian accounts of political ontology found in the work of thinkers like Jean-Luc Nancy and Philippe Lacoue-Labarthe as to the affirmative and vitalist political ontologies of authors like Jane Bennet, William Connolly, or new materialism more broadly. The theory of judgment plays a unifying function in Stiegler's work, as it provides a way to conceive of the conditioning of undecidability within a totalizing context (Hughes 2014, 51; Ieven 2012, 83–84; Voela and Rothschild 2019, 63). More widely, it also requires a less prescriptive relationship with our understanding of the political than that found within political ontology, as these judgments are open to non-totalizing transformations that may escape the criteria that such ontologies establish.

One consequence of this a-transcendental theory of political judgment that combines totalization with non-totalization is that the limits of undecidability cannot be known. While I previously defined the political as the response to pharmacological problems, this minimal definition does not stipulate what the boundaries of the political must be in any particular context. Stiegler's understanding of political judgment implies a plurality of ways of understanding the distinction between the political and the non-political that escape the categorization of any single political ontology. Political judgment, if it is to be pharmacologically curative, must totalize a particular set of political conditions while nevertheless maintaining an openness to the possibility of its suspension. This applies as much to the activity of political theorists as it does to concrete political decisions. I now turn to theories of the impolitical and to the ontological turn in anthropology to build on this consequence of Stiegler's understanding of judgment.

Technics and the Impolitical

Stiegler is not an explicit theorist of the "impolitical," the non-political sphere that lies beyond the boundaries of politics. However, by claiming that political concepts are conditioned by organological and pharmacological conditions, he implies that the criteria of selection that inform what counts as a political judgment in a particular context require an accompanying decision on what is not political. The conditionality of political concepts leads to a plurality of possible ways of dividing the political from the non-political. This outside of the political is explored by two distinct approaches within contemporary political theory, each of which characterizes the political with one of the tendencies toward non-totalization or totalization.[7] Theories of the impolitical give a non-totalizing account of the political, as they conceive of politics as engendered by its separation from the impolitical. Politics can never be fully totalized because its impolitical ground bars such closure. Theories of apolitics, in contrast, attempt to define a completely apolitical space that cannot be reduced to the impolitical condition of politics. Unlike the impolitical, the apolitical plays no role in constituting politics. I now give an account of these two tendencies in contemporary political theory that clarifies how Stiegler's theory of judgment embodies these tendencies toward both totalization and non-totalization in a way that pluralizes the line between the political and the non-political.

Roberto Esposito is perhaps the most prominent thinker of the impolitical. The impolitical is not a particular space or concept but an unrepresentable ground that is the condition of politics. In his words: "The impolitical *is* the political, as seen from its outermost limit. It is the *determination* of the political, in the literal sense that it makes visible its *terms*" (Esposito 2015, 13). As a negative, unrepresentable ground, the impolitical forms the outermost limits of what can be considered as political. Understood as such, consideration of the impolitical is not a retreat to a field untouched by politics in the sense of a pure outside. Instead, it undermines the totalizing "political-theological valorization of the political" that attributes a-historical or essentialist values to politics (Esposito 2015, 78). Politics emerges from a decision that both binds and separates the political and the impolitical by determining "what that city leaves at its margins" (Esposito 2015, 198). Any attempt to think politics must be attentive to the impolitical field from which it separates itself. Here we hear an echo of the default of origin in Esposito's understanding of the impolitical. In chapter 1 I demonstrated that Stiegler claims that the default leaves politics devoid of "oughts" and that the meaning of politics must be invented in all situations of decision (Stiegler 1998, 201). I have expanded on this need to invent the political by exploring the simultaneously conditioned and conditioning nature of political judgment; however, from the perspective of the impolitical, it is clear that the default that underpins this form of judgment also acts as a ground from which politics must distinguish itself. Stiegler recognizes this similarity between his understanding of the default and Esposito's impolitical understanding of community.[8] This can be seen most clearly when Esposito defines the impolitical in terms of the link between politics and technology: "the impolitical recognizes the perfectly co-originary nature of technology and politics" and that "there is no *praxis* that is prior to *techne*" (Esposito 2015, xxvi). Politics, as a field of action and *praxis*, is only made possible on the condition of an originary default that is sutured to the field of the political by way of a decision mediated by technicity. The impolitical forces a judgment on the nature of the meaning of the political, which makes it impossible to totalize the political as such.

For those who advocate for a concept of the apolitical, the impolitical represents an attenuated method for thinking the outside of politics that reduces it to a sharpening of the meaning of the political. Laurent Dubreuil begins from a similar point to Stiegler and Esposito by defining apolitics against the political "responsibility of ordering" (Dubreuil 2016, 16). Rather than defining apolitics as something that allows the full meaning of the political to be discerned—even if this is by way of a tracing of its limit—he perceives it as a more radical refusal of this principle of order: "apolitics would be a *deictic refusal* that allows the *affirmation of an irreducible outside*" (Dubreuil 2016, 22). From this perspective, Esposito's understanding of the impolitical reduces it to its role in constituting the political itself. As Viriasova notes: "The impolitical is never radically beyond politics, it is not unpolitical, insofar as it shares, coincides with, and differentiates the domain of the political, cuts it open without ever leaving it" (Viriasova 2018, 83). Like Dubreuil, Viriasova challenges the capacity of the impolitical to truly break from the gesture of totalization that political ontology engages in; the impolitical is only valuable because of the way it modifies how we view the political. In doing so, both suggest it is possible to identify areas of life that are severed from political reason of any kind.

These positions represent two approaches to thinking the beyond of politics. For Esposito, political concepts must be understood in relation to an impolitical ground from which they are separated. For Dubreuil and Viriasova, any such gesture toward de-totalization, which they see as ontological, must also be totalizing, as it provides an a priori grounding for the political. These positions are opposed; however, something can be taken from both to show how Stiegler's theory of judgment forces us to see the political as the result of multiple decisions regarding the separation between the political and its outside. For Esposito, judgment is a precondition of the political because it must separate itself from the impolitical. For Dubreuil and Viriasova, any such gesture effects a totalization of the political field. Judgment is necessary to form the political, and as such the political will always be totalizing. Drawing inspiration from Esposito, I also argue that because the political is separated from an impolitical default, it will never be fully present to itself, perpetually holding the status of fiction. While Dubreuil and Viriasova try to roll back the totalization of life by politics, any attempt to define the "beyond" of politics will also lapse into totalization, as it expresses a definitive judgment on where the political begins and ends. Instead, I claim that there is no single "outside" of politics, as this sphere is relative to the decision that constitutes the line between the political and the non-political.

This position can be seen to be implicit within Stiegler's conception of political judgment. Political judgments are both generated from and generative of the a priori criteria of selection unique to particular regimes of psychic and collective individuation. These judgments must be fictional, as they separate themselves from the impolitical default that necessitates a decision in the face of the pharmacological problems that characterize an a-transcendental field. Political decisions always fail in their attempts at totalization, however. Judgments give meaning to an idiomatic locality, but this totality is short-circuited by the pharmacological undecidability of the impolitical default and the conditions of iteration found within individuation. The decision precipitated by the impolitical must necessarily create a boundary between the political and the non-political, informed by particular criteria of selection and the nature of a particular pharmacological problem. The dividing line between the political and the non-political is a product of judgments conditioned by the patterns of support and criteria of selection unique to a particular a-transcendental field. This totalization is ongoing, open, and recursive because judgment participates within and transforms an existing process of individuation.

The consequences of this association of Stiegler's understanding of political judgment with this literature on the impolitical are twofold. First, political decisions do not simply subject particulars to universals. Instead, judgment participates in the active creation and transformation of an a-transcendental political field. The second and perhaps more radical consequence is that this also applies to the activities of political theorists. Totalization is unavoidable, as any description of the political must also act as a judgment that responds to a set of pharmacological and a-transcendental conditions. As in Stiegler's criticisms of Heidegger, political ontology represents a proactive set of judgments that place constraints on what can be thought of as political. Despite the open and post-foundational status of much political ontology, it must at some point engage in the closure of what can be considered as political. One brief example illustrates this point well. Oliver Marchart tries to separate the conditions of politics from explicit political judgments by distinguishing between political theory, which defines the nature of politics, and political ontology, which considers the post-foundational ground of the political. He expresses a preference for the language of antagonism when articulating the irreducibility of the political to a decisionism of the kind articulated above because of its presumption of the contestability of political concepts, "for the name may, or may not, assume plausibility within a particular politico-theoretical context and tradition" (Marchart 2018, 167). This would appear to suggest the kind of pluralism with respect to the political being pursued here, for Marchart recognizes the conditionality of the conceptual language of antagonism. Nevertheless, he is also assertive when articulating the necessity of thinking antagonism as the condition of the political: "antagonism is the ultimate referent of any name, political ontology needs to name antagonism" (Marchart 2018, 166). The contrast between these two statements demonstrates the aporia of post-foundational political ontology. It articulates a non-totalizing account of the political while using the totalizing language of ontology. While he seeks to avoid decisionism and totalization by equating antagonism and conceptual indeterminacy, Marchart nevertheless makes a judgment on the nature of the conditions of the political.

This point does not rule out ontology as a tool available to political theorists. Instead, it is intended to show that when understood from Stiegler's perspective, the activity of political theory is not exempt from the totalizing conditions of judgment. If judgment is both conditioned by, and a response to, the pharmacological problems of a particular a-transcendental field, it is not plausible to conceive of theorizations of the political as somehow free of this conditioning. As Martin Crowley puts it, "Stiegler . . . thematizes the decision as itself political" (2022, 140). Within the account given above, which emphasizes the importance of the a-transcendental for the concept of judgment found in the philosophy of technics, Stiegler offers a pluralization of the concept of the political both within individual political theories and at the metapolitical level of the activity of theorizing itself. Not only are there a plurality of conditions for political decisions, but, more significantly, any attempt to define the political in theoretical terms also takes on the status of an a-transcendental, totalizing fiction. A final condition of this position is the irreducibility of the variety of forms of thinking represented by the a-transcendental to a single frame that might explain and encompass all possible divisions between the political and the non-political. I now draw on the ontological turn in anthropology to articulate such a position.

Anthropology and the Conditionality of Political Judgment

Above I have argued that ontology is the product of a judgment that enacts a particular totalization of the political by engaging with pre-existing judgments that correspond to an a-transcendental field. There is a diversity of possible political judgments and conceptions of politics that are irreducible to a single set of structures, decisions, or ontologies. The recent turn to ontology within anthropology allows me to expand on this claim, as the thinkers within this ontological turn all attempt, in various ways, to show how the diverse ontological classifications of entities made by human groups are not reducible to a single philosophical position.[9] These authors perceive the diversity of schemas that constitute social and political relations to be real iterations of particular worlds, rather than relativistic interpretations of a singular reality reducible to a homogenous standard of corrigibility. In the below I develop this claim in a-transcendental terms: each possible ontological world is the product of the progressive and collective production of an a priori set of conditions that are constantly modified by a posteriori judgment. Here I argue that the ontological turn represents an a-transcendental conception of ontology that encompasses both political judgments and the activities of political theorists in this way.[10] Ontological or cosmological frameworks express one of a multiplicity of possible distinctions between political and non-political judgments, conditioned by an a-transcendental pattern of support. The consequences of Stiegler's argument regarding the framing of thought by technicity share features with the ontological turn that facilitate my conclusions regarding the role of ontology in continental political thought after the philosophy of technics.

Anthropology's ontological turn consists of a challenge to the dominance of the concept of culture within social anthropology. When understanding human behavior, "cultural" and "societal" factors take precedence over those perceived to be beyond historical diversity whether they be biological or transcendental (e.g., Clifford and Marcus 1986). The culture of both the observer and the observed play a role in constituting anthropological knowledge. Those within the ontological turn argue that an underrecognized consequence of this epistemological claim is that the very conceptual frames by which one understands such diversity, "culture" and "the social," should be subject to the same scrutiny as different "cultures." As Marilyn Strathern argues, the concept of cultural and social determination of behavior "derives from Western ways of creating the world. We cannot expect to find justification for that in the worlds that everyone creates" (Strathern 2001, 4). Strathern alleges that the focus on social and cultural shaping of behavior presupposes the necessity of culture as a concept and entails presumptions about the worlds of the observed that may not represent the accounts they give of themselves, insofar as they may not do so through the lens of cultural difference.

Those sympathetic to this gesture ask what anthropology would look like if the philosophical premise of the human as a socially and culturally determined being was either relativized or abandoned (Rees 2018; Holbraad and Pederson 2017, 5–6). In making this claim, the thinkers of the ontological turn argue that the distinction between nature and culture—on which the constructivism of cultural anthropology rests—cannot be seen to be universal. Various iterations of this claim exist, but a particularly clear instance can be found in the work of Philippe Descola. If anthropology is pursued as "the project of understanding the relations that human beings establish between one another and with nonhumans . . . we need first to show that the opposition between nature and culture is not as universal as it is claimed to be" (Descola 2013, xviii). If the distinction between nature and culture is just one particular way of classifying entities, then it is impossible to fall back on the social as an explanatory mechanism for divergent human behaviors. What counts as a social or political relation cannot be assumed to precede ontological presuppositions that generate those relations.

On the face of it, this appears alarmingly transcendentalist. How could such presuppositions exist if not as an eternal characteristic of the mind? However, taking influence from Stiegler, they can be understood to be a-transcendental. Baptiste Gille gives a definition of the relationship between ontological propositions and ontological discourses that resembles the a-transcendental relationship between individual judgments and the prejudgments that they draw from and intervene within. What he calls "ontological propositions" are "singular propositions that signal a shift up in generality and which strive to give definite descriptions of their objects, requiring an ordered distribution of properties." He continues to define "ontological discourse" as "any discourse that sets out to stabilize the attributes of an event by organizing a set of ontological propositions in a systematic way" (Gille 2017, 306). The relationship between ontological propositions and discourses is transductive; propositions exist within a discourse that stabilizes a particular view of reality to which they refer, while these discourses are meaningless without such a set of propositions. Here Gille redefines ontology as the active constitution of reality through decisions regarding the relationship between ontological propositions. Ontological reasoning is a *practical* activity (Maniglier 2016). These ontological discourses are maintained not just by the utterances that make them intelligible through language but also through the actions that presuppose them: "Major ontological premises are *indicated* by silent mechanisms of confirmation rather than *demonstrated* by appeals to greater generality . . . not only to discursive practices, but to a certain pre-reflexive, first person way of feeling, confirmed by actions or by *schemas of practice*" (Gille 2017, 313). Ontological propositions do not have a free-floating existence but both inform and are supported by practices and the institutions that they constitute. Within Stiegler's lexicon, such a position would be considered as a-transcendental. Criteria of selection govern the generation and ordering of ontological propositions that form and transform the rules and the social practices that they make possible. Political ontology, and the judgments it carries with it, should be considered as one such schema of practice.

If ontology is produced by transductive relationships between individual propositions and their institutional and technical codification, then it is clear that some ontological propositions and their institutional orderings are irreducible to others or to a single principle that accounts for all ontological perspectives. Ontological pluralism in anthropology seeks to show how other modes of classifying entities might come to suspend existing conceptual judgments in this way. Despite the variety of methods and approaches that characterize it, this aim is shared across the ontological turn. Descola defines anthropology as "a novel form of understanding the otherness of others . . . without paying an unnecessary tribute to the dogmatic wrapping with which we try to justify its legitimacy" (Descola 2005, 72–73). Similarly, Eduardo Viveiros de Castro refers to anthropology as "a conceptual practice whose aim is to make alterity reveal its power of alteration" (Viveiros de Castro 2011, 10), which makes possible what Patrice Maniglier calls "a redescription of ourselves in the light of alterity" (Maniglier 2014, 40). By recognizing the contingency of the conceptual frames by which reality is codified, the ontological turn attempts to make possible "the permanent decolonization of thought," which continually suspends existing categories and makes room for the possibility of new modes of existence (Viveiros de Castro 2014, 40).

Read through the a-transcendental conception of political judgment found in Stiegler's work, ontology is both totalizing insofar as it forms a schema of practice that makes a particular ensemble of relations intelligible, and also non-totalizing, as it can become subject to suspension in the light of other classificatory practices. If the political is formed by its separation from an impolitical ground that implies an apolitical sphere, then ontological speculation within political theory must delineate a space outside politics in a totalizing manner. Matei Candea concludes as much in his own account of the irreducibility of the informant's conceptions of politics and those of the anthropologist. If the observed may make claims about the nature of the political that conflict with the presumptions of the anthropologist, then we must recognize that the "distinction between the political and the non-political is crucial in enabling the political itself" (Candea 2011, 317). Such distinctions are not universal—they can come into conflict in unexpected and irresolvable ways. Whether thought of in terms of "politics" or "the political," the political field posited by political ontology is constituted by such exclusions. Within the theory of political judgment I have derived from Stiegler's philosophy of technics, the political necessitates a decision or judgment on its boundaries that engages with existing patterns of support and delineates the existence of non-political spaces, theories, and ideas. As the thinkers of the ontological turn argue is the case with the work of anthropologists, the activity of political theorists is not exempt from this conditioning.

Conclusion: Judgment and the Challenge of Non-Totalization

Reading Stiegler's theory of judgment alongside theories of the impolitical and the ontological turn in anthropology clarifies the task set by the a-transcendental. Doing justice to the a-transcendental requires the development of a conception of the political that does not account for the plurality of the political as such, but that recognizes the possibility of the existence of political judgments that do not correspond to the ontological and conceptual lexicon in which we define politics. I have argued that Stiegler's philosophy of technics goes a long way toward achieving this goal insofar as it establishes the conditionality of the human, links politics to distinct pharmacological problems, understands the political as generated from within organological conditions, and sees the way that we attach ourselves to those conditions as the product of processes of individuation. These claims are represented, respectively, by the concepts of the default of origin, the *pharmakon*, organology and individuation, and desire. Judgment unites these ideas within Stiegler's work, as it is necessary to respond to the *pharmakon* and give meaning to a particular process of individuation in the face of the default of origin, while simultaneously individuating and transforming that locality.

I have also argued that understanding judgment in this way unifies the ramifications of Stiegler's philosophy for the role of ontology within political theory. Doing so allows us to reduce these consequences to two claims. First, any political judgment requires a distinction between the political and the non-political that draws on the patterns of support and the criteria of selection constitutive of a particular locality. Political judgments may involve the application of criteria that are not necessarily considered to be political from within the perspective of another ontological schema. These schemas are not static, however. Political decisions are totalizing because they give meaning to a process of individuation by participating within the ongoing, recursive individuation of the presuppositions of a particular context that eludes ontological exhaustion. The second claim elevates this point to a metapolitical level. Political theorists engage with the patterns of support and criteria of selection characteristic of a particular process of individuation, and therefore cannot articulate ontological claims that would encompass the potentialities represented by the possible diversity of divisions between the political and the non-political. This curtailing of the explanatory power of ontology within political theory derives directly from the a-transcendental perspective found within Stiegler's philosophy. Concepts are conditioned by technicity, its pharmacological problems, and the image of the non-inhuman within a particular process of individuation. Judgment, therefore, has served to unify my account of both Stiegler's philosophy of technics and its consequences for political ontology.

In contrast to the commitment to non-totalization within continental political theory more widely, Stiegler advocates for the necessity of this practice of totalizing political judgment. This is both a methodological and a political claim. Methodologically, he suggests that we cannot account for the nature of social and political life without acknowledging its contingency. If, as Stiegler claims, "when we try to theorise on the origin of the human we stumble across an accident every time," then it is necessary to consider how responses to this accidentality constitute totalizing yet local answers to the question of the origin (Stiegler 2017c, 111). Methodology overlaps with politics here. Whether intended or not, ontologies are laden with values and assumptions that engage in this meaning-giving activity. As Isabelle Stengers puts it, to adjudicate between ontological judgments is to "ratify" or "disavow" such presuppositions, either explicitly or implicitly (Stengers 2018, 83). To express a conceptualization of the political—even if this takes the form of an open and non-totalizing political ontology—is to totalize the space of politics. By reading Stiegler's theory of political judgment through the concept of the impolitical and the ontological turn, I argue that the political theorist should be understood as inhabiting a web of ontological propositions, practices, and institutions that support their judgments. This is not to denigrate political theorists. What is presented here is a work of political theory, and Stiegler emphasizes the urgency of judgment and decision in the face of pharmaka. Totalizing judgment is necessary to give meaning to the problems posed by "the accidentality of the *pharmakon*" in a curative and open way (Stiegler 2013f, 41). An absence of judgments that acknowledge their quasi-causality and indeterminacy concedes judgment to positions that do not make space for the transformative and open nature of political decisions. This danger is represented most clearly for Stiegler by societies of control under twenty-first-century capitalism that attempt to totalize human behavior within the calculating demands of the profit motive. Avoiding the task of critically assessing one's totalizing judgments, as I argue political ontology does, fails to challenge this situation by providing concrete alternatives to these problems.

Stiegler's a-transcendental theory of judgment reveals the interplay between totalization and the non-totalizing nature of the indeterminacy that underpins it. If the central problem of political judgment is the assessment of whether particular decisions regarding the character of politics balance totalization with non-totalization, then this perspective should also be used to assess Stiegler's political claims. In the following three chapters I engage in an immanent critique that considers the balance between totalization and non-totalization within Stiegler's explicit judgments on politics. In chapter 4 I introduced this problem within the concept of proletarianization, and I now possess the framework to explain it more fully. Does Stiegler allow non-totalization to inhabit his politics, or does he engage in a form of political judgment that closes the space for alterity?

6

Judgments on the Impossible:
Otium, Antigone, Amateurs

Across the previous five chapters I have argued that Stiegler's philosophy is characterized by his commitment to balancing totalization with non-totalization within judgments on the nature of the non-inhuman and of the political. This was established across my account of a range of concepts that represent Stiegler's reconciliation of the continental critique of non-totalization with totalizing judgment: the default of origin, the a-transcendental, *différance*, individuation, repetition, organology, quasi-causality, and desire. I have also argued that this balance between conceptual closure and openness within judgment acts as a limit on the ability of political ontology to exhaust the range of ways that the decision might constitute the political within diverse, organological localities and in response to a range of pharmacological problems. While Stiegler's wider philosophy is characterized by a commitment to this balance between both totalization and non-totalization, it has not been established whether his own political judgments uphold these standards. In these final three chapters I engage in an immanent critique of his political judgments based on the framework established so far. In this chapter, I consider how Stiegler develops consequences for politics in his development of the concept of the impossible. As the first political concept in my immanent assessment of Stiegler's political judgments, I show that his use of the impossible holds to the balance between totalization and non-totalization that his philosophy demands.

This case is made through an account of Stiegler's development of the concept of the impossible through his use of the work of Maurice Blanchot and Georges Bataille, and an articulation of the link between the impossible and the political concepts of *otium*, the Antigone complex, and the amateur. Much like the generation of French philosophers who preceded him, and like continental political theory more widely, Stiegler is concerned with conceptualizing how the impossible that underpins first principles escapes totalizing conceptual determination (Gutting 2011; Floyd 2016; Donahue and Ochoa Espejo 2016; Arnold 2020). Figures most clearly associated with this attentiveness to indeterminacy, such as Jacques Derrida and Gilles Deleuze, are not central in his account of the impossible, however. Instead, Stiegler draws on the work of Blanchot and Bataille to articulate his understanding of the impossible as conditioned by technicity. Derrida and Deleuze are most commonly associated with Stiegler's philosophical and political positions, through the concepts of *différance* in the case of Derrida and repetition, the quasi-cause, and societies of control in the case of Deleuze. I have shown the influence of both of these thinkers on Stiegler's work and the importance of his use of their concepts: however, Blanchot and Bataille hold greater significance with respect to his understanding of the impossible, as they provide him with a way to conceptualize how impossibility is experienced through particular practices of the improbable. Links are made to Derrida and Deleuze below; however, here I emphasize the importance of the currently underrecognized role of Blanchot and Bataille in Stiegler's politics. This is due to their significance for his claim that a commitment to a non-totalizing and conceptually elusive understanding of the impossible requires acknowledging the centrality of totalizing conditions to the experience of this default, which underpins open and pharmacologically curative forms of individuation.

Developing this conception of the impossible becomes a political concern for Stiegler in the face of the elimination of space for the incalculable within societies of control. As shown in chapter 4, Stiegler's attention to the problem of control societies arises from his claim that the formation of desire requires indeterminacy. In the absence of space for diachrony, the pharmacologically curative tendency toward open and intermittent non-inhuman forms of individuation is destroyed. For Stiegler, the "impossible can and *must* be realized," for "to fail to achieve it would be to condemn non-inhumanity to disappear" (Stiegler 2019d, 162). *Otium*, the Antigone complex, and the amateur are judgments that are made in response to this threat of disappearance and represent three attempts to replace a culture of consumption and disconnection with one of non-totalizing and active engagement with totalizing heritage and tradition. Within these three political interventions, the impossible finds its meaning within a set of determinate conditions. *Otium*, a form of creative and intermittent free-time, arises from the interstices of *negotium*, or occupied time. The meaning of the law requires a transgression that nevertheless holds to its spirit by reconstituting it, as Stiegler argues in a reading of Antigone. Finally, artistic invention results from the repetition of a tradition of artistic inheritance by amateurs. In each case, the impossible underpins a quasi-causal and indeterminate form of non-inhuman action that engages with and transforms its totalizing conditions through repetition. As a set of political judgments, I argue that these three concepts do not predetermine the way that this combination of totalization and non-totalization occurs. They therefore hold to the pharmacologically curative and open form of political judgment that Stiegler advocates.

This argument is made in several steps. I first introduce Stiegler's reading of Blanchot and Bataille. Both suggest that experience of the impossible is conditioned by practices of the improbable, claims that Stiegler takes on to argue that there is no direct access to indeterminacy outside an a-transcendental set of technical conditions. Like his use of Freud, Calum Watt has argued that Stiegler's reading of Blanchot is disparate and allusive (Watt 2016, 317), a comment that also applies to his readings of Bataille. Consequently, part of the task of this chapter is to reconstruct Stiegler's adoption of their work. Following this reconstruction, I then, second, introduce the three political figures who expand on this condition. *Otium*, the Antigone complex, and the amateur are judgments made by Stiegler in response to the problem of control, and they share the presumption of the necessity of impossibility for political engagement. Because of their reliance on determinate conditions, each of these concepts maintains that the content of engagement with the impossible cannot be defined in advance. As political judgments, *Otium*, the Antigone complex, and the amateur articulate the composition of the impossible with totalizing practices of the improbable, holding to Stiegler's reconciliation of totalization and non-totalization.

Impossibility and Technics

The importance of Blanchot and Bataille to Stiegler's philosophy can be seen clearly in a passage from *The Age of Disruption*, where he links both to his understanding of Kantian aesthetic judgment, which I introduced in chapter 5. Aesthetic judgment always encounters something "unimaginable" that does not represent its "failure" but rather "its interminable condition," which he understands "in Blanchot's sense." Art that is subject to judgment, moreover, gives access to "the infinite sublime of excess and of the default," which "is also Bataille's question" (Stiegler 2019d, 182). This fleeting reference to both Blanchot and Bataille in the context of judgment allows me to expand on Stiegler's repeated allusions to both. Blanchot's understanding of literature and language draws our attention to the impossibility that faces any attempt to articulate universal aesthetic judgments, and Bataille demonstrates that particular practices and rituals are required to mediate the experience of this impossible and sublime condition. Language and ritual, reinterpreted by Stiegler through technicity, highlight the role that a-transcendental context plays in facilitating access to the indeterminacy and impossibility that he valorizes as the source of pharmacologically curative forms of individuation. If one hears echoes of Stiegler's reading of Derrida and Deleuze here, it is precisely because he uses Blanchot and Bataille to situate Derridean *différance* and the Deleuzian quasi-cause within the a-transcendental conditions that mediate access to the impossible. While Derrida and Deleuze are more immediately perceptible influences on Stiegler, Blanchot and Bataille provide a way to concretely situate his non-totalizing account of politics within totalizing conditions as they claim that the impossible is only accessible through particular practices of the improbable.

Stiegler distinguishes between the impossible and the improbable primarily through his reading of Blanchot. In an interview that sets out his interest in Blanchot's work, he states that "everything important is absolutely improbable, as Maurice Blanchot said, absolutely improbable . . . the things that really count don't exist. Only the things that don't exist count, and they're not reducible to the calculations of probability" (Stiegler 2012a, 181–82). While Stiegler goes on to use the impossible and the improbable to distinguish between the absolute condition of this deferral and the conditions in which it takes place, here he does not yet differentiate them clearly. To trace his development of the difference between the impossible and the improbable, I first briefly introduce how Blanchot understands impossibility.[1] Blanchot argues that language, by dint of its drive to order and conceptualize, reduces the unknown to the known. He asks, however, whether experience can escape language's indexical function (Blanchot 1993, 43). He answers this question not by asserting the exceptionality of such an experience, but by claiming that any experience of this unknown must take place through language, and therefore that the unknown is the condition of all language, as it must be codified for there to be expression (Blanchot 1993, 45). This radical impossibility that is beyond, yet supportive of, language is irreducible to ontological speculation: "must we not also say: impossibility, neither negation nor affirmation, indicates what in being has always already preceded being and yields to no ontology? Certainly, we must!" (Blanchot 1993, 47). Language's condition, in Blanchot's account, is an impossible unknown irreducible to philosophical speculation.

Blanchot's wider project concerns how writing can provide access to this unknown. Stiegler associates this link between writing and the impossible with his conception of the default that underpins technicity. A short essay by Blanchot, titled "The Beast of Lascaux," is crucial for Stiegler's interpretation here, as it collapses speech and writing into technicity: "The impersonal knowledge of the book . . . does not ask to be guaranteed by the thought of any one person, since this is never true and can constitute itself as truth only within a world inhabited by all and by virtue of such a world. And any such body of knowledge is bound to the development of technology in all its forms, and it treats speech, and writing, as technology" (Blanchot 2000, 9). For Stiegler, "'the impersonal knowledge of the book' is a product of the process of grammatization," or the gradual discretization and production of impersonal collective knowledge that is not tied to a single individual (Stiegler 2015b, 115). Here impossibility takes on the meaning attributed to the default at the heart of the technical condition (Stiegler 1996, 27; 2009a, 20; 1998, 134–35). If, for Blanchot, writing gives access to the impossible that it attempts to codify, then for Stiegler technics plays this role insofar as it gives meaning to the default that underlies the non-inhuman.

Impossibility becomes more immediately political in *Automatic Society*, where Stiegler clearly distinguishes between the impossible and the improbable. This distinction helps to identify how algorithmic governmentality characteristic of societies of control eliminates the potential for access to the impossible by way of practices of the improbable: "It is this improbable—that is, incalculable—quasicausality that totally computational capitalism tends to *systemically* eliminate" (Stiegler 2016a, 76–77). Practices of the improbable that grant intermittent access to the impossible are incompatible with the calculation required by control. To make this distinction between impossibility and improbability, Stiegler refers to a section of *The Infinite Conversation* where Blanchot claims that the improbable is "a meeting point between possibility and impossibility" (Blanchot 1993, 41). Whereas the impossible is a radically inaccessible default at the heart of language, the improbable is the point at which one might experience this impossibility through the concrete practice of writing. Following his expansion of Blanchot's theory of writing to technicity, Stiegler takes the improbable to refer to practices that are open to the indetermination of the impossible, which control and calculation eliminate by reducing them to the possible: "algorithmic governmentality disintegrates in advance any intermittence, and therefore liquidates the impossible (unpredictable and unanticipatable) possibility of the improbable that it can neither correlate nor identify" (Stiegler 2016a, 116).[2] Considered in this way, impossibility and improbability refer respectively to the condition of conceptual indeterminacy and the means of access to that indeterminacy.

Stiegler's turn to practices of the improbable signifies that engagement with quasi-causality and *différance* can only occur within a set of totalizing conditions that inform access to the impossible. Conceptual judgments that underpin decisions, such as those on the nature of the political, emerge from within these practices and represent attempts to reduce the impossibility of the default to the known. Concepts are subject to *différance* because, "having never been present," they are "always yet to come" because of their translation of an unknowable default into conceptual fixity (Stiegler 2018c, 229). They are also subject to the condition of quasi-causality because they give necessity to the "impossible and improbable possibility that is the originary default of origin" (Stiegler 2016a, 119). Distinguishing between the impossible and the improbable allows Stiegler to conceptualize how impossibility is unthinkable outside local and totalizing conditions. Blanchot's facilitation of this claim suggests that he is as important to Stiegler's work as more recognized influences such as Simondon, for he "provides not only a better understanding of what Simondon says, but also a more refined critique of what he means" (Stiegler 2012b, 70). Expanding on his critique, seen in chapter 3, of Simondon's association of the pre-individual with nature, Stiegler argues that this move halts the interminable dialogical movement of the individuation of concepts. Contrastingly, for Blanchot, all concepts must be turned "into the quasi-cause" that transforms the impossibility at the heart of language, or the "endless end in the incessant (as Blanchot says)," into a fiction that gives meaning to the non-inhuman (Stiegler 2022, 280). Preference for Blanchot to Simondon here suggests that for Stiegler, the totalizing conditions of the a-transcendental take precedence over any positive philosophical conception of indeterminacy or impossibility, in the same way that they bar direct access to the pre-individual understood as nature.

Stiegler's interest in Bataille arises from his attempt to do justice to this claim by expanding on the link between the context of judgment and the practices that form its conditions. General economy, Bataille's attempt to conceptualize the role of excess, waste, and indeterminacy within economic relations, is adopted by Stiegler to make a case for the role of the impossible within concrete political and economic judgments. Space for indeterminacy and impossibility, which Bataille understands with reference to a specific understanding of the sacred, is necessary for social systems to function. Here society is split into two poles: one characterized by the homogeneity of rules, prohibitions, and norms, and another characterized by heterogeneous acts that transgress their limits and open onto experiences irreducible to order (Bataille 1985, 143). Sacred experiences arise from heterogenous activities incommensurable with the mundane and profane world. The character of heterogenous experience is not predetermined by Bataille, however. Experiences of the sacred are reliant on the prohibitions of the profane world, from which it distinguishes itself in the form of an exceptional experience that is "meaningful only in that context" (Bataille 1991, 90). Like Blanchot, Bataille highlights the importance of something ineffable and impossible that underlies social order but is nevertheless accessed by way of the totality represented by rules that form the profane world.

General economy conceptualizes economic relations from this perspective. As a form of restricted economy, capitalism seeks to reduce all activity to predictability and profitability, thereby expelling heterogenous and sacred experiences from human activity. Opposed to this are the principles of general economy that recognize the need for sacred experience and expenditure without calculable profits. Bataille draws on Marcel Mauss's identification of the logic of gift giving in potlatch rituals to develop this understanding of general economy. Mauss saw the potlatch, a form of gift giving characteristic of Indigenous peoples of the Pacific Northwest of the American continent, as a form of expenditure lacking immediate return: "Consumption and destruction of goods really go beyond all bounds. In certain kinds of potlatch one must expend all that one has, keeping nothing back" (Mauss 2002, 47). For Bataille, potlach rituals represent an experience of the sacred that "withdraws useful products from profane circulation" (Bataille 1988, 76). The social function of the potlatch is an example of the need for unproductive expenditure to give meaning to profane existence. Expenditure plays a social function, but it is nevertheless irreducible to mere profitability. This claim informs Bataille's critique of calculation and utility within capitalism. He contrasts capitalism's "unreserved surrender to *things*, heedless of consequences and seeing nothing beyond them" with a general economy that "requires that at an ill-defined time and place growth be abandoned, wealth negated, and its possible fecundation or its profitable investment ruled out" (Bataille

1988, 136, 182). Unpredictable expenditure is necessary because of the role that heterogenous and sacred experience plays in giving profane existence meaning. Stiegler adopts Bataille's anthropological point, claiming that "societies are based on the great divide between human activities subject to the life of subsistence and those devoted to consistences. These two modes of life, distinct yet inseparable, form what Bataille called a general economy." This division is supported by "intellectual and spiritual practices, religions, beliefs and the life of the spirit" (Stiegler 2008a, 40). General economy recognizes the structural role that experience of impossibility, in the form of consistence, plays in binding individuals to collective individuation because it totalizes that process while leaving it open to transformation. Echoing Bataille, Stiegler argues that "one cannot build an economy the way one changes a wheel—at a certain moment, the potlatch must be inserted into it" (Stiegler 2012c, 13).[3] Commitment to a conception of general economy is thus central to both Bataille's and Stiegler's critiques of capitalism, for it structurally constrains the unpredictable activity that constitutes social bonds.

As a theory that accounts for the role of incalculable expenditure within human existence, Stiegler's adoption of general economy provides an opportunity to refine his criticism of societies of control. Stiegler argues that "a human society without festivities [fêtes] is not possible. And yet, the psychotechnologies of the twentieth century have destroyed festivities, because all festivities have become an opportunity for marketing. And so there are no more festivities" (Stiegler 2010a, 473). In reducing opportunities for excess to marketing opportunities, control eliminates "the difference between consistence and existence." Political responses to this collapse of consistence must adopt "a *general economy*, that is, a political economy that renews the question of the belief in politics," for belief requires incalculability (Stiegler 2011a, 92). This perspective is necessary because "a control society" reduces existence to "usages" and establishes a situation where "there is no longer any belief in nor possibility of a pursuit of individuation" (Stiegler 2011a, 96). Here Stiegler deploys the contrast between profane homogeneity and sacred heterogeneity within his philosophy of technics. Because of the pharmacological nature of the relationship between technicity and human behavior, profane order can both form practices of the improbable and facilitate the poisonous totalization of behavior within the logic of calculation.

One might ask at this point what Blanchot and Bataille have added to Deleuze and Derrida's influence on Stiegler's politics. Quasi-causality and *différance* both point to the impossibility underlying conceptual invention that is threatened by societies of control. Their contribution can be perceived within Stiegler's claim that the poststructuralist generation of thinkers failed to address the question of how desire is produced by foregrounding a form of political resistance generated by an ontologically productive form of desire, as seen in chapter 4. In doing so, they neglected that the experience of the impossible, which would provide resistance to the totalization of capitalism, is produced within specific totalizing conditions (Stiegler 2015a, 72). Blanchot's account of the improbability that constitutes access to the impossible and Bataille's theory of general economy provide Stiegler with two versions of the claim that it is only within totalizing conditions that *différance* operates or that quasi-causal conception invention can occur. To combat control requires the active cultivation of judgments on practices that facilitate incalculable forms of desire, rather than the advocation of resistance to totalization that sees order as a constraint on creativity. Blanchot and Bataille's understandings of language, the sacred, and general economy allow Stiegler to break with the attribution of value to the impossible *itself* that he perceives as the fault of the politics of poststructuralism.

This reading of Blanchot and Bataille takes them to affirm the necessity of thinking deferral, indetermination, and difference from within the fixed conditions of a particular technological horizon. It is the task of political judgment to set out fictions that grant meaning to the impossible through particular practices of the improbable. As Dan Mellamphy and Nandita Biswas Mellamphy argue, Stiegler's politics revolves around the articulation of fictions as a form of artifice that facilitates individuation by constituting the "world" within which such individuation takes place (Mellamphy and Mellamphy 2015, 134–35). This constructive understanding of judgment within Stiegler's adoption of the language of the impossible rests on his wider distinction between becoming and the future. Becoming refers to indifferent temporal progression, whereas the future requires the unification of processes of individuation within a project that gives meaning to the brute reality of subsistence. Politics concerns this "*transformation of becoming into future* that is always the question of any noesis qua passage from facts to laws, that is: qua projection of existences onto the plane of consistences" (Stiegler 2016a, 136). In Tracy Colony's words, Stiegler thinks "futurity at once from within the horizon of a technologically factored becoming but at the same time as figured by a difference that is not reducible to that becoming" (Colony 2017, 65). Political decisions are underpinned by impossibility, quasi-causality, and *différance*, but they take place within the totalizing conditions of a particular projection of the future that establishes the irreducibility of consistence to the predictable becoming of control.

Here the political stakes of the impossible within Stiegler's work are clear. Impossibility is constrained by the totalization of control, but political responses to control societies cannot simply oppose totalization. Instead, they must support practices of the improbable that cultivate access to the impossible in the face of the reduction of existence to the profane world of calculation. While this issue becomes more politically salient within Stiegler's later discussions of calculation from *Automatic Society* onward, it is present from the beginning of Stiegler's major writings. Colony has highlighted how the English translation of the first volume of *Technics & Time* occludes a crucial mention of the decision in the context of the nonprogrammed. The distinction between the future and becoming concerns "becoming qua the bringing into play of the nonprogrammed, the im-probable, and destiny qua nonpredestination, the decision" (Stiegler, 1998 172, in *Colony* 2017, 80).[4] Once these last two words have been returned to this citation, it is clear that from the beginning of his work, Stiegler considers the nonprogrammed, or the impossible, to take place through the totality of particular decisions. *Otium*, the Antigone complex, and the amateur all represent political judgments that insert the impossible back into individuation in this way. In doing so, they attempt to balance the totalization necessary to facilitate access to the impossible with the non-totalization that it engenders. For the remainder of this chapter, I give an account of how each of these concepts represents Stiegler's attempt to rethink the political in terms that facilitate access to impossible and non-totalizing forms of judgment.

The "*Otium* of the People"

Otium is a form of leisure that Stiegler defines with reference to the incalculable expenditure that underpins Bataille's understanding of general economy. In its most simple form, *otium* is time distinguished from *negotium*, work required to meet the needs of subsistence: "otium is the time of leisure free of all negotium, of all activity connected with subsistence: it is the time of existence" (Stiegler 2013c, 420). Rather than a distinction between free and occupied time, the *otium/negotium* distinction maps onto the difference between sacred and profane experience. *Otium* consists of practices that lead to experience that is "*out* of the ordinary" (Stiegler 2011a, 100), as it "embraces the incalculable, what has no price, what cannot be measured by accounting" (Stiegler 2016b, 162). As is well established within commentary on Stiegler, the difference between these two terms should be understood as lying between time that is available for the invention of incalculable singularities (*otium*) and time that is subject to calculation (*negotium*), rather than simply free and occupied time (de Beistegui 2013, 187–88; Mellamphy and Mellamphy 2015, 137). *Otium* represents a non-totalizable use of time irreducible to the calculating constraints of *negotium*.

Congruent with the rest of his work, Stiegler does not oppose these two tendencies, for "*otium* cannot simply be opposed to *negotium*" (Stiegler 2011a, 123). *Otium* gains its meaning by distinguishing itself from *negotium* within a specific context and specific set of constraints on the use of time. As a political term, *otium* concerns the time available for the production of consistences, and futures, out of particular a-transcendental horizons through practices of the improbable. This point can be made clear by considering Stiegler's critique of Michel Foucault's understanding of *hypomnemata*. Stiegler defines *hypomnesis* as the practices and artifices that support *anamnesis*. *Hypomnemata*, for Foucault, are more precisely defined as the written practice of diary writing, which Stiegler subsumes under the concept of *otium* or time free for unproductive leisure and reflection. These *hypomnemata* form a "material record of things read, heard, or thought, thus offering them up as a kind of accumulated treasure for subsequent rereading and meditation" (Foucault 1997, 209). Stiegler sees the record constituted by *hypomnemata* as necessary for the incalculable reflection represented by *otium* (Stiegler 2011a, 83). This means that *hypomnemata* cannot be opposed to other technical practices, as they are, like all forms of technicity, bound up with psychic and collective individuation: "*hypomnemata* are technologies of individuation, such that individuation is psychic and collective, that is, social and political" (Stiegler 2011a, 77). *Hypomnemata* refer to the techniques, technologies, and practices that support psychic and collective individuation in general. *Otium* finds its origin within these totalizing technical conditions. In contrast, Foucault, according to Stiegler, distinguishes between wider political techniques of power, control, and discipline and the ethical cultivation of the self represented by *hypomnemata* (Stiegler 2011a, 78). Separating the exceptional practice of *hypomnesis* as *otium* and the standardized exercise of technical power, Foucault fails to consider "what, within the context of this standardization (and thanks to it), could be produced as *extra*ordinary" (Stiegler 2010e, 118).[5]

This critique of Foucault may be challenged, but for my purposes it clearly highlights that for Stiegler, *otium* is not a practice that arises within a particular historical context so much as a general anthropological category that accounts for how unproductive and exceptional activity arises from calculated and totalizing circumstances. Stiegler does concur with Foucault's finding of an initial definition of the practice of *otium* within ancient Greek and Roman life, where a strong distinction was made between *negotium* and self-cultivation.[6] Defining *otium* as the practice of consistence beyond calculated *negotium* that is nevertheless inextricable from totalizing conditions, Stiegler empties it of historical content and redefines it as practice that supports experience of the impossible.[7] The a-transcendental status of this claim is made clear when Stiegler states that "no society has ever existed that did not contain practices comparable to what the Roman nobility called otium" (Stiegler 2011a, 118). Therefore, as both de Beistegui and Sophie Fuggle argue, *otium* is not a call for a return to an ancient Greek or Roman conception of leisurely activity (de Beistegui 2013, 187; Fuggle 2013, 206). Instead, Stiegler's advocation of *otium* asks us to recognize the role of impossibility within psychic and collective individuation more generally.

Impossibility is pivotal to this conception of *otium* because the former is the condition of the engagement with consistency found in the latter.[8] As a political judgment, *otium* encompasses the conditionality associated with the impossible: one can only access the time of *otium* on the basis of specific, a-transcendental practices of the improbable. Stiegler does not determine what *otium* looks like, but simply determines that "it is the discernment of a difference—of a difference that only exists to the extent that one *believes* in it, and that one only believes to the extent that one *makes* it" (Stiegler 2011a, 99). While *otium* represents a specific political judgment that responds to the eradication of time dedicated to consistence within societies of control, it also attempts to account for the possibility of a plurality of political judgments that arise from reflection on consistence within particular pharmacological circumstances. A late restatement of the principle of *otium* in relation to the *pharmakon* presents it as such: "*Otium* and *negotium* constitute the bipolarity constitutive of the tension characteristic of the pharmacological situation . . . of the non-inhuman being" (Stiegler 2018c, 74). *Otium* is the pharmacologically curative tendency of the balance between the time of consistence and *negotium*, the time of subsistence, and represents Stiegler's commitment to non-totalizing practices that foster access to the impossible by way of particular, totalizing conditions.

The Antigone Complex

If *otium* is defined by time dedicated to the space for judgment on consistences, then it is conceivable that this reinterpretation of consistence may conflict with the norms that guide an existing process of psychic and collective individuation. Stiegler openly endorses this possibility and defines politics as "*a sublime form of transgression*" (Stiegler 2013b, 31). This transgression is underpinned by the impossibility found within Bataille's understanding of the sacred, as an exceptional experience that is nevertheless conditioned by a set of totalizing taboos. Understanding the sacred in this way requires "the reconciling of what seems impossible to reconcile, respect for the law and the violation of the law, the taboo and its transgression" (Bataille 1986, 36). Establishment of new political judgments conditioned by the impossible requires the reconciliation of totalizing conditions and their recursive modification by transgression. Stiegler develops this conception of politics in a reading of Sophocles's *Antigone*.

Set in the aftermath of a civil war in Thebes during which Antigone's brothers Eteocles and Polyneices are both killed fighting for opposing sides, *Antigone* revolves around the eponymous character's resistance to the illegitimacy of political authority that fails to recognize its contingent foundations. Creon, who emerges as king of Thebes after the war, will only perform burial rights for Eteocles, declaring that Polyneices should be left unburied as a traitor to the city. Pledging to provide Polyneices with the correct burial rites, Antigone decrees the laws of the gods more important than the laws of the city and affirms the existence of justice beyond the law. While Antigone affirms the irreducibility of the laws of the gods to the laws of humans, Creon affirms that "the city *is* the king's—that's the law!" (Sophocles 2015, 34). Antigone's conflict with Creon represents a difference between generations within which laws become sedimented and subsequently challenged. As political forms mature, they form the foundations of positive law that "limits or even proscribes singularity"; however, Antigone's appeal highlights that these "distinctions are never definitively acquired" and "must always be interpreted anew" (Stiegler 2013b, 35). Rather than a transcendental principle, the law to which Antigone appeals is the impossible non-origin of human law that requires constant reinterpretation through new judgments.

In contrast to Creon, Antigone perceives the tragic condition of the law: it can only exist on the basis of the impossibility that underpins it. Definitive laws are impossible, but they are nevertheless the source of non-totalizing judgments that engage with and recursively alter the way that they structure social life. Stiegler's point here is twofold. First, the authority of the law rests on its critique: "justice, insofar as it consists (and this consistence is its *only* authority), clearly proceeds from the critique of law . . . and from its capacity to discern and judge (within) the law—to discern and judge what is just" (Stiegler 2013b, 38). Second, this critique and the judgment it entails are given form by a particular institutional setting: "Authority is the condition of all consistence: it designates consistence in general; it is the general structure through which consistences are possible" (Stiegler 2013b, 45). Law, understood as this hypomnesic prescription of the structure of consistence, is a particular practice of the improbable that harbors the impossible.

Totalization and non-totalization are reconciled within the Antigone complex, as Stiegler conceives of law as both structurally open to critique and as the foundation of critique itself. Judgments that do not recognize their contingency in this way surrender their legitimacy, as the impossible is the very condition of the consistences that form the totalizing nature of law. Conflict between generations represented by Antigone and Creon is "structurally necessary" for the production of belief in the law because it attests to the impossibility that underpins it (Stiegler 2015a, 26). It is through this intergenerational process of critique that the impossible can underpin pharmacologically curative practices of conflict that challenge the poisonous imposition of totalizing judgments without recognition of their default. Greta Thunberg's criticism of the failure of national and international organizations to address climate change represents, for Stiegler, a contemporary example of this Antigone complex (Stiegler 2020c, 13–51). Thunberg's intergenerational criticism is directed at the carelessness of those responsible for an economic system founded on the inability to recognize the contingency, and ultimate fragility, of its structuring principles in the face of climate change. Carelessness is substituted with a sense of responsibility and an appeal to the laws of science that consist beyond those structures. While the Antigone complex is developed by Stiegler within the context of a reading of Sophocles, his identification of Thunberg's activism with this intergenerational critique shows that he sees this diachronic criticism and transformation of synchronic principles as structuring all social systems. This reinforces my claim that, for Stiegler, any political judgment is formed by a particular set of totalizing conditions and can be superseded by judgments that appeal to the interpretability of its consistences. The Antigone complex attests to the balance between totalization and non-totalization and the recursive relationship between them.

"Everyone an Artist": Amateurs and Aesthetic Politics

This process of conflict is ultimately the source of invention, which Stiegler endorses more widely through his advocacy of an artistic mentality characteristic of the amateur. While both *otium* and the Antigone complex are immediately anthropological—referring to the tension between *otium* and *negotium* and the law and its critique—the amateur is a more immediately polemic concept, mobilized within Stiegler's critique of aesthetic disconnection within consumerism. Under capitalism, conditions for widespread engagement with aesthetic judgment and invention, which are characteristic of an amateur's engagement with their craft, are replaced with standardized cultural products and practices; "the '*amateur*,' the art-lover, comes to be replaced by the consumer suffering from a dazed cultural obesity" (Stiegler 2013b, 90). In contrast to the consumer, the amateur is not someone who casually learns a hobby or the opposite of a professional, but rather someone "who is no longer anything like a consumer and who *wants to know*—to be individuated" (Stiegler 2010e, 70). An amateur is an individual who is dedicated to a particular practice and participates in the production of consistences through their engagement with it.

In contrast to the more general time of impossibility represented by *otium*, the *otium* of the amateur is centered around artistic practice and engagement. Proletarianized consumers are deprived of the skills necessary for engaging with the impossible, a state that Stiegler thinks can be remedied by the development of amateur practice, as "the manual reproduction and technical mastery it requires are conditions for the formation of judgment, and therefore of transindividuation" (Stiegler 2017e, 42). Amateurs judge by practicing and individuating a particular field of expertise. As Martin Crowley summarizes, an amateur is "a non-professional, of course, but crucially, one who practises an art, or a skill, out of love for the activity. . . . Amateurs repeat—practise scales, say, or copy out a score—in order to maintain their love of these objects; through such repetition, they continually become who they are, in relation to and distinct from the collective inheritance they are engaging with, perpetuating, and modifying" (Crowley 2013b, 128–29). Here we return to the importance of repetition and recursivity within Stiegler's philosophy. Amateurs recursively modify a process of individuation by engaging with the practices that support it to transform them through repetition. Repetitive practices of the amateur-artist are opposed to cultural automation without the space for dreams that might engender new processes of individuation (Chalmers 2020). In light of Stiegler's reading of Blanchot, this repetition informs practices of the improbable that facilitate access to the impossible default that underlies consistence to generate extraordinary and unexpected judgments.

Amateurs are not simply political because of their polemical opposition to the figure of the consumer, but also because of their engagement with transindividuation. Circuits of transindividuation are "symbolic systems" that "form, weave, hatch and frame spaces and critical times of decisions that life must always take when, having become the form of technical life, it is always in some way a *critical* life" (Stiegler 2013c, 70). Stiegler's focus on the amateur is not simply the investment of individual aesthetic activity with political value. It represents a broader concern with the fundamental aesthetic and symbolic nature of human existence. As Crowley argues, for Stiegler, "participation in the life of the senses, articulated in dialectics of synchronic/diachronic, individual/collective symbolization, becomes indispensable to any human existence beyond the level of mere physical subsistence" (Crowley 2013a, 49).[9] Amateurs embody the symbolic basis of individuation by repeating, practicing, and transforming the technical practices that support the consistences that orient it. A totalizing context is necessary for this amateur practice, but the amateur's engagement with the impossible opens this context to non-totalizing judgments. As I demonstrated in chapter 5, the decisions generated within these aesthetic practices are analogous to political judgments. If the amateur's practice involves the cultivation of singularities that reinterpret consistences, then these judgments and interpretations are bound up with the totalizing contexts that form political judgment. Art and politics are united by this cultivation of singularity. Aesthetic judgment is inherently political, as it concerns "the *experience* and the *support* of this sensible singularity as an invitation to symbolic activity, to the production and discovery of traces in collective times" (Stiegler 2014e, 6). As with *otium* and the Antigone complex, the amateur is situated within a particular totalizing context but represents a non-totalizing engagement with these a-transcendental conditions. Stiegler maintains the openness of the nature of amateur practice insofar as it takes its meaning from the singularities and consistences produced within a distinct organological locality.

In defining the amateur as the individual who participates in aesthetic circuits of transindividuation, Stiegler translates Joseph Beuys's declaration that everyman is an artist into the lexicon of his philosophy of technicity. Beuys's position on creativity is close to Stiegler's, as he sees it as reliant on the sculptural relationship between human existence and its tools and materials: "Thought is a sculptural process, and the expression of the thinking forms in language is also art. This totality of humankind's creativity—beginning with feelings and thoughts and their expression in a special material, the language material, for which you need your body and physical tools, your tongue, larynx, lungs, the air, the sound waves, the ear of the other person—all have to do with the idea of sculpture in the future" (Beuys

1990, 73). For Beuys, this artistic practice is formative of human existence: "art alone makes life possible" (Beuys 1990, 87). Stiegler interprets this sculptural and artistic definition of the human as "a Beuysian organology" (Stiegler 2015b, 75). Artistic practice is formed by the immersion of the human within the material world and, for Stiegler, the technical supports that are the organized forms of these inorganic materials.[10] The amateur is a figure who, in contrast to the consumer, actively engages with the sculptural condition that Beuys claims defines the human by pursuing individuation for the sake of singularity, and partakes in practices of the improbable that allow for the impossible production of new consistences.[11]

As Beuys claims, we are all artists because human individuation involves an irreducibly aesthetic component. Amateurs engage with symbols, rituals, practices, and techniques that underpin individuation to reinterpret the consistences that form the conditions of that individuation, and are therefore intimately concerned with the collective basis of political judgment.[12] Because the repetition of these practices can never be purely identical, like political judgment, "*every* aesthetic practice is a *putting into doubt*" that challenges an existing set of prejudgments (Stiegler 2015b, 161). As Crowley and Robert Hughes both argue, the symbolic and aesthetic character of transindividuation is central to articulating the link between the *I* and the *We* insofar as it mediates the disjunctive unification of particular instances of psychic individuation within a single process of collective individuation (Crowley 2013a, 49; Hughes 2014, 61–62). Understood in this way, Stiegler's advocation of the amateur is not just a political judgment that opposes the creative repetition of a totalizing set of aesthetic conditions to the uncritical totalization of aesthetic control under capitalism. It is also an open judgment that makes space for the variety of ways in which this political relationship between aesthetic judgment and its conditions might unfold.

Conclusion: The A-Transcendental and the Impossible

As political judgments, *otium*, the Antigone complex, and the amateur all embody Stiegler's commitment to the reconciliation of totalization and non-totalization. In each case, the access to the impossible that underpins conceptual invention, interpretation, and judgment is facilitated by particular practices of the improbable found within leisure time, the development of the law, and aesthetic practice. These three judgments all represent, as Ross Abbinnett puts it, the diverse ways in which the "heterogenous temporalities of spirit" can have "unforeseen effects" (Abbinnett 2018, 150). By advocating for a politics of improbable practices that facilitate access to this impossible wellspring of transformation, rather than valorizing the impossible itself, Stiegler shows that he is concerned with the multiplicity of forms that such a politics might take. For Richard Beardsworth, this is precisely what distinguishes Stiegler from figures within twentieth-century French philosophy and poststructuralism, like Derrida and Deleuze, who are concerned with the impossible. For Stiegler, "the alterity of the indeterminate, so rightly targeted and prized by post war continental philosophical reflection as a major object of philosophical reflection, demands work" (Beardsworth 1998a, 80). In this chapter I have argued that Stiegler's commitment to this work in his use of Blanchot and Bataille underpins his focus on the concrete practices of the improbable that condition access to undecidability in this way.

It is this focus on the practice of improbability that gives rise to improbability, rather than the impossible itself, that lends *otium*, the Antigone complex, and the amateur an a-transcendental character. As conceptions of political activity, they have no content besides the stipulation that one engage with the impossible through a particular set of practices, the character of which will depend upon the a-transcendental horizon in which they are formed. The political judgments that arise from this engagement with consistence do not rule out the possibility of suspension by changes to pharmacological problems, contrary judgments, or evidence of anthropological alterity that upend our certainty about the political value of particular practices of the improbable. As a political category, the impossible maintains a tension between the totalizing judgments that form the political through decisions that separate it from the indifference of the default while also maintaining the situated and non-totalizable character of these decisions. In contrast to a political ontology of the indeterminate that privileges the impossible in itself, Stiegler's conception of the impossible allows for the postulation of a plurality of political judgments that totalize while maintaining the space for the suspension and critique of their totalization.

7

Neganthropology and the
Problem of Judgment

Critical accounts of climate change and the associated turn to the language of the Anthropocene have presented a fundamental challenge to humanist accounts of political agency. Embedded within ecological conditions, the human is less a master of nature than part of a global climate system that it cannot treat according to its whims. This challenge has been met by those committed to non-totalizing accounts of the political. One response has been to provide images of human agency founded on ontological conceptions of the human's relation to nonhuman agents, an approach prominent within new materialist accounts of the Anthropocene (Randazzo and Richter 2021). Another has been to claim that the scale of the effects of human agency "stretches our capacity for interpretive understanding" and undermines the "sense of ontology" attributed to humanity. Dipesh Chakrabarty argues that this represents the necessity of "nonontological ways of thinking the human" (Chakrabarty 2012, 13). Given the Anthropocene's entanglement with global capitalism and the crisis of judgment that it presents for politics, it is not surprising that Stiegler's late work was deeply concerned with a response to this problem. Do his judgments on the politics of the Anthropocene combine totalization and non-totalization in a way that accords with the need for "nonontological" understandings of the human? Or does Stiegler articulate a totalizing and ontological understanding of the agency required to solve these problems, thereby falling into the trap of associating a particular ontology with a necessary path out of the Anthropocene problematic?

In this chapter I argue that Stiegler falls prey to the latter tendency in the "neganthropology" that he poses as the solution to the Anthropocene.

Neganthropology serves as a response to Claude Lévi-Strauss's polemic claim that "'Entropology'" should replace the study of anthropology because of the destructive effects of humans on their natural and social environments (Lévi-Strauss 1961, 397). Like Lévi-Strauss, Stiegler adopts the language of thermodynamics to account for the negative ecological impact of humanity. In contrast, he does so to account for both the entropic tendency toward disorder and a contrary, negentropic tendency that resists physical inertia. Through his use of the concepts of entropy, negentropy, and anti-entropy and his accounting for the transformation of these physical terms by technicity with the concepts of anthropy, neganthropy, and anti-anthropy, Stiegler develops his "neganthropology" to claim that a "neganthropization of the world breaks with the careless and negligent anthropization of its entropic effects—that is, with the essential characteristics of the Anthropocene" (Stiegler 2016a, 14). Neganthropology represents an attempt to understand how knowledge is characterized by a pharmacological tendency toward entropy, and its epistemological and political project is to support forms of social organization that maintain neganthropic structures with the potential for intermittent, anti-anthropic moments of "bifurcation" that respond to pharmacological problems, the Anthropocene chief among them.

At first glance, Stiegler's transformation of the language of entropy furthers his commitment to the local nature of political judgment and to cultivating a plurality of non-inhuman forms of existence. In response to the exacerbation of the pharmacological tendency toward anthropic disorder within societies of control, he argues that anti-anthropy must be cultivated within practices that support intermittent judgments in response to moments of crisis like the Anthropocene. A local and contextual approach to thinking, or "noodiversity," is the condition of the improbable bifurcations to be induced by these judgments (Stiegler 2020a, 244). Here I ask whether the language of thermodynamics is appropriate for supporting noodiversity, or whether it represents a set of ontological presuppositions that constitute a totalizing judgment without openness. By pursuing this question, I further Ashley Woodward's claim that Stiegler's use of the concept of entropy is metaphysical when considered from the perspective of his own philosophy of technicity (Woodward 2016, 100; 2017, 129–30). I contend that Stiegler's assertion of the necessity and universality of the language of thermodynamics constitutes a commitment to a totalizing and non-suspendible ontology that brings with it a set of totalizing propositions regarding the nature of the human.

This claim is developed in three steps. I first introduce Stiegler's use of thermodynamic language, paying particular attention to his distinction between the conceptual triads of entropy, negentropy, and anti-entropy and anthropy, neganthropy, and anti-anthropy. This account is situated within Stiegler's claim that thermodynamics represents an epistemological shift in favor of the local constitution of knowledge, and his political claim that escaping the Anthropocene requires the cultivation of local noodiversity. I then, second, consider how Stiegler presents neganthropology as a universal political problematic that contradicts its purported aim of supporting plurality, with respect to both his use of terms derived from the ontological presuppositions represented by the language of entropy, and the status of the human as a universal subject of neganthropology. Third, I argue that this ontology presupposes a totalizing conception of the human as an unruly animal prone to destructive behavior in the absence of social bonds. This claim is made by elaborating on the relationship between anthropy and Stiegler's use of the Freudian language of drives. In the absence of negentropic and neganthropic order, humans are liable to regress to destructive and violent drive-based behaviors. These two consequences suggest that Stiegler's political development of the language of entropy does not maintain the balance between totalization and non-totalization that I argue his thought demands.

Epistemology and Politics after Entropy

Stiegler's turn to the language of entropy should be understood in the context of the role that it plays in redefining epistemology and politics within the Anthropocene. Thermodynamics extends the basic presuppositions of the philosophy of technics into the language of energy, its preservation, and its dissipation, and returns us to the concept of exosomatization first introduced in chapter 3. Exosomatic organs form an organological relationship to biological and social organs, and in doing so they transform the relationship between entropic disorder and the negentropic tendency of life to resist dissipation. By extending the task of resisting entropy to exorganisms, Stiegler places the problem of energy at the center of his philosophy of technics. It should be recognized that he is by no means the first thinker in the continental tradition to draw on the language of entropy and negentropy.[1] However, Stiegler's version of the consequences of entropy shows a commitment to the systematic integration of the language of thermodynamics with his wider philosophy. Introducing this position and its consequences for epistemology and politics first requires a summary of the general usage of entropy and negentropy that Stiegler adopts and diverges from.

Entropy first becomes a conceptual problem amid the industrial revolution. The first law of thermodynamics, the conservation of energy across its transformation from one state to another, met an impasse in the reality of steam engines. Steam engines required the irreversible transformation of fuel into heat and exhibited the loss of some of that heat to their surroundings; the efficient transformation of heat into work came up against the tendency of energy to move toward equilibrium conditions (Daggett 2019, 42–44). Heat will always transfer its energy to cold material by tending toward equilibrium and away from a non-equilibrium state required to produce work. Without interference from the outside, the second law of thermodynamics refers to this tendency of a closed system to move inexorably toward equilibrium. Generalized by Ludwig Boltzmann to statistical probabilities applicable to the cosmos as a whole, entropy signifies the "steady degradation of energy until all tensions that might still perform work and all visible motions in the universe have to cease" (Boltzmann 1974, 19). While its consequences are still subject to scientific debate, entropy is nevertheless taken to refer to this inevitable dissipation of ordered matter into more probable, disordered states.

Two issues that arise from the discovery of entropy are important here because of the attention that Stiegler pays to them. First, entropy posed a fundamental challenge to classical mechanics within physics. Newtonian conceptions of reversibility and the potential prediction of the future with the knowledge of all interacting forces are replaced by irreversibility, because of the dissipation of energy, and the stymieing of exact prediction by the role of probability within entropic movement (Prigogine and Stengers 2017, 213–32). After entropy, universal, reversible, and deterministic principles expressed by Newtonian, classical mechanics must compete with local, irreversible, and non-deterministic processes. The second issue concerns the relationship of entropy to the reality of order within the universe. Norbert Wiener gives an evocative account of these cosmological consequences: "As entropy increases, the universe, and all closed systems in the universe, tend naturally to deteriorate and lose their distinctiveness, to move from the least to the most probable state, from a state of organization and differentiation in which distinctions and forms exist, to a state of chaos and sameness" (Wiener 1989, 12). While the tendency toward entropy characterizes this slow heat death of the universe as it moves inexorably toward equilibrium, it is evident that order does exist. Negative entropy, or negentropy, has been proposed by a range of thinkers as a solution to this problem. Erwin Schrödinger used negentropy to account for the organism's capacity to maintain a level of organization against threats posed by its environment

(Schrödinger 1992), and in Wiener's cybernetics, negentropy represents the stability of information within communication in contrast to entropic noise (Wiener 2019, 17). While entropy induces anxieties at the cosmological level—the loss of universal, deterministic laws and the fatalistic eventuality of heat death—it also draws attention toward a relational universe, where essences are replaced by the transfer and transformation of energy within local negentropic conditions.

Stiegler's development of the language of thermodynamics revolves around the epistemological import of its relational view of the universe and the problem that entropy poses for technical forms of life. Entropy's epistemological challenge to Newtonian mechanics undermines the possibility of articulating an ontologically stable, linear, and determinist view of the universe, which Stiegler associates with the modern calculative imaginary (Stiegler 2020b, 74). This point becomes politically salient later, as it is this primordial improbability that is negated by societies of control. More importantly for now, Stiegler emphasizes the need for an epistemological focus on locality as a result of this challenge to classical mechanics. While the macroscopic consequence of thermodynamics is a "renewed thought of the cosmos," the vision of the universe engendered by the science of combustion is "relative, but it leads to *conceiving of the cosmos in its totality on the basis of this position*" (Stiegler 2016a, 11). Entropy and negentropy cannot be understood without reference to relations and differences that signify the proximity or distance of a particular system from equilibrium. Hence, Stiegler sees his turn to the language of thermodynamics as eluding the fixity represented by ontology (Stiegler 2020c, 368) and demanding the examination of negentropic potential from a local perspective (Stiegler 2019d, 306–7).

The lack of ontological determination represented by thermodynamics leads Stiegler to claim that local, relational claims and judgments must take place in relation to the cosmological and universal scale. This claim rests on two gestures that concern the relationship between entropy and life: the adoption of the concept of anti-entropy from the work of Francis Bailly, Giuseppe Longo, and Maël Montévil, and the differentiation of the tripartite distinction between entropy, negentropy, and anti-entropy within life from the tendencies toward and against dissipation within technical life, which Stiegler calls anthropy, neganthropy, and anti-anthropy. In *Automatic Society*, his earliest extended discussion of the problem of entropy, Stiegler had not fully developed the third concept of anti-entropy or completely distinguished between entropy and the string of terms that follow from the concept of anthropy. Here he adopts Schrödinger's distinction between entropy and negentropy as the condition of life in general. Negentropy is, for Schrödinger, the way that "the organism succeeds in freeing itself from all the entropy it cannot help producing" (Schrödinger 1992, 71). According to Stiegler, this struggle against entropy is "the *crucial problem* of the everyday life of human beings and of life in general, and, finally, of the universe in totality for every form of life" (Stiegler 2016a, 11). Neganthropology, at this point in Stiegler's work, refers to the articulation of "negentropic criteria" that would govern human life by resisting entropy (Stiegler 2016a, 14).

Several points accompany this initial turn to the concept of entropy. The most important of these is a clear link between Stiegler's earlier philosophy and his turn to entropy, found in his claim that negentropy and *différance* are connected. Associating it with the deferral of presence and stability, Stiegler argues that *différance* should be understood as the process by which entropy is deferred: "what Derrida called *différance*, if we may indeed relate negentropy to this concept, is first and foremost a matter of economy and detour" (Stiegler 2018c, 57).[2] *Différance* refers to the non-presence of an organism to itself because of its exposure to degradation and its organizational responses to the tendency toward dissipation: "*life defers its entropic disappearance via the play of mnesic traces* of all kinds: psychic, social and technical" (Stiegler 2019d, 54). Here Stiegler's adoption of entropy fits with his broader commitment to thinking the human in nonhumanist terms because of the integration of technicity with the entropic tendencies of its environmental conditions.[3] However, this conceptual shift engenders two problems. If negentropy maintains a level of order by deferring entropic disorder, then how can the quasi-causal and unpredictable interventions that Stiegler associates with non-totalizing political judgment be accounted for? Moreover, how can the relationship between entropy and negentropy in life and within the technical condition be meaningfully distinguished?

Anti-entropy provides a way to differentiate negentropic stability and the production of stability by moments of invention that create new possibilities for the organism. For Bailly and Longo: "anti-entropy is correlated to the formation of *multilevel, integrated and regulated organization*, and *not only* to the appearing of order corresponding to a lowering of physical entropy" (Bailly and Longo 2009, 92). Anti-entropy is distinct from negentropy insofar as it occurs, to use a term that Stiegler adopts from Bailly, within the "extended critical situation" of living matter (Stiegler 2020a, 306). If entropy constantly threatens the negentropic stability of the organism, then anti-entropy refers to the capacity of organisms to respond to this ongoing critical moment by producing new functions that are integrated into existing negentropic structures. Anti-entropy consists of "functional innovations that appeared in the past" and "the production of functional innovations" that contribute "to the ability of biological objects to persist over time by contributing to their organization in a given context" (Montévil et al. 2021, 56). Metastable negentropic relations are produced by anti-entropic bifurcations that emerge from particular localities, reorganizing them to produce new possibilities for the organism's individuation.

Adoption of the concept of anti-entropy comes with the challenge of distinguishing between anti-entropic invention at the level of the organism and at the level of technical life. Like with *différance*, Stiegler must differentiate between anti-entropy within life in general and anti-entropy within technical life. Two gestures constitute his response to this challenge. The first is a distinction between entropy, negentropy, and anti-entropy and anthropy, neganthropy, and anti-entropy: "the three-phases of vital individuation take place between entropy, negentropy and anti-entropy," whereas the "the three-phase psychotechnosocial individuation operates between anthropy, neganthropy and anti-anthropy" (Stiegler 2020c, 271). This division is analogous to the distinction Stiegler makes between *différance* within life and the *différance* engendered by the technical object. A qualitatively distinct play of disorder, order, and invention to that within life in general is engendered by the relationship to the technical object, which is represented by anthropy, neganthropy, and anti-anthropy.

Stiegler's second gesture is to codify this shift by turning to a distinction, and relationship, between endosomatic and exosomatic organs across which anthropic, neganthropic, and anti-anthropic relations operate. The concepts of exosomatic organs and of exorganisms who use these organs, which I introduced in chapter 3 to elaborate on the interaction between local conditions of individuation at different organological scales, are developed by Stiegler from the work of the biologist Alfred Lotka and the economist Nicholas Georgescu-Roegen. Lotka argued that within human evolution, endosomatic organs are supplemented by "artificial aids" that "might be termed *exosomatic evolution*" (Lotka 1945, 188). Exosomatic evolution allows humans to increase the amount of energy available for the pursuit of life by extending energy conservation through artificial means. As Georgescu-Roegen clarifies in his adoption of Lotka's distinction: "Exosomatic instruments enable man to obtain the same amount of low entropy with less expenditure of his own free energy than if he used only his endosomatic organs" (Georgescu-Roegen 1971, 307). Economic principles, for Georgescu-Roegen, are derived from the interaction between these two types of organs. In this bioeconomic perspective, humans produce the energy needed for survival through the maintenance of negentropic structures that utilize exosomatic organs.

Stiegler adopts this terminology from Lotka and Georgescu-Roegen to distinguish between entropy, negentropy, and anti-entropy and anthropy, neganthropy, and anti-anthropy while simultaneously ensuring that they are co-extensive with evolution at the endosomatic, or biological, level. A clear statement of this dual purpose can be found in *The Age of Disruption*: "Exoso-matization is not 'natural,' that is, derived from the 'laws of nature,' nor is it simply 'artificial,' at least if . . . we consider that the process of exteriorization and the artifactual organogenesis in which it consists delimit the technical form of life" (Stiegler 2019d, 96). Exosomatic evolution allows Stiegler to identify a specifically human relationship to entropy that does not rely on exceptionalism, as it "harbours new entropic and negentropic possibilities for non-inhuman life, new possibilities other than those stemming from the organogenesis of endosomatic life" (Stiegler 2019d, 275). Anthropy is one such possibility that concerns a homogenizing tendency toward disintegration and dissipation found within technical and social forms of organization. Neganthropy refers to the metastable differences that resist anthropy and possess the potential for anti-anthropic bifurcation. The distinctiveness of anti-anthropy consists in the non-biological nature of its inventions and the role that they play in organizing a broader social and technical, rather than simply organic, system: "Anti-anthropy is distinguished from neganthropy in that it diachronizes a synchronic neganthropic order. These (neganthropic and anti-anthropic) values are produced by *locality* as such, which they characterize and, in so doing, *delimit*" (Stiegler, Vignola, and Azar 2021, 29). Themes that I have emphasized across Stiegler's work return here in his transforma-tion of the language of entropy. Within non-inhuman life, neganthropic stability establishes totalizing localities that are themselves the product of the exosomatic and recursive anti-anthropic invention of exorganisms. It is the invention of relationships between the various neganthropic levels of these organisms that necessitates totalization, but only on the condition that these systems are open to non-totalizing bifurcations.

I am now in a position to properly qualify the epistemological and political stakes of Stiegler's turn to the language of entropy. Viewed from the neganthropological perspective, knowledge is not the attribution of cer-tainty to beliefs but a means of establishing relations between exorganisms that provide the opportunity for anti-anthropic bifurcation: "Neganthropology and neganthropic production, which result from exosomatization, are concretized only through the knowledge that they require. These forms of knowledge produce tastes, differences, noodiversified nuances through which the exosomatic being constantly raises itself toward a noesis that is more than human" (Stiegler 2017d, 94). Neganthropological knowledge does not concern energy as such, although it will certainly address humanity's relationship to entropy and negentropy. More fundamentally, within the neganthropological perspective, knowledge concerns the establishment of relations between simple and complex exorganisms at various scales that can regulate the production of neganthropological metastabilities that support anti-anthropic bifurcation. Local totalities that support diverse forms of knowledge, therefore, condition the non-totalizing and singular judgments that form part of the a-transcendental conditions for individuation.

Georges Canguilhem and Alfred North Whitehead are particularly important for this epistemological perspective. Both refuse to distinguish knowledge from its local conditions, which for Stiegler are eminently technical: "As for Whitehead and for Lotka, knowledge is for Canguilhem a vital function in the form of technical life that is exosomatized life" (Stiegler 2020c, 347). Canguilhem outlines this perspective as follows: "Knowledge, including (and perhaps above all) biology, is one of the ways by which humanity seeks to take control of its destiny and to transform its being into a duty. For this project, man's knowledge about man is of fundamental importance. The primacy of anthropology is not a form of anthropomorphism, but a condition for anthropogenesis" (Canguilhem 2008, 19). Knowledge constitutes the non-inhuman, as it gives meaning to its being and establishes conditions for its individuation. This knowledge is necessarily local, for "negentropy is always defined in relation to an observer . . . it is always described in relation to a *locality in time as well as in space that it, as such, produces*, and that it *differentiates*." Consequently, knowledge is bound up with the question of locality, as "what appears entropic from one angle is negentropic from another angle," but it nevertheless moves toward totality because it "is *always a way of collectively defining what is negentropic in this or that field of human existence*" (Stiegler 2019b, 44). Neganthropology is the project of supporting the constitution of non-inhuman existence as a form of life that develops through knowledge of itself, on the condition that this knowledge is simultaneously totalizing and open insofar as it is local.

This reconciliation of openness and totalization within the epistemological perspective established by neganthropology becomes clearer in the context of Stiegler's adoption of Whitehead's understanding of reason. For Whitehead, "Reason is the organ of emphasis on novelty. It provides the judgment by which realization in idea obtains the emphasis by which it passes into realization in purpose, and thence its realization in fact" (Whitehead 1929b, 20). Like Canguilhem, "reason is for Whitehead a *vital function* in the processuality of the universe, which is to allow the reasonable being to *participate in its concrescence*" (Stiegler 2020c, 195). Whitehead defines concrescence in similar terms to individuation: "the process, or concrescence, of any one actual entity involves the other actual entities among its components" (Whitehead 1929a, 7). Within "each process of concrescence a regional standpoint in the world, defining a limited potentiality for objectifications, has been adopted" (Whitehead 1929a, 67). In Whitehead's process philosophy, reason participates in the establishment of relationships between entities, or in the construction of concrescences. Exosomatic organs are not possessed of inherent purpose or function outside their concrescence within metastable organological relationships by anti-anthropic invention, a task that Stiegler claims constitutes the function of reason.[4]

Here I return to themes discussed already. In Stiegler's reading of Whitehead, the function of reason is to quasi-causally give meaning to the relationship between exosomatic organisms that constitute a particular process of individuation. Understood in this way, reason rests on quasi-causality, which is redefined as "the *veridical power of anti-anthropy* in the process of exosomatization" (Stiegler 2022, 275). This position deepens the a-transcendental framing of thinking that I introduced with respect to organology and the work of Gaston Bachelard in chapter 3. Knowledge is produced by the performative dimension of anti-anthropy that renders thinking inherently local insofar as it constituted within the relationship between exosomatic organs: "Reality is always already exosomatic: the real cannot be thus conceived, that is to say observed *as such*, as real, and distinguished from what is not (*not yet*) real, only from the poetic and pharmacological experience of the production of *pharmaka* that are exosomatic organs" (Stiegler 2018a, 102–3). As an epistemological project, neganthropology seeks to draw further consequences from the disruption of Newtonian universalism by thermodynamics. Knowledge is constituted by the local, totalizing, and a-transcendental conditions of a particular set of exosomatic organs, but these contexts are themselves rendered non-totalizing by their relationship to the recursive production of their conditions by anti-anthropic bifurcations.

As a political project, neganthropology regulates the relationship of these intermittent, anti-anthropic forms of invention to the *pharmakon* that acts as their condition. Implicit within Stiegler's reading of Lotka, Georgescu-Roegen, Canguilhem, and Whitehead is a political conception of knowledge: it forms a quasi-causal response to the mere facts of exosomatic and endosomatic evolution by totalizing and giving meaning, or function, to existing neganthropological conditions. Anti-anthropic judgment is political because it responds to the pharmacological problems unique to a particular exosomatic context: "Technics is itself a process of exosomatic individuation *both supporting and threatening* psychic individuation and collective individuation, and *supported by what it threatens*: technical individuation requires the psychic and social individuals that it threatens. This amounts to a primordially pharmacological situation" (Stiegler 2021b, 246). Exosomatic evolution supports individuation in an organological manner, and in doing so takes on characteristics attributed to technicity elsewhere in Stiegler's work. In particular, the relationships between entropy and negentropy and anthropy and neganthropy are aligned with the pharmacological character of exosomatization. Because of "the ambiguous character of exosomatic organs," they "make possible both the production of new neganthropic forms and a massive increase in the rate of entropy" (Stiegler 2018c, 77). Neganthropology represents the translation of Stiegler's earlier claims regarding the necessity of judgment upon pharmacological problems into the language of the duality represented by entropy and negentropy. As seen in chapter 5, this "knowledge is always critical in the broad sense: it discerns, and exercises judgment, *to krinon*" (Stiegler 2018a, 104). To respond to entropy and anthropy requires this sorting and discerning activity that is resolutely political because it responds to the generation of entropy and anthropy by pharmaka.

Consequently, judgment is central to the neganthropological political project insofar as Stiegler distinguishes between the entropic becoming of the universe and the establishment of a neganthropic future that is irreducible to a state of fact. If the future is negentropic and becoming entropic, then judgment establishes "an interpretation of ends such that they rise above analysis only on the condition that they break with it, and do so as decision, that is, as bifurcation" (Stiegler 2018c, 74). Such judgment is political because it forms *"an anti-anthropic knowledge that can contribute to modifying the spontaneously reigning neganthropic order"* (Stiegler 2020c, 179). Here it is clear how neganthropology represents both a novel development and a unification of already existing themes within Stiegler's work: the balance between totalization and non-totalization found within the a-transcendental, the quasi-causal nature of judgment, and the plurality of forms of human thought, action, and existence represented by the non-inhuman. "Quasi-causality is neganthropological causality par excellence" because it represents the unpredictable emergence of these anti-anthropic judgments from their a-transcendental conditions and the wider condition of being in default (Stiegler 2019d, 346, n.64). Because of the importance attributed to this anti-anthropic quasi-causality in Stiegler's philosophy, negentropy becomes, as Tracy Colony has put it, an "evaluative criterion" for the quality of political decision making (Colony 2017, 83). Neganthropology classifies as curative those judgments that support local systems that resist entropy and anthropy, and associates totalization that imposes on locality with pharmacologically poisonous decisions.

The language of entropy is modified in this way to provide a therapeutic conceptual framework that responds to two particular threats to the diversity of forms of the non-inhuman within the Anthropocene era: the entropic collapse threatened by climate change and the eradication of the kinds of judgment needed to respond to this pharmacological problem within societies of control. At its broadest level, neganthropology concerns the opening of an exit from climate change within the Anthropocene. For such an exit to be found, Stiegler argues that "noodiversity" is necessary "to effect a bifurcation in the Anthropocene" (Stiegler 2020b, 72). This diversity is politically necessary because of the prior epistemological claim that the invention of new functions that integrate entropic becoming into a future requires anti-anthropy, which is improbable, unpredictable, and quasi-causal. Diversity of thought is necessary to produce solutions that meet the function that Canguilhem and Whitehead attribute to reason. This claim regarding the exit to the Anthropocene coheres with Stiegler's earlier claims regarding the organological nature of judgment. If reason is "a specific negentropic capacity to 'realize' an order in struggling against this 'anarchic element,'" then it is to general organology that Stiegler turns to as the method that "investigates the conditions of possibility of a political and noetic *decision*" (Stiegler 2017a, 144, 146). While anthropogenic climate change represents a singular moment in the history of exosomatization, where the entropy and anthropy produced by technical life might culminate in its extinction, Stiegler nevertheless integrates this singularity with his existing claims about the nature of political judgment.

Understood in this way, it is capitalist totalization that represents the second, and perhaps greatest, threat to the possibility of any exit from the Anthropocene because it eliminates the diversity of judgment through calculation and control. In chapter 4, I explored why Stiegler argues that under societies of control the incalculability that is required for desire to function is destroyed by the calculation of capitalist marketing. Within the

Anthropocene this argument is elevated to a higher level; the biosphere is gradually replaced by a technosphere that integrates technological forms of automation and calculation on a global scale. Within this "age of full and general automation," Stiegler argues that "biological automatisms, physiological automatisms, psychic automatisms and social automatisms—or what remains of them—are rearranged with and progressively trans-formed by . . . technological automatisms, then de-formed by them, and eventually replaced by them" (Stiegler 2021b, 241). This generalized calculation has two consequences. It deepens the general proletarianization of judgment because of the mass replacement of improbability with probable and calculated forms of rationality. Put simply, "control undertakes the mechanical liquidation of discernment," as it delegates judgment to automated processes (Stiegler 2020a, 17). In addition to destruction by delegation, the type of reasoning that calculation engages in is of a different nature from the kind exercised by anti-anthropic invention. In Stiegler's words: "Automatic calculability involves a delegation of the analytical function of the understanding to an automatic retentional system that leads to a hypertrophy of the under-standing and to a regression of reason in the Kantian sense—as the faculty of deciding, operating through a synthesis that is also called judgement. In his post-thermodynamic resumption of these Kantian questions, Alfred Whitehead revived this singularity of a synthetic function that would not be soluble into the analytical faculty" (Stiegler 2020b, 73). Inventive reason can only operate synthetically for Stiegler, by integrating and uniting existing neganthropic relationships into new forms and functions. While not inherently poisonous, analytic truths that are abstracted from these localities form the basis of calculative reason that imposes upon the local and synthetic function of reason. The dominance of this thinking levels local and neganthropic heterogeneity into anthropic homogeneity. This denial of the synthetic function of locality is the source of the destruction of noodiversity and the forms of thinking and invention required to exit the Anthropocene.

In sum, the political stakes of neganthropology revolve around the development of the concepts of the non-inhuman, the a-transcendental, and judgment with respect to the pharmacological dualities between entropy and negentropy and anthropy and neganthropy. The "non-inhuman" is "absent from the technosphere" constituted by the Anthropocene because it is incompatible with the anthropic form of calculative reason that control relies on (Stiegler 2018a, 369). This anthropic leveling eliminates judgment by totalizing without openness, because judgment requires anti-anthropic bifurcation and noetic diversity. Exiting the Anthropocene requires us to *"to reintroduce, between exosomatization and exomemorization, the conditions for a variability capable of reconstituting a noodiversity"* (Stiegler 2020b, 76). These conditions will necessarily be both totalizing, because they give function and meaning to the human in the form of the a-transcendental, and non-totalizing, insofar as differences must be maintained to support future anti-anthropic bifurcations. Stiegler's turn to the language of thermodynamics here forms yet another chance for him to stake out his political differences with the poststructuralist tradition, insofar as the epistemology that he derives from the thermodynamic revolution requires this transition from locality to a form of open universality exercised by political judgment (Stiegler 2018a, 47). This claim rests on the delimiting of ontology by locality. Noodiversity cannot be reduced to a set of ontological conditions precisely because a single ontology would represent just one anti-anthropic account of the neganthropic condition of the non-inhuman. Neganthropological thinking, therefore, is intended to act as a post-ontological epistemology that responds to the political need for noodiversity to generate solutions to the pharmacological problems of the Anthropocene.

Metaphysics and the Subject of Neganthropology

I now turn to an immanent critique of whether neganthropology lives up to these intentions. The most immediate problem sits with respect to the ontological status of entropy. As Ian James has argued, while the claim that the thermodynamic revolution constitutes a significant transformation of epistemological conditions coheres with the organological framing of knowledge within the philosophy of technics, the nature of the relationship between the scientific and non-scientific uses of entropy within Stiegler's work is less clear (James 2019b, 206–7). Two options seem available here: either the naturalistic reduction of anthropy to entropy or the maintenance of a separation between the scientific and psychosocial iterations of the second law of thermodynamics. James highlights that a naturalistic reduction of the two realms would represent what Stiegler sees as inhuman simplification of the diversity of thinking to calculable and computational categories (James 2019b, 212). In *Automatic Society*, he argues that "the *computational model* of this algorithmic governmentality combines with the *naturalistic model* of current cognitivism, so that noetic life as well as biological life is reduced to a calculation" (Stiegler 2016a, 119). This resistance to naturalism is also exhibited by Stiegler's distinction of his position from Wiener's concerns about the homogeneity of entropy. For Wiener, "The dominance of the machine presupposes a society in the last stages of increasing entropy, where probability is negligible and where the statistical differences among individuals are nil" (Wiener 1989, 181). Despite recognizing the similarity between this claim and his own, Stiegler is at pains to assert that Wiener's position is based on a metaphysical, and thus anthropic, understanding of entropy (Stiegler 2020a, 79). Exploring the reasons behind the distance that Stiegler puts between Wiener's position and his own will provide grounds for questioning whether he avoids reducing thermodynamics to an ontological and totalizing ground.

In chapter 1, I demonstrated that Stiegler's critique of metaphysics rests on the claim that it ignores accidentality by articulating a-historical and transcendental claims that repress their technical conditions. It is worth reiterating this claim in his own words here, and in terms that build on my account of judgment in his work: "*Metaphysics* weaves itself as the *ideal text* or the *ideal library*, which is to say the text or the library that defines, *like a dictionary*, what are the *right criteria* to be deployed as principles of selection by and in the retentional system, and which, as foundational, would themselves be *indisputable*, that is . . . non-textual, *and therefore non-hypomnesic*" (Stiegler 2020a, 100). Wiener's cybernetic lingua franca would represent one such "indisputable" set of foundational principles for acting as criteria of selection for thinking, judging, and acting across human, biological, and machinic realms. In contrast, Stiegler's understanding of thermodynamics represents what he sees in Socratic, pre-Platonic, and tragic thought as an "archi-criterion, *the criterion that enables criteria to be established.*" Tragic thought subsists below the level of ontological reasoning because it "prepares the way for the coming of archi-criteriology, ontology, the history of being and the difference between being and beings" (Stiegler 2020a, 112). Neganthropology is intended to act as such an archi-criterion for a Nietzschean reevaluation of values in the face of the anthropic leveling of calculation: "If we are to think the Anthropocene as giving rise to the devaluation of all values, then we must think with Nietzsche: the vital task for all noetic knowledge in the Anthropocene is the transvaluation of all values" (Stiegler 2018c, 38). This transvaluation would be achieved by fulfilling the anti-anthropic function of reason that Stiegler finds in both Canguilhem and Whitehead.[5]

Despite accusing Wiener of metaphysical thinking, in his late work Stiegler also grants thermodynamic language a form of philosophical priority when thinking this transvaluation. He shares with Wiener the dramatization of the struggle against entropy on the backdrop of a "cosmological stage," as Katherine N. Hayles puts it (Hayles 1999, 105). Neganthropology develops an epistemology in which locality moves toward generality and universality in an a-transcendental way; the local cannot be abstracted from or eliminated, but it must also be integrated with larger exorganisms. Does elevating neganthropology to a cosmological principle not contradict this aim by ontologizing the conditions of local noodiversity? Stiegler stresses that the development of the language of entropy is conditioned by the locality represented by the European industrial revolution (Stiegler 2019b, 33). However, he also claims "that the *entropy/negentropy relation is the vital question par excellence*" and that, to return to a passage already cited, "the *question* of entropy and negentropy among human beings [is] the *crucial problem* of the everyday life of human beings and of life in general, and, finally, of the universe in totality for every form of life" (Stiegler 2016a, 10–11). Here Stiegler is caught between an organological conception of thermodynamics and the reduction of the thinking of noodiversity to an archi-criterion that would be metaphysical *on his own terms*.

Stiegler seems to have begun grappling with but did not resolve this uncertainty. With reference to the language of entropy, he states that he aimed to "requalify the metaphysical terms in which those concepts were elaborated after thermodynamics" (Stiegler 2020a, 79). Nevertheless, he also claims that "the living, insofar as it is not immortal, nor therefore divine, *always returns* to cosmic entropy" and that the political project required to resist this phenomenon at the human level is "necessarily also a neganthropology" (Stiegler 2020a, 44, 47). Seen in this light, the language of neganthropology would appear to be less a tragic archi-criterion for the establishment of criteria for judgment and more a totalizing set of metaphysical criteria of judgment that rest upon ontological presuppositions that are not open to suspension because of their necessity. If "repressing the *pharmakon* and its toxicity, is also repressing the problem of *anthropy*," then it must entail that the language of thermodynamics is a central principle of the philosophy of technics in this late period of Stiegler's work because of the essential link between pharmacology and anthropy (Stiegler 2020c, 261). This criticism is not intended to support a total rejection of any use of the language of thermodynamics within a critical political project. Instead, I am claiming that when considered against Stiegler's criteria for political judgment, it would seem that it constitutes a metaphysical set of criteria for judgment in the form of the totalizing ontology represented by the thermodynamic nature of being. These claims are not open to suspension because of the essential link between the repression of the question of technicity qua *pharmakon* and the repression of the problem of anthropy.

The totalizing nature of these claims is made starkly apparent by Stiegler's criticism of others for neglecting the political importance of thermodynamics. Above I argued that the language of neganthropology furthers the commitment to judgment that distinguishes Stiegler from the poststructuralist tradition. This goes beyond a commitment to totality and judgment; he also chastises "'continental'" or "'French'" philosophy for "forgetting" the importance of thermodynamics (Stiegler 2019d, 261). This can be read, to some extent, as a performative gesture—Stiegler concedes that some of these thinkers did consider thermodynamic questions in passing, and, as Woodward points out, figures like Lyotard were deeply concerned with questions of entropy and negentropy (Woodward 2017, 130). It seems that Stiegler's allegation of poststructuralist forgetfulness is directed at the lack of a systematic conceptualization of thermodynamics: the poststructuralists failed to articulate the civilizational and cosmological stakes of the pharmacological struggle between entropy and negentropy. This simplifies the problematic posed by the thermodynamic revolution by resolving the problem of locality and relationality into a problem of good (neganthropy and anti-anthropy) and evil (anthropy) (Woodward 2017, 130–31). Even though the "good" of reason and anti-anthropy is purged of substantive content, this ought seems to be derived from a particular is, this being, as Woodward puts it, "the drama of energy in the universe" (Woodward 2016, 100). While Stiegler does not oppose anthropy to neganthropy insofar as they are aligned with the irreducible pharmacological duality between poison and cure, they are nevertheless associated with undesirable and desirable responses to the *pharmakon* that, in the context of his wider claims, *must* be recognized. This political and ethical gesture seems even more fraught with difficulty in the context of the polyvalence of thermodynamic language. Entropy is not always opposed to information, and, as Cecile Malaspina notes, "The difference between information and noise is . . . rarely ready-made" (Malaspina 2018, 64). Where elsewhere the epistemological and political valence of entropy is unclear or undecided, within Stiegler's philosophy it takes on an unnegotiable connotation of evil that presupposes the "ready-made" nature of the distinction between entropy and negentropy.

This metaphysical slippage seems all the more important when we consider who acts as the subject or agent of neganthropology. Stiegler answers this question in undeniably universal terms: "Whoever *we* are, we *all* today face the 'question concerning technology'" that is represented by the Anthropocene (Stiegler 2020b, 67). Because of the increasingly global nature of the technosphere and its effects, neganthropology is a response to a challenge that impacts "Humanity as a whole" (Stiegler, Vignola, and Azar 2021, 19). I do not wish to deny the scale of the problem of climate change here; it is unequivocally a universal problem. However, despite his attention to noodiversity, Stiegler presents the neganthropological problematic as a unifying account of the Anthropocene. As many have noted, the Anthropocene not only undermines humanist conceptions of agency but also accounts of a unified human subject that would be responsible for responding to climate change (e.g., Chakrabarty 2009; 2012; D. Kelly 2019, 109). This problem also extends to the periodization of the Anthropocene. It is not my aim to situate Stiegler's claim within these wider debates regarding when and where the Anthropocene began, but it is worth considering one particular account of this problem insofar as it pertains to the question of agency.[6] Jason W. Moore takes issue with the language of the Anthropocene, as it provides a "meta-theory of humanity as a collective agent, without acknowledging the forces of capital and empire that have cohered modern world history" (J. W. Moore 2015, 171). To reflect the role that capitalism has played in the generation of the Anthropocene, Moore proposes the adoption of the nomenclature of the Capitalocene to account for how the accumulation of capital by a particular class, originally local to the European and Anglo-American worlds, has driven climate change. From this perspective, even though he does associate capitalist totalization with the problem of the Anthropocene, Stiegler's falling back on the language of universality abstracts from these conditions by positing a universal responsibility for enacting neganthropological transformation. My criticism of the concept of general proletarianization articulated in chapter 4 returns here. The problems of the Anthropocene are enforced by generalized proletarianization, a condition that ultimately concerns the inability to articulate anti-anthropic judgments experienced by humanity as a whole rather than as a differentiated subject of history characterized by a diversity of relations to power (Stiegler 2018c, 79; 2020b, 72). Within the calculative rationality of the Anthropocene, "we *all* become auxiliaries—that is, proletarians—of this vast automaton" (Stiegler 2021b, 242).

Stiegler's response to Moore's argument falls back on a line of reasoning that will by now be familiar. Moore claims that the Cartesian dualism between mind and body represents a clear example of the epistemological bedrock of the distinction between humanity and nature that underpins capitalist exploitation (J. W. Moore 2015, 19–20). Characteristically, Stiegler argues that capitalism and Cartesian dualism are but moments in a broader trajectory inaugurated by the repression of technics by philosophy. Rather than within capitalism, "it is at the beginning of what is called the history of metaphysics . . . that we must locate the dogmatism which will lead to the eschatology of the Anthropocene era" (Stiegler 2020c, 217). Entropy may have only been discovered with the thermodynamic revolution, but this marks a crucial moment within a broader struggle between metaphysics and the philosophy of technicity. This gesture reinforces both the ontological status of the language of neganthropology and the universal scope of the human whom it considers as its subject. While some might object that, like the cybernetic rendering of thermodynamics, Stiegler is concerned here with the complexity necessary for local and meaningful political decisions in the face of informational entropy (Bates 2020), here I make a meta-theoretical claim about the philosophical decision lying behind this argument. For Stiegler, the language of thermodynamics is ontologically necessary for coming to terms with the proletarianization that engenders the Anthropocene. We are all equally implicated in this politics because it represents a broader struggle between metaphysics and the technical conditions of the human, now understood in thermodynamic language. Paradoxically, after his turn to neganthropology, Stiegler articulates his critique of metaphysics in the language of a metaphysical archi-criterion that encompasses all of humanity: the ontology of thermodynamics within the wider history of the repression of technicity. When seen in this light, neganthropology takes on the status of a totalizing judgment without room for suspension, despite its intended role as a support for noodiversity.

Neganthropology, the Unruly Human, and the Politics of Order

The totalizing nature of the ontological necessity of entropy appears even more starkly in the context of Stiegler's account of how this universal subject of the long history of the Anthropocene is impacted by the form that the duality between good and evil takes within it. This duality can be found in the association that he establishes between the pairs of anthropy and neganthropy and drives and desire. As demonstrated in chapter 4, drives are transformed into desire within processes of psychic and collective individuation that allow for singularity and incalculability and are

186 | Returning to Judgment

unbound by calculation that eliminates the space for the unpredictability of desire. Calculative reason characteristic of the Anthropocene is massively anthropic because it homogenizes social life and in doing so engenders the mass destruction of desire, an inability for the anti-anthropic integration of singularity within neganthropic order, and the widespread failure of the binding of the drives. Prediction and calculation represent a process that "is entropic and leads to disindividuation" (Stiegler 2016a, 91). While disindividuation is necessary for new processes of individuation to emerge, the systemic disindividuation induced by anthropy prevents this production of singularities that give meaning to individuation. As a result, the "groups struck by collective disindividuation are, and will increasingly be, prone to losing every reason for living" (Stiegler 2019d, 29).

It is the destruction of desire that induces this loss. Whereas the "composition of tendencies" integrates processes of individuation with the singularities of desire, the "decomposition" of these tendencies by calculation leads "to the reign of the drives, that is, to spiritual misery" (Stiegler 2014b, 3). Neganthropy is explicitly opposed to this decomposition insofar as responding to this loss of desire requires a new "libidinal economy as the possibility of moving beyond the drive-based stage of consumerist capitalism and as constituting an economic system founded on the valorization of negentropy translated into neganthropology." Stiegler states this even more explicitly when he continues to argue that "the binding of these drives through what Freud described as identification, idealization and sublimation . . . is always a neganthropic process" (Stiegler 2020a, 48). A clear association is established here between the language of thermodynamics and the language of psychoanalysis, as the desire necessary to bind oneself to particular images of the non-inhuman is opposed to the entropy of the drives. The cause of the dissolution of drives into desire also lies behind the rise in anthropy.

One consequence of this move is the necessity of a politics centered around the opposition between entropic disorder and negentropic order. This rests on the postulation of a transcendental image of the human that arises from the diagnosis of a collective loss of reasons for living in the Anthropocene, which compounds the universality of the subject of this process within neganthropology. Prior to his turn to the language of thermodynamics, Stiegler argues that without attachment to collective totalizing fictions provided by the singularity of desire, "We become less than 'barbarians,' beasts and, worse than beasts, a pure destructive power" (Stiegler 2009a, 47). This leads to "the worst expressions of mere instinct" because it prevents the production of singularities from common social bonds

(Stiegler 2011a, 48). Consequently, calculation leads to "the liquidation of the social as such: to barbarism" (Stiegler 2013b, 23). This language becomes increasingly hyperbolic after Stiegler's turn to the global problem of the Anthropocene. Without addressing the challenge that it poses, we run "the risk of a global and social explosion consigning humanity to a nameless barbarism" (Stiegler 2019d, 8). The Anthropocene question is "part of a *libidinal diseconomy* characteristic of 'overconsumerist' capitalism, resulting from the disintegration of intergenerational relations, unbinding the drives through systemic desublimation, and causing regressions, disintegrations, persecution of scapegoats, addictions, auto-intoxications, suicides, new forms of crime and hyperviolence" (Stiegler 2020c, 118). These consequences all arise from the anthropy-inducing calculation that unbinds the neganthropy necessary for the integration of social relations via the function of reason. Hence, the appeal to the drives within societies of control is also an appeal to entropic and anthropic destructiveness induced by the loss of the social, which Stiegler argues impacts humanity as such rather than the non-inhuman. The evils of entropy and anthropy are equated with the destructiveness of the drive.

Diagnosing the problems of the Anthropocene in this way leads Stiegler toward totalization without openness not just because he generalizes this analysis across all humans and all social problems, but also because this diagnosis rests on a totalizing image of the human as an unruly animal that is kept in check by the order social convention provides. Without the socialization necessary for the production and maintenance of neganthropic structures, the human turns to inhuman and destructive drive-based behaviors. Here Stiegler adopts a metaphysical image of human nature that serves as the archi-criterion of much modern political thought, in which the destructiveness of individual and un-socialized self-interest is opposed to the social bonds by which they are curbed. In Marshal Sahlin's words, this forms a vision of "human nature so avaricious and contentious that, unless it is somehow governed, it will reduce society to anarchy" (Sahlins 2008, 1). This is not a vision restricted to the human. Whether this anarchic animal is subdued by constraint or by the reconciliation of particular "interests" with "common interests," this political problem is resolved by "a totalized metaphysics of order, for the same generic structure of an elemental anarchy resolved by hierarchy or equality is found in the organization of the universe as well as the city" (Sahlins 2008, 1–2). Sahlins's point here is that the political problematic of the unruly animal takes place on the backdrop of an ordered vision of the universe that the human should be brought into line with. Entropy plays a similar role within neganthropology: the general struggle against entropy within the cosmos as a whole is replayed by the human insofar as it must maintain conditions that produce neganthropy rather than violent anthropy.

This parallel between Stiegler and the modern political imaginary can be seen clearly by a brief comparison with Thomas Hobbes's *Leviathan*. While Stiegler does not advocate for the same political and institutional mechanisms as Hobbes, his argument nevertheless relies on similar principles when considering the relationship between order and disorder. The crux of Hobbes's argument is the need to transfer individual rights and freedoms possessed by nature to a sovereign in exchange for security from the absolute freedom of others in a state of nature where government is absent. Important here is that humans are not just violent in the state of nature because of a lack of institutional restraint on individual freedom, but also because of the lack of common measure or value by which disagreements over the exercise of freedom may be resolved. For Hobbes, reason is "nothing but *reckoning* . . . of the consequences of general names agreed upon, for the *marking* and *signifying* our thoughts" (Hobbes 1996, 28). Of the threats to order, one of the most significant is the claim "*that every private man is judge of good and evil actions*," a condition that is "true in the condition of mere nature, where there are no civil laws" (Hobbes 1996, 214). Violent insecurity is both a characteristic of human nature as such, and a product of the lack of social conventions for keeping that nature in check.

Stiegler reiterates the basic structure of this argument insofar as he claims that the social bonds produced by neganthropy and desire are dissolved within the homogeneity produced by the calculation that unleashes anthropic drives. The totalization of the cosmological drama between the good and evil tendencies of neganthropy and anthropy, which applies to all humans within the Anthropocene, is also part of a metaphysical commitment to the need to produce political order by constraining the drive-based barbarism that underlies the non-inhuman. The early modern concern for order that Stiegler mirrors here also extends into the thermodynamic era, where the growth of entropic disorder "seemed to threaten modernity itself" (Rabinbach 1992, 147). Dissipation of energy threatens the orderly and efficient extraction of value from both workers and the environment at large. This "energopolitics," as Cara New Daggett puts it, is one that associates order with productivity (Daggett 2019, 127). This is precisely the perspective that Stiegler opposes with his vision of neganthropology; however, it bears a similarity to it insofar as entropy is opposed to the neganthropic potential for anti-anthropic invention. One might argue here that the concern for order represented by the post-thermodynamic politics of capitalism is distinct from Stiegler's argument in favor of the "conservation of . . . negentropic potential" for anti-anthropic bifurcation is irreducible to the totalization of control societies, which is itself part of a reconsideration of the social role of work and productivity (Stiegler 2016b, 163). This is indeed the case. However, while this conception of order as conservation of potential for individuation is aimed at the production of noodiversity, it nevertheless poses a universal conception of what occurs when this order lapses into disorder in the form of a metaphysical conception of uncontrollable, anthropic drives that underpin neganthropic forms of desire. Thus, while the broader political goals of modern and industrial concerns about disorder are distinct from Stiegler's, he nevertheless shares with them a conception of the effects of that disorder: the unleashing of a violent and unruly component of human nature. Entropy as disorder acts as an archi-criterion for discerning and judging upon the correct path of action within the Anthropocene that imposes on the local, organological, and a-transcendental conditions of judgment that may be incompatible with this universal image of the unruly human.

My argument here hews closely to criticisms made by a range of commentators on Stiegler's work, which revolve around the claim that he is committed to a kind of political conservatism. On the more generous end of the spectrum formed by these criticisms, Dominic Pettman suggests that Stiegler "does sound like a nostalgic aesthete" in his analysis of the impact of television, social media, and other technologies that he associates with capitalist calculation (Pettman 2011, 173). Pettman does propose, however, that this resolves into the aim of "*protecting* the libido from extinction" rather than an endorsement of order as such (Pettman 2011, 177). On the harsher end of this spectrum, Sophie Fuggle and Chris Turner argue that Stiegler's argument regarding the disruption of social structures, by what I refer to here as the entropic tendencies of calculation, leads him to advocate both a traditional model of the family and an uncritical image of educational and carceral public institutions (Fuggle 2013, 199–201; C. Turner 2010). Of particular concern is the lack of attention paid to the norms and exclusions that such institutions can embody and perpetuate in the name of order. These criticisms are focused on comments Stiegler makes regarding the establishment of maturity through French educational institutions established by Jules Ferry in the late nineteenth century (Stiegler 2010e, 51–52) and do not pertain to the general conditions of order within neganthropology. I do not have space to fully assess the historical details of this critique, but I simply want to note that Fuggle's, Pettman's, and Turner's criticisms revolve around the assumption, also developed here, that within parts of Stiegler's work there is a tendency toward the conservation of a particular image of what it means to be human, and of how that concept of the human relates to social order.[7] This is particularly clear in the context of Stiegler's explicit rejection of the influence of the politics of 1968 on poststructuralism, which I introduced in chapter 4. The dissolution of authority is not a viable political position, for it neglects the formation of desire required to access the incalculable by forms of totalizing authority. While throughout this book I have argued that Stiegler's philosophy attempts to balance this commitment to totalization with non-totalization, within the context of neganthropology, totalization is integrated with a set of ontological claims that resist non-totalizing suspension. Consequently, as a political judgment, neganthropology proposes a particular conception of politics that is necessary for resisting the universal inhuman consequences of entropy, which take the form of the barbarism of the unruly human.

These criticisms that are directed at the political consequences of Stiegler's work can also be found in disagreements with the foundations of his philosophy. For Mark Hansen, Stiegler is focused on exposing the "dependence of human becoming on technics *without rethinking the process of human becoming itself*" (Hansen 2017, 186). The consequence of such a position is a commitment to a particular image of the human that comes to be disrupted by technicity.[8] The account of the philosophy of technics given across this book does not follow Hansen's position here because of the importance I have given to the concepts of the a-transcendental and the non-inhuman as ways to grapple with the constantly changing nature of political judgment within the human-technical relationship. However, within the context of the political project of neganthropy, Stiegler does fall back on the claim that certain universal and a-historical characteristics of the human are impacted by technicity, as argued above. The human is presented as an unruly animal characterized by an entropic tendency toward disorder that is exacerbated by calculation within the Anthropocene. Without the negentropic order and stability provided by social systems, the human will inevitably, for Stiegler, fall into destructive behavior. I am claiming that, by his own standards, this image of the political totalizes it in a metaphysical manner. Not only is the language of entropy an ontological necessity for comprehending the universal human subject of the Anthropocene, but it also appears that all humans experience the problems of this conjuncture in the same way because of the shared propensity toward violence.

Conclusion: An Energetic Conservatism?

Across this chapter, I have argued that Stiegler's analysis of the Anthropocene is wrought by a tension that leads him to totalize without space for openness or suspension. While the language of anthropy, neganthropy, and anti-anthropy is advanced to support the development of noodiversity and new forms of knowledge that can induce a bifurcation that opens an exit from the Anthropocene, the philosophical commitments associated with the language of entropy lead Stiegler to articulate this problematic in a way that short-circuits this plurality. This is found in the related claims that, first, the language of entropy is ontologically necessary and therefore used in an appeal to a universal subject of human history, and, second, that the human is possessed of a tendency toward violent, anthropic disorder that is unleashed by the destruction of social bonds by calculation. The balance between totalizing judgment and non-totalizing openness that I have suggested Stiegler's a-transcendental method demands is not held to by these political judgments. They assume that the problem of entropy can and *needs* to be reversed (Lynes 2019), even if debates regarding the nature of entropy suggest that it is not necessarily an impediment to meaning, social value, or cohesion. As Malaspina summarizes, such a position risks surrendering "novelty, unpredictability and hence also complexity of information to the imperative of certainty at any cost" (Malaspina 2018, 68). Definitional and conceptual ambiguity surrounding the language of entropy suggests that it could be a source of the kind of novelty and invention that Stiegler values, but this possibility is negated by the association of negentropy with the positive values of order and stability. I suggest here that the language of neganthropology may have a similar constraining effect in the political realm. While Stiegler resists the epistemological consequences of certainty that he associates with computational capitalism, he does nevertheless seek a form of certainty in the political world. To put this claim in another conceptual dyad of Stiegler's, the synchronic appears to take on political value *in itself,* whereas the diachronic only appears to be politically valuable insofar as it contributes to the gradual construction of the synchronic (Withers 2019). Hence, I agree with Woodward when he argues that "philosophy which attempts a political and cultural critique must do more than simply adopt scientific principles such as entropy and negentropy as avatars of 'good' and 'evil' " (Woodward 2017, 130). One might highlight, as Stiegler himself does, that the language of neganthropology is intended to act as a therapeutic concept appropriate for a particular pharmacological problematic as opposed to a metaphysical or ontological system (Stiegler 2019c, 108). However, these therapeutics, insofar as they respond to pharmacological problems, possess the status of political judgments. As suggested in chapter 5, all such judgments carry ontological commitments. Here this means that while entropy and negentropy are subject to pharmacological undecidability and the deferral of *différance*, they are also raised to the level of a political judgment above challenge insofar as they require the acceptance of the thermodynamic image of the universe. This therapeutic prescription totalizes the space of what counts as a meaningful political judgment within the Anthropocene by restricting the foundations of critique to the language of the critic, that of neganthropology, while simultaneously assuming a universal vision of the experience of the problem of climate change.[9]

A consequence of this critique is the suggestion that Stiegler's work constitutes a kind of energetic conservatism, implied by Fuggle, Pettman, and Turner, in which order is required to constrain the destructive drives that underpin human nature. Some readers, like Ross Abbinett and Christina Howells, have rejected accusations of romanticism or conservatism directed at Stiegler because of his reticence toward the appeal to origins (Abbinnett 2018, 114–16; Howells 2013, 150). Gerald Moore has tempered this stance somewhat by acknowledging that Stiegler's reliance on anecdotal evidence and the metaphysical implications of Freudian language invites "his reputation as a nostalgic conservative and excitable panic merchant" (G. Moore 2018, 191). I do not want to weigh in on this debate here with a decisive answer to the problem of whether Stiegler fits into the mold of a conservative thinker.[10] Instead, I simply wish to highlight that order plays a role within neganthropology that appears as universal, insofar it applies to all, and is concerned with constraining the inherent violence of an unruly human. Such a philosophical position is not conducive to pursuing noo-diversity if the diverse forms of knowledge that such a position is meant to cultivate might conceptualize the problem of the Anthropocene in ways that are irreducible to the language of thermodynamics or the necessity of constraining anthropic violence. While Stiegler attempts to avoid totalizing metaphysical judgments on the nature of the human and of the political, his neganthropological response to the Anthropocene fails to fulfil this task.

8

The *Polis* as Judgment
on the Origins of the Political

In the second half of the twentieth century, many figures within French philosophy adopted ancient Greek thought as a central theme within their reflections on the political. As Miriam Leonard has detailed, the literature, myth, and philosophy of ancient Greece "became the focal point of a questioning of the nature of ethical choice and political action in so-called structuralist and post-structuralist thought" (Leonard 2005, 5). Despite his attempts to distinguish himself from his poststructuralist predecessors, Stiegler inherits and furthers this dimension of their work. His references to ancient Greece are unique, however, because of the extent to which he takes the *polis* as a historical reality through which the political must be understood, rather than simply a philosophical influence on his account of politics. Contemporary politics, he argues, requires a recognition of the Athenian *polis* as the origin of the political in the context of the eradication of the space for individuation, judgment, and bifurcation by calculation and totalization. This chapter furthers my immanent critique of Stiegler's political judgments by exploring the consequences of this claim for the reconciliation between totalization and non-totalization in his work.

At first glance, this gesture appears positive for the development of an a-transcendental theory of the political, as it conceives of politics as a form of individuation dependent on specific, historical conditions. I argue that instead of underpinning the diversification of political judgment across local contexts, Stiegler's claim that the political finds its origins within the ancient Athenian *polis* represents a totalization of the space of politics that does not contain the opportunity for non-totalizing transformation. By restricting the criteria for political activity to the written codification of law inaugurated within the *polis*, Stiegler adopts a specifically Greek conception of politics, as other commentators have argued (Beardsworth 2010, 187–88; Davis 2013, 175), which represents a closure of the space for openness by a particular, local judgment. I articulate this problem as part of an investigation of a wider ambiguity in the philosophy of technics regarding the political status of the concept of individuation. Individuation can be seen to be inherently political because of its perpetual deferral of the completion of identity, or it might also be argued that a specifically political regime of individuation exists, represented for Stiegler by the *polis*. I argue that both options are insufficient for balancing totalization and non-totalization. Rectifying this situation requires a rejection of both possibilities to develop the claim that responses to the *pharmakon* produce a local divide between what counts as political and non-political within a particular process of individuation.

I return to the pharmacological nature of the political first introduced in chapter 2 to resolve this problem. By associating the *pharmakon* with the political, Stiegler suggests that technics, and therefore individuation, is only political insofar as it is shaped by local pharmacological problems. However, by restricting political individuation to the historical trajectory initiated by the *polis*, he also excludes vast swathes of human history from the non-inhuman condition represented by the political response to pharmacological problems. The alternative claim that individuation itself is political, moreover, totalizes the space for conceiving of the nature of the political in the same manner as ontological judgments on politics. If the pharmacological basis of the political is taken seriously, it provides a way out of this dilemma: individuation is political insofar as it responds to a local pharmacological field of problems and an a-transcendental set of prejudgments that determine what counts as a political decision. Individuation renders these judgments open to contestation, but these challenges are nevertheless tied up with local and totalizing judgments regarding the boundaries of politics. This claim avoids the dual problems of ontological totalization, represented by the claim that all individuation is political, and the historical totalization of the argument that the political begins with the ancient Greek *polis*. The question of the origin of political individuation can never be answered definitively because it is conceptualized within a local field of prejudgments that totalize and shape this judgment.

This argument is made across three steps. First, I establish Stiegler's position regarding the *polis* as one of two political readings of the concept of individuation found in his work in order to establish the shortcomings of both. This involves both the reconstruction of Stiegler's claim that the *polis* represents the origin of politics, as this position is not articulated in one text and stretches across his published work, and the distinction of this historical totalization of the political from the ontological totalization represented by the claim that all individuation is political. Second, I further explore the totalization represented by Stiegler's restriction of the origin of politics to the *polis* by demonstrating how it contradicts his statements on the pharmacological nature of the political. I focus more extensively on the problems of this particular answer to the question of the political nature of individuation, as it forms part of Stiegler's concrete judgments on contemporary politics, and because my objection to the claim that individuation is political in itself aligns more closely with the limits to political ontology articulated already. This allows me to show the totalizing and exclusionary nature of Stiegler's claims regarding the *polis*: judgments that could be considered as political because of their character as a response to pharmacological problems are not considered to be because they do not follow the totalizing criteria set by the Greek "invention" of politics. Third, despite the unique nature of historical and totalizing judgments on the nature of politics, I claim that they have the same consequences as ontological judgments on the political. Stiegler's views on the *polis* conflict with the local, a-transcendental, and non-inhuman conception of the political developed from his work across this book, as they fail to balance totalization and non-totalization. I conclude, therefore, that the political does not have a single origin because it is formed by local fictions regarding the nature of the non-inhuman. Individuation is not inherently political, nor does it find its political form in the *polis*. Instead, it is rendered political by a diversity of local judgments that respond to pharmacological problems.

The Two Political Forms of Individuation

As this book's argument has suggested, the concept of individuation has significant political ramifications.[1] Here I examine two versions of these consequences in Stiegler's work to further my immanent critique of his politics and to advocate for a conception of the political that balances the tension between totalization and non-totalization. The first consists of the claim that everything is political, as the principle of individuation undermines fixed identity. I first introduced the principles behind this claim in chapter

3; everything is political because identity is perpetually deferred within the processes of psychic and collective individuation engendered by the technical condition. Certainties regarding identity are permanently open to challenge, contestation, and transformation, as the unity between psychic and collective individuation is never stable: "this projection is never concretized except *by default*, in other words by ceaselessly *deferring* this completion" (Stiegler 2009a, 4). Because of this spectral relationship between the *I* and the *We*, "individual identity . . . is never clearly constituted as such," for it rests on the changing "identity of technical objects and of all already-constructed artifices in general" (Stiegler 2011c, 97). All forms of human activity are political, as they are constituted by this permanently adjusting transductive relationship between psychic, social, and technical organs. The very act of thinking individuation is political because it intervenes within these processes of individuation: "knowledge, insofar as it is always already a psychosocial individuation, and in that sense practical, is also—and irreducibly—political" (Stiegler 2015d, 71). All individuation is political because identity is formed through individuation, and to know individuation is to intervene within it.

The problem with this particular understanding of the nature of the political has already been preempted. Chapter 2 began with Emily Apter's criticism of the claim that everything is political: within this perspective, politics cannot be rigorously differentiated from any other activity (Apter 2018, 1). I also argued that the claim that all individuation is inherently political presents a totalizing perspective on the nature of politics insofar as a particular philosophical position provides a way to account for all political activity. Inna Viriasova's critical account of this gesture within political ontology makes this point clear. If everything is political simply because of the ramifications of a particular ontological claim, here the principle of individuation, then such a gesture absolutizes and totalizes the space of politics by rendering all refusals of the political as secret affirmations of an underlying political truth or ground, even if this ground is intended to be non-totalizing (Viriasova 2018, 61). Seen in this way, this first reading of the political value of individuation runs against the claim that political space is produced by totalizing yet open judgments that separate it from the non-political realm.

Stiegler also argues that political individuation begins within the ancient Greek *polis*. No single text articulates this second understanding of the political value of individuation; however, it is present from Stiegler's earliest to his last works. Across two articles first published at the beginning of his career in the 1980s, Stiegler argues that politics begins with the emergence of the written codification of law and the subsequent possibility for the democratic contestation of knowledge within the *polis*. In "Technologies of Memory and Imagination," Stiegler claims that "the 'negotiability' of power and at the same time a new form of the elaboration of knowledge, rests on the possibility of publication and characterises political society . . . as essentially profane" (Stiegler 2018b, 35). More than just a change from religious to profane justifications of power that might be perceived elsewhere, this transformation represents a genuine and novel historical shift unique to particular conditions. In "Programs of the Impossible, Short-Circuits of the Unheard-Of," Stiegler claims that "the historical and the political are indeed dated. They can be characterized here in the following way: political community makes calling its laws into question a principle . . . *Politicity* and historicity figure this form of community (insofar as it is essentially secular) in clear opposition to a society that is tribal or mythological or sacred" (Stiegler 2014d, 96). Within this second perspective, individuation is not inherently political, as politics is a particular process of individuation that emerges from within specific historical conditions.

These early claims are repeated across Stiegler's writing up until his last publications. One important development within his position is the argument that the Greek *polis* is the origin of the trajectory taken by Western political institutions: "Political societies arose with the Greek *polis*, which was grounded in public law, itself declared, described, and made explicit according to a strict set of rules in the sense that they were grounded in citizenship . . . *which itself was formally declared and based on public law* which was simply the entry condition into a social group called *polis*, and then *civitas*, and finally *nation*" (Stiegler 2013d, 23). This trajectory toward the nation represents the growth of the founding principle of the *polis*: that "the citizen is the individual who bears the legitimate right to *interpret and transform the law*" (Stiegler 2018c, 131). Critical discussion and interpretation found politics "because logical disputation replaced war between the clans" (Stiegler 2015a, 189). The figure of the citizen as the agent of this conflict of interpretations is the archetype of the political subject, as "politics is configured in the Occident through the *polis* as it constitutes a *politeia*—formed by the *politou*, the citizens, themselves defined by their equality of rights and duties within the framework of a law made public" (Stiegler 2020c, 178–79). Individuation is only political when citizens have the right to interpret the law that emerges in the *polis* and develops within Western political institutions. Hence, the *polis* "constitutes a new process of individuation" (Stiegler 2014f, 49).

The exclusive nature of this claim does not have to be inferred. Stiegler consistently restricts politics to the Greek context and its historical legacy. The anthropologist Pierre Clastres is invoked as a representative of opposition to this position:

> Clastres' opposition springs from his resistance to the ethno-centrism that sees aboriginal societies as communities without power. However, this is another ethnocentrism that sees power only in its political form—the origin of the word here is not without importance. If Clastres admits there is a rupture in terms of time with the appearance of writing and history, why not also recognize a rupture in terms of space—as if the one were possible without the other? I believe that political space is dated. (Stiegler 2014d, 105, n.75)

I return to the question of ethnocentrism below, as my point here is to emphasize Stiegler's commitment to the claim that "humanity is not political in general" (Stiegler 2018b, 60). He argues that "politics appears with the *polis*, and is then spread more widely via Christianity" and therefore that "there is no 'political' power in Indian chiefdoms, for example, contrary to what Pierre Clastres assumes" (Stiegler 2016a, 284, n.77). Not only does Stiegler imply that the political is restricted to the historical development of a particular process of individuation, but he also actively makes this claim in a totalizing manner.

Two points need to be clarified before I can fully explore the consequences of Stiegler's claim that the *polis* represents the origin of the political: what he means by the written systematization of politics and the significance of his opposition to the work of Clastres. Alphabetization enables the codification of law and opens the possibility of a community capable of legal interpretation and critique. "Communitization calls for the possibility of interpretation," which arises from the fixity provided by "exact identification" that "instigates the sudden appearance of *a* difference and imposes infinite difference on any reading" (Stiegler 2009b, 39). "Infinite difference" is imposed by the default of origin and its deferral of presence; however, a specifically political form of deferral emerges with alphabetization that makes equal interpretation of the law possible. In Stiegler's words: "space becomes political when it becomes a literate community—when the citizen is reading and writing. Political memory requires a literal/literate memory technology, and the city is the network through which written materials circulate" (Stiegler 2009b, 145). Community qua politics is found within social groups that possess written regulations for individual conduct that are open to scrutiny and interpretation because of the literacy of its members. Intelligibility, therefore, is a constitutive part of political agency: "A political statement is not understandable by someone who did not receive citizenship education" (Stiegler 2013c, 78). Alphabetization and literacy transform the more general reflexive deferral of identity found in psychic and collective individuation into a specifically political form.

This gesture leads Stiegler to distinguish between political and apolitical forms of society. He explicitly situates political individuation within the conditions of individuation represented by alphabetization, the formation of individual agency and autonomy in relation to the law, and the development of these conditions across Western history. In his words: "By political *or* apolitical, I mean: in *or* from the process of psychic and collective individuation that has opened up history as individuation of the West" (Stiegler 2012e, 187). The political and the apolitical are distinguished here to pose the possibility of a process of individuation that might follow the West's. Apolitical thought addresses the overcoming of Western political individuation, as opposed to a non-political realm outside of politics. Here Stiegler differentiates between the presence of political societies, apolitical forms that follow their individuation, and non-political realms outside this historical process. If politics begins with the *polis*, then life prior to and outside political individuation must be non-political. Political community can be distinguished from apolitical forms that might follow it and non-political forms that both precede and coexist alongside politics. Stiegler is clear that the trajectory inaugurated by writing consists of a totalizing judgment on the nature of politics that may come to an end, but the uniquely political status of this process of individuation is not itself open to non-totalizing suspension. It is in this sense that the *polis* forms the conceptual boundaries of the political.

Stiegler's repeated rejections of Clastres's position demonstrate this point clearly. For Clastres, claims that classify as non-political those societies that do not possess the same institutions for the production of consensus, legitimacy, and debate that emerge with the *polis* do not hold up to ethnographic evidence. He resists the conclusion that it is only with writing that reflection on the problems that affect a group can be adequately solved:

> Peoples without a writing system are no less adult than literate
> societies. Their history has the same depth as ours and, short of

racism, there is no reason to judge them incapable of reflecting on their experience and of discovering the appropriate solutions to their problems. Indeed that is why it will not do to state that in those societies in which the command-obedience relation is unknown (that is, in societies devoid of political power), the life of the group is maintained through *immediate social control,* adding at once that this control is *apolitical* (Clastres 1988, 20).

Here Clastres defines the political as a problem-solving operation. Politics occurs wherever the problem of power is present, and therefore the political cannot be restricted to institutions that we associate with literate societies: "Even in societies in which the political institution is absent, where for example chiefs do not exist, *even there* the political is present, even there the question of power is posed" (Clastres 1988, 22–23). Where Stiegler identifies political societies with the written embodiment of law, Clastres finds the political within the omnipresent problem of power.

Here I return to the two political conceptions of individuation that I began with. Clastres represents a position, also found in Stiegler, that holds that all human societies are political. In Stiegler's version of this argument, all individuation is political because of the deferral of identity that it entails. He simultaneously claims, through his rejection of Clastres's argument, that political individuation represents a specific process of individuation that began with the Greek *polis.* In the second volume of *Qu'appelle-t-on panser?* both of these claims are articulated in close proximity. Stiegler argues that "not all power is political" and then goes on to state, "There is politics because there is psychic and collective individuation" (Stiegler 2020c, 178, 181). One might make the case here that these statements are not contradictory, as psychic and collective individuation represents a necessary but not sufficient condition for politics. I return to this point below when considering the problem that the *pharmakon* poses for Stiegler's position on the *polis.* For now, I simply wish to highlight Stiegler's emphasis on the claim that there is a particular form of individuation that constitutes politics in order to account for the loss of the capacity of citizens to engage in the critical interpretation of the law that begins with the Greek *polis:* "In the 21st century, these *defining conditions* of *citizenship* are still *formally* true, but they are *actually* false" (Stiegler 2020c, 182). While from the perspective elaborated here both positions on individuation totalize the political—by either reducing politics to a single philosophical perspective or by restricting the political to a particular historical trajectory—the delimitation of politics to the consequences of the ancient Greek *polis* takes priority within Stiegler's work insofar as it represents his attempt to judge and respond to the pharmacological problematic represented by control societies. Moreover, to state that all is political because all is individuation is to make a similar gesture to the ontological totalization found within neganthropology, as argued in the previous chapter. Therefore, I now more extensively consider the nature of the historical form of totalization represented by Stiegler's claim that the *polis* is the origin of the political.

The Pharmacological Origins of the Political

To do so, I return to the political status of the *pharmakon* to deepen my immanent critique of Stiegler's Greek conception of politics. Beyond the question of the consequences of individuation for the political, we have already seen that Stiegler gives a third definition of politics as the response to the problems posed by the *pharmakon*. Politics prescribes " 'social therapeutics' for the shocks caused by technological pharmaka" (Stiegler 2015b, 6). This definition of the political underpinned my response to the problem of the relativization of the political induced by the default of origin in chapter 2. Technics is political not because the technical condition defers all identity, but because it distinguishes the human from life in general by situating pharmacological problems at the heart of this difference. Subsequently, in chapter 5 I argued that political responses to pharmacological problems occur within the context of a set of prejudgments that distinguish them from their non-political outside. Within this position, which I am arguing constitutes the significance of Stiegler's work, the political cannot be exhausted by a single, totalizing conceptual framework, as it is produced and separated from the non-political by judgments that respond to a local set of problems. It is already clear how Stiegler's claims about the *polis* contradict starkly with this understanding of the political. It is axiomatic for Stiegler that all human societies are technical and that all technical objects are pharmacological. To claim that political individuation emerges with the *polis* is to inaugurate a distinction between groups that can articulate political responses to the *pharmakon* and those who respond by other means. Within this perspective, large parts of human history are perceived to have regulated society through the category of apolitical social control criticized by Clastres. Such a judgment totalizes politics without incorporating the constitutive role that openness plays within the political decision and without recognizing the plurality of forms of political organization that are engendered by pharmacological locality.

One might argue that this problem arises from an uncharitable interpretation of an ambiguity regarding the status of the *polis* in Stiegler's work. It is unclear whether it is intended to be a literal claim regarding the origins of politics or a metaphor for critically assessing political institutions. Stephen Barker argues that "for Stiegler, the *polis* is both city, in the largest sense . . . and the metaphoric 'associated milieu' of individuation" (Barker 2012b, 24).[2] While the *polis* is the actual origin of political individuation, it is also a heuristic tool for exploring the nature of politics more widely. As Barker continues:

> A proper understanding of *polis* as Stiegler defines the term . . . requires our keeping in mind that all of these terms are themselves *pharmaka*, as is the potential "enchantment" that is possible through the associated milieu of the *polis*. This fascination, the magic spell, the irresistible charm of *le grand polis*, the world, in an age of industrial *hypomnēmata*, can liberate or imprison, depending on whether *in the end* they result in association or dissociation; this is *the* political question as such. (Barker 2012b, 25)

From this perspective Stiegler does not claim that all individuation is political, nor does he restrict politics to the *polis*. Instead, the *polis* becomes an archi-criterion for thinking about how consistences motivate psychic and collective individuation by associating and binding individuals to collective individuation within particular localities. Like the apparently therapeutic status of the language of neganthropology, one might suggest that the *polis* acts in a similar way. It is a therapeutic metaphor for assessing the political nature of particular processes of individuation. As suggested above, here Stiegler can be understood as claiming that psychic and collective individuation is not itself political but the underlying condition of political forms of association that are assessed through the metaphorical heuristic of the *polis*, rather than by their proximity to or distance from the historical conditions of the *polis* itself. This begs the question of whether Stiegler himself falls afoul of the "irresistible charm of *le grand polis*." To what extent does using the *polis* as a metaphorical heuristic for judging political decisions leave this totalization open to other judgments on the nature of politics?

Whether used literally or metaphorically, when referring to the *polis*, Stiegler distinguishes between political societies and those that are purely social or, as I have suggested, non-political. Such a distinction implies that political responses to pharmacological problems are not present outside the literal or metaphorical conditions set by the *polis*. Here Stiegler echoes Hannah Arendt's use of the *polis* as a model for politics. For Arendt, the fundamental consequence of the Greek distinction between the political and the social is that action and speech represent faculties that render humans as political animals in contrast to the mere fact of social coexistence (Arendt 1998, 22–28). This is not the place to extensively assess this claim; however, one particular element of it is pertinent because of its applicability to Stiegler's understanding of the political. Exclusion from political existence applies to groups who are outside the historical trajectory inaugurated by the *polis*, but also to realms of human existence that do not conform to its model—the household, for example. Arendt herself states this division clearly: "Where men live together but do not form a body politic—as, for example, in tribal societies or in the privacy of the household—the factor ruling their actions and behavior is not freedom but the necessities of life and concern for its preservation" (Arendt 1960, 30).

By rejecting the existence of political individuation outside the *polis*, Stiegler engages in a similar gesture. The social, or the realm of necessity, is a de facto non-political space because political agency entails a response to the *pharmakon* in the form of the interpretation of the law. Some readers of Arendt have defended her idolization of the *polis* as a metaphorical device for highlighting the importance of appearance and judgment in political action (e.g., Marshall 2010; Tsao 2002). As Barker suggests, a similar tendency can be seen in Stiegler's focus on the struggle between sophistry and citizens capable of philosophical reflection as the key lesson of the *polis*. For Stiegler, "the social becoming induced by grammatization, in the form of the birth of the *polis* (that is, the process of Western individuation), was already, at the same time, the site of a conflict, expressed in the struggle between sophistry and philosophy—that is, a conflict about the status of mnemotechnics" (Stiegler 2011a, 39). As a metaphor, the *polis* refers to this battle between the sophistic manipulation of tradition and a properly political engagement with its pharmacological tendencies.[3] From this perspective politics denotes those activities that attempt to bind a group together by giving it meaning in a way that is open to reinterpretation rather than through sophistic control that reduces it to a merely social body. This supports the suggestion that Stiegler does not restrict politics to the historical trajectory inaugurated by the *polis*, but instead that he uses it as a heuristic for assessing the political character of diverse processes of individuation that might not conform to its model.

Metaphorical use of the figure of the *polis* falls short of this goal because of a further ambiguity in Stiegler's account regarding the distinction between the political and the social. Stiegler attempts to articulate an absolute distinction between politics as rule informed by critical judgment and total social control. Within "imperial societies, individuals were subjected to autocratic royal power that controlled collective individuation in its totality" whereas within "the *polis*, psychic individuation . . . of the citizens . . . becomes the dynamic principle of *collective* individuation" (Stiegler 2014f, 49). Judgment is associated with this political form of association: "a *literate collectivity* becoming *precisely in this way* a *polis* and forming a *critical time and space*, thus a true *politeia*, an *individuation of citizens* that could be qualified according to their ability to judge, in other words to criticize" (Stiegler 2009d, 42). This characterization of judgment as collective and thus as political "opens up a specific space and time where strictly ethnic pro-grammings are suspended and interrupted" (Stiegler 2014d, 85). Here Stiegler hews closely to the distinction, criticized by Clastres, between political control and non-political social control. Moreover, by distinguishing between politics and social control, it would seem that Stiegler restricts not just politics but the very capacity for critical judgment to a particular process of individuation. Stiegler's defense against this accusation would be that he is indeed engaging in such a gesture, but to do otherwise would be to fall into the trap of ethnocentrism. Stiegler argues that "there is no ethnocentrism in that claim, insofar as the political thus understood is valorized no more than the devalorized non-political" (Stiegler 2014d, 105, n.75). However, the distinction between these political and non-political spheres is not as clear as it first seems. This ambiguity leads Stiegler to implicitly endorse a position akin to ethnocentrism in his attempt to separate the political and the social, which renders it as an arbitrary distinction rather than a decision based on justified criteria of judgment that balance totalization and openness.

This problem is found in his discussion of the impact that the formalization of social relations by technicity can have on social groups. Stiegler takes two examples, from the work of Claude Lévi-Strauss and Benjamin Lee Whorf, where the subjects of ethnographic research, the Nambikwara and the Hopi, resisted the formalization of their language by anthropologists (Stiegler 2013d, 23). Apparent awareness of the pharmacological nature of grammatization played a key role in the reticence of these groups: "the Hopis didn't want their language to be grammatized: they knew it would destroy their very culture" (Stiegler 2013d, 24). Stiegler's earlier distinction between politics and social control begins to break down because of two value judgments at work here. First, the Hopi's reticence is not perceived to be political, as it does not meet Stiegler's standards for a critical interpretation of tradition codified in writing. In contrast, according to the criteria I have developed from his work, it is clear that a judgment is made by the Hopi in response to the pharmacological threat posed by grammatization, which represents the articulation of a decision from the position of a set of prejudgments that codify what is and isn't open to political contestation. Elsewhere Stiegler argues that politics takes the form of the intermittent passage to noetic action in response to pharmacological problems: "To think is to engage in politics" (Stiegler 2014b, 16). It is clear that the Hopi's reticence toward grammatization engages in this intermittent process whereby a judgment is made on the nature of the non-inhuman within a particular locality, binding a process of individuation to a particular set of decisions and prejudgments within that context. This represents "the intermittent fruit of noesis" that "produces a singular difference in becoming, irreducible to its laws" (Stiegler 2018c, 62). While these prejudgments are not written, they inform a decision regarding what counts as a pharmacological threat and attempt to unify a process of individuation in response to that threat. Excluding these decisions from the realm of the political, particularly when they meet the standards of my minimal definition of this term, would be to engage in the ethnocentrism that Stiegler argues his definition of politics avoids.

This is compounded by Stiegler's second judgment on the Hopi's intransigence toward grammatization. He asks: "Wouldn't Hopi society . . . have had a better future if anthropology had been able to offer another modality of grammatization, that is, a discretized formalization of its relational flows—the kind of flows through which social networks arise which constitute a social group?" (Stiegler 2013d, 24). Little is offered in the way of a definition of what this modality of grammatization would look like, but the presupposition is clear—written codification is perceived to be more effective at preserving culture because of its political nature. It is unclear that a better form of grammatization would have helped preserve the Hopi's way of living in contrast to an absence of empire, colonialism, and the encroachment on Indigenous ways of life by Western institutions. As I argued in chapter 4, Stiegler's political judgments tend to privilege the question of knowledge over those of power and violence. Similarly, here it seems that Stiegler bases his conceptualization of what counts as a political judgment on the question of the efficacy of a distinct form of knowledge as opposed to the concrete power relations at stake within a particular context. Resisting grammatization may not have been the most effective way to preserve Hopi culture, but this does not make this judgment any less *political*. If judgments that unite the social body are intermittent examples of noesis, and "intermittence is what ensures the possibility of existence and the necessity of consistence within the necessity of subsisting," then it seems that decisions regarding consistences that are based on written interpretation are determined to be uniquely political on the basis of criteria that privilege the literate form of politics inaugurated by the *polis* (Stiegler 2016a, 75). Understood in this way, the difference between political and social forms of control breaks down, as it seems less a philosophical distinction that accounts for a diversity of political judgments, and more a judgment based on Stiegler's totalizing preference for a particular form of political action. Even when used metaphorically to comprehend these necessary conditions, the analytical lens of the *polis* cannot help but obscure political judgments that do not conform to Western forms of political individuation.

Consequently, even if the *polis* is conceived of as a metaphorical tool for analyzing forms of social integration rather than a historical argument, it is not a productive one for conceiving of the diversity of forms that the origin of the political can take. It might be argued that the separation between the political and the social is not intended to be literal and that Stiegler's adoption of the metaphor of the *polis* is part and parcel of his broader concern for the urgency of the political situation to which he was responding. This is indeed the case, and the influence of Clastres on the anti-totalizing politics of poststructuralism from which Stiegler tries to distinguish himself goes some way toward explaining his motivations here.[4] Nevertheless, this particular fiction has consequences that are unacceptable for any development of a pluralist conception of the political from Stiegler's work. The metaphor of the *polis* ends up blurring the distinction between political and non-political societies, and the only way of distinguishing between them is to make an arbitrary decision on what counts as a political judgment according to its proximity to this model.

As Stiegler himself claims, responses to the *pharmakon* are political, as they take the form of totalizing judgments that respond to the problems unique to a particular a-transcendental field. To suggest that politics begins with the *polis* is to remove decision-making outside its historical trajectory from the category of the political, implying that large parts of humanity have been incapable of responding to the problems that constitute their very nature. This is because such claims rely on a pure vision of politics represented by the *polis*, whether understood as the literal origin of politics or as metaphor. Attention to the pharmacological origin of the political deepens the initial problem with the totalizing claim that the *polis* represents the origin of politics, as it conflicts with Stiegler's open definition of the political derived from the intermittent character of the non-inhuman. If the human judges in a way that is accidental and intermittent, because of the default of origin, then there can be no transhistorical criteria for distinguishing a purely political form of judgment because it would constitute one such intermittent sphere of decision. If the political is to be tethered to the intermittent need to respond to the pharmacological nature of technical objects, then political judgment must emerge from the problems specific to a local and a-transcendental field. To balance totalization and non-totalization within conceptions of the political, we must concede that there is no single origin of politics, understood either in terms of the political nature of individuation in general or a specific regime of political individuation, but as many origins as there are pharmacological problems and conceptions of the non-inhuman.

Historical Judgments and the Totalization of the Political

When read in this way, Stiegler's claim that the *polis* signals the origin of political individuation fails to balance totalization and openness. As with his adoption of the language of thermodynamics, a particular judgment totalizes the space of the political while simultaneously barring the possibility of anthropological suspension—here seen in Stiegler's clear rejections of forms of politics that do not conform to the model of the *polis*. The question that lingers is whether this historical judgment is functionally different from totalization within ontological conceptions of the political. Across this book I have considered how Stiegler's perspective demonstrates that political ontology, even if it is committed to pluralism, totalizes the space of politics. Here this position has been represented by the claim, present in Stiegler's work, that all individuation is inherently political. However, his argument that the *polis* represents the origin of the political is not ontological, for it takes the form of a literal or metaphorical claim about the status of particular historical forms of social organization. In what way can a distinctly non-ontological form of totalization be said to exhibit the same totalizing tendencies as ontological claims?

Oliver Marchart provides an account of this historical form of totalization in Stiegler's work. He argues that the historical understanding of the political significance of the *polis* subordinates the political to its technical and ontic conditions and neglects its ontological character. Marchart criticizes the distinction, made in volume one of *Symbolic Misery*, between two kinds of discord in the Greek city: *stasis*, representing conflict and civil war; and *eris*, representing political disagreement. Only the latter is "the characteristic game of the agora," which Stiegler defines as the interpretation enabled by the written codification of law (Stiegler 2014e, 97). Without this translation of *stasis* into *eris* we are left with war, which occurs "with the failure of political pacification" (Stiegler 2014e, 11). For Stiegler, conflict must be expelled from the *polis* for politics to take place. Marchart takes issue with this gesture, for it prioritizes the historical and technical conditions of politics over an ontological conception of conflict as the post-foundational ground of political dispute. This disagreement is analogous to the distinction between the two political consequences of individuation already introduced. Individuation is political because it renders identity as subject to deferral and conflict on a primordial ontological level, or because a specifically political regime of individuation can be identified that represents a significant ontic shift within broader ontogenetic conditions. Marchart takes the first of these two paths. He claims that the post-foundational understanding of ontology renders being itself political, whereas Stiegler prioritizes technicity over this ontological understanding of being, as "particular techniques, including rhetorics and the art of politics, have to be differentiated from a more general or ontological *technicity*, not . . . from an ontological politicality" (Marchart 2018, 72–73). *Stasis* represents a fundamental antagonistic and political understanding of being that Stiegler neglects by situating the birth of the political within the historical translation of conflict into eris. As a result, "the intrinsic and inseparable link between the ontic dimension of politics and the ontology of the political is cut off" (Marchart 2018, 75). Stiegler's historical judgment totalizes politics, as it elides a more general ontological judgment on the nature of conflict.

In contrast to Marchart's critique of his historicism, I argue here that Stiegler's claim regarding the *polis* does render the conditions for political individuation as a transhistorical constant. Particular ontic conditions represented by the *polis* provide totalizing criteria for evaluating political judgment. The similarity between Stiegler's use of the *polis* and that found within the work of the historian and classicist Jean-Pierre Vernant makes this clear. According to Leonard, Vernant's critique of the application of the modern conception of the will to the ancient Greek context slips from the register of a historical corrective into a broader philosophical claim regarding the nature of agency. Within ancient Greek politics, action did not find its source in the self as it was formed by the human's relationship with the divine: "In making a decision a subject did not exercise a power of auto-determination truly his own . . . Swept along in the current of human life, action turned out to be illusory, vain, and impotent without the help of the gods" (Vernant and Vidal-Naquet 1990, 82–83). Regardless of the veracity of Vernant's claim about the difference between ancient Greek and twentieth-century conceptions of agency, Leonard argues that in articulating the above position regarding classical agency, he ends up endorsing a tragic conception of action in which we can never escape heteronomy and find full autonomy. In doing so, Vernant's claims about the otherness of ancient Greek agency are caught up with "structuralist preoccupations" regarding the relationship between the individual and the structures that they inhabit (Leonard 2005, 40).

It is beyond my purpose to examine Vernant's position or the accuracy of Leonard's critique.[5] What Leonard does demonstrate, however, is how a historical point regarding the nature of a concept at a particular point in time can slide into a transhistorical claim that imposes upon the accuracy of a historical reading, or transposes and advocates for that concept within the contemporary. For Leonard, Vernant does both; he reads the otherness of tragic conceptions of agency through a structuralist lens and then advocates for that conception of agency in the contemporary. A similar operation is at work in Stiegler. As demonstrated above, whether it is taken as a historical moment or a metaphor, the invention of politics within the *polis* takes the form of a transhistorical constant against which politics is judged. What Leonard identifies in Vernant—the ossification of history in a transhistorical ideal—is also made manifest in Stiegler's claim that the *polis* possesses characteristics that are historical yet also necessary for establishing the nature of politics. Moreover, they are deemed necessary for any response to the dire state of political institutions within societies of control.

These two criticisms move in opposing directions, and I cannot endorse Marchart's position from the perspective of my attempt to limit ontology by way of the reconciliation of totalization and non-totalization within Stiegler's approach to continental political theory. However, a single insight can be taken from them both. Both Marchart and Leonard, insofar as Leonard's critique of Vernant can also be applied to Stiegler, are united in criticizing totalizing uses of ancient Greek politics. For Marchart, the focus on the specific technical conditions of politics represented by the *polis* occludes a broader theorization of the general condition of politics. While I cannot follow this claim to its ontological conclusions, it is possible to adopt the point that Stiegler focuses on a single historical moment to the detriment of other possible conceptions of politics. My expansion of Leonard's criticism of Vernant suggest that this gesture is also generalized by Stiegler as a conceptual model for understanding the nature of politics. While these two positions work toward a critique of history and ontology respectively, they are united on the problem of totalization: to limit the nature of politics to the emergence of the *polis* is to engage in a form of totalization that constrains the space for open judgments that might suspend and transform the political in a non-totalizing manner.

Conclusion: The Many Origins of the Political

In this chapter I have argued that while one might claim that Stiegler endorses the dated nature of political space as an alternative to ethnocentrism, or that he uses the *polis* as a metaphorical tool for assessing political judgment, neither of these positions holds when his view on the *polis* is considered from the perspective of the balance between totalization and non-totalization found elsewhere in his work. Stiegler's definition of politics as a response to the problems posed by the *pharmakon* conflicts with this historical totalization of politics, as the latter excludes forms of social organization from the category of the political if they do not conform to the criteria developed from the *polis*, even though they might reasonably be conceived of as a response to pharmacological problems. If to be non-inhuman is to engage with the technical object qua *pharmakon*, then to restrict politics to the *polis* is to conceive of major parts of humanity as incapable of responding to the poisonous tendencies of the a-transcendental fields in which they exist. From within Stiegler's philosophical system this judgment regarding the *polis* is inconsistent with his own statements on the nature of politics. Rather than a model for political judgment, the *polis* represents just one form that responses to pharmacological problems might take. In the context of my interpretation of the two possible ways of perceiving the political value of individuation within Stiegler's work, I claim that individuation cannot be political in itself because of the ontological totalization that this position implies, nor can it be seen to become political with the *polis*. Individuation only takes on a political character within the intermittent responses to the need to provide meaning to a particular non-inhuman context. If Stiegler holds that we are only non-inhuman intermittently and accidentally, then he must accept that we act politically in potentially unpredictable ways. The nature of politics will depend on the pharmacological problems and system of prejudgments that define possibilities for political judgment and action within a particular locality.

Within this a-transcendental and non-inhuman conception of the political, not only is Stiegler's judgment regarding the *polis* inconsistent with his wider philosophy. It is also incompatible with the pluralist conception of the political that I have developed from his work across this book. I have argued that any conception of the nature of politics requires a judgment that totalizes the space of what can be considered as political by defining parts of human existence as non-political. This totalizing operation is foundational for the operation of political theory. If we are to balance this totalization with the non-totalizing perspective that renders political judgment dynamic, recursive, and open to transformation, then these judgments must make space for their suspension by the evidence of existing or possible anthropological alterity. To claim that individuation is inherently political or that political space begins with the *polis* is to negate the possibility of this pluralist conception of the political. Instead, I have argued that the default of origin leads to a default of the political that underpins the possibility of forms of political judgment that are unimaginable from within any single a-transcendental horizon. Politics has no origin besides the local conditions in which it finds its genesis. From this perspective, Stiegler's judgment that the nature of politics arises from the *polis* forecloses the unforeseen possibilities that the concept of the political may herald.

Conclusion

A Pharmacology of the Political

Across this book I have given an account of Stiegler's work that presents the reconciliation of totalization and non-totalization as the unifying theme of his philosophy of technics, and I have claimed that this represents a significant break with existing approaches to the problem of totalization within continental political theory. Stiegler suggests that we should not just critique totalization, but articulate totalizing political judgments that maintain the space for the incalculable and for their own suspension. Judgments of this kind carve out the difference between the political and the non-political within a particular locality by engaging with the pharmacological problems unique to an a-transcendental horizon. This understanding of judgment is situated, local, and totalizing, but is also open to non-totalizing transformation, because of the recursive and diachronic nature of its synchronic conditions. Stiegler's explicit, and more well-known, political concerns regarding capitalism arise from this underlying framework regarding the relationship between totalization and non-totalization. He argued that open and non-totalizing judgments that constitute the non-inhuman are under threat from the totalizing nature of capitalism, which eliminates noodiversity in the pursuit of calculable profits. Continental political theory's critique of totalization could not come to terms with this problem, for Stiegler, as it failed to return to the task of articulating a form of totalizing judgment that reconciled itself with non-totalization because of its reticence toward questions of judgment and totality. By establishing this position he casts a critical light on, and tries to break from, the mid-twentieth-century French tradition of continental philosophy that is so influential for his work: "those were indisputably exceptional years, but we must not try to duplicate the allure of their style and craft" (Stiegler 2009e, 103).

213

214 | Returning to Judgment

In addition to claiming that the reconsideration of the problem of totalization plays a unifying role in Stiegler's work, I have argued that his philosophy also has significant consequences for contemporary continental political thought that participates in the various forms of the ontological turn. The retreat from judgment into ontology leaves us unable to address the need for the articulation of totalizing judgments that make space for their critique and suspension in the face of pharmacologically poisonous forms of totalization. We are unable to engage in this task if we simply adopt the tools of political ontology, as post-foundational and immanent ontological reasoning represents a form of totalization that lacks an explicit framework for critically assessing its impact because of its reticence toward judgment. I approached this claim obliquely across the first four chapters in my account of the core concepts of Stiegler's philosophy. The default of origin and the undecidability of the *pharmakon* cannot be exhausted by a single ontology, as ontological claims are generated from within a particular process of individuation and in response to its distinct pharmacological problems. Political ontology undercuts its own pluralist aims because, as I argued in chapter 5, *all* political judgments are totalizing insofar as they give meaning to the non-inhuman within a particular process of individuation. Other ontological commitments and positions might come to suspend existing judgments, and as such it is necessary to explicitly acknowledge and engage with totalization rather than propose ontological conceptions of politics that try to elude totalizing judgment. This gesture localizes the activity of political theorists themselves, and not just the political events, actions, and agents they describe.

Here I want to conclude by considering what it means to articulate political judgments that engage critically with totalization. Some preliminary answers to this question can be approached by renaming the problematic represented by the reconciliation between totalization and non-totalization in Stiegler's work as a pharmacology of the political. If the political takes the form of a judgment that responds to the pharmacological problems of a particular context, then that judgment forms part of a set of a posteriori judgments that go on to form the a priori conditions of future individuation. Understood as such, concepts of the political are part of a recursively constituted problematic that conditions individuation and therefore can be treated as pharmacological and subjected to pharmacological critique. This pharmacologically reflexive form of critique considers the extent to which totalizing judgments on political problems necessitate a particular language, set of concepts, or responses that negate the potential for other ways of thinking about and responding to the questions posed by the *pharmakon*. The previous three chapters began to engage in such a critique of Stiegler's work to demonstrate how his political judgments embody the tension between totalization and non-totalization that his philosophy draws our attention to. The concepts I associated with the role of the impossible—*otium*, the Antigone complex, and the amateur—all develop a balance between totalization and openness. In contrast, Stiegler's political judgments on the necessity of thermodynamic language within his neganthropological response to the Anthropocene, and regarding the origins of the political in the *polis*, both constitute totalizing ontological and historical claims that do not leave space for their suspension.

Despite the critique of political ontology that has been developed alongside my account of Stiegler's work, this does not mean that ontological reasoning within political theory must be completely abandoned. My claim is that the limit to political ontology lies in its inability to exhaust the possibilities represented by the pharmacological formation of political problems and its lack of recognition of its role as a totalizing judgment that circumscribes our understanding of the nature of politics. The task of a pharmacological approach to the political is to engage with the consequences of these totalizing judgments and not to simply rule out particular methodologies. Stiegler's philosophy of technics provides both a philosophical framework for considering this problem and a set of judgments that demonstrate this tension in practice. A political theory committed to pluralism in the form of noodiversity does not need to abandon ontology, but instead must consider the practical and "therapeutic" consequences of its ontological commitments. Do they totalize the political in a way that makes room for conceptual individuation that might arise from technical change, new pharmacological problems, or encounters with other localities?

Read as such, Stiegler's work demands a kind of intellectual modesty that is in tune with the pluralist ethos of continental political theory but at odds with its methods. He implores us to rethink noodiversity at the level of the intellectual tools used to conceptualize the political, but he also combines this modesty with a renewed commitment to thinking the connection between the local and the general, the particular and the universal, the open and the totalizing, in order to respond to problems posed by global *pharmaka*. Stiegler's pharmacological approach to totalization equips continental political theory with a set of tools for returning to the task of articulating totalizing judgments that address large-scale problems while maintaining the importance of locality in the genesis of those judgments.

A rejection of totality in favor of locality neglects the important role that the latter must play in addressing increasingly large-scale political problems. This particular gesture, as I suggested in the introduction, is characteristic of both post-foundational approaches to political ontology and immanent, vitalist, and monist approaches to the political found within new materialism. Uncritical totalization has its shortcomings, but the same can be said of localism that does not consider the necessary passage to totality and generality.

I suggest, then, that Stiegler's work empowers continental political theory to pursue questions of totality and judgment. While continental political theory has never been reluctant to draw on other fields beyond its own boundaries, this will also require collaboration with areas of political theory with which it has tended not to converse. For example, comparative political theorists might provide insight into the disconnections and connections between local traditions that might underpin the pharmacological consideration of the passage to generality (Jenco 2011), while analytical political theory might provide an opportunity to widen the resources applied to pharmacological problems (Arnold 2020). Anna Jane Gordon has argued that such an approach would constitute a "creolization" of political theory, as "an act of teleological suspension through which we recall a larger *telos* . . . a galvanizing concern with understanding and protecting a distinct domain called political life. Rather than treating our discipline as if it were never born and can never die by ontologizing it (or treating it as isomorphic with Being itself), we must recenter difficult questions over the methods that would determine in advance what can and cannot be asked" (Gordon 2014, 200). Gordon's point here is that the very nature of political theory is constituted by the encounters between local problems and perspectives, and the challenge of diversifying the discipline must not neglect the critical task of continually constituting the general project that we refer to as politics. The invention that arises from the interaction between localities, which Gordon calls creolization, is a constitutive part of political theory as opposed to a new project that has emerged with recent, and urgent, concerns for plurality and diversification within the discipline. The limit to political ontology is its equation of this political project with being, and therefore its neglect of the pharmacological question of how political judgments are constituted, how they relate locality to totality, and whether those passages to generality provide the opportunity for their own suspension.

While Stiegler himself does not engage in a discussion of creolization, Gordon's methodological claims present a position close to what I argue represents his significance for continental political theory in particular.

As we have seen in our examination of concepts like organology, Stiegler advocates for engagement with the sciences in way that fits the model of creolization. Moreover, the concepts of the non-inhuman, the *pharmakon*, and the a-transcendental force us to recognize both the accidental and situated character of philosophical thought while also imploring us to find ways to reconcile the local with general forms of political judgment without reifying or essentializing those judgments. Rather than abandoning totalization, Stiegler argues that we must articulate totalizing, generalizing, and universal projects that integrate within them a pharmacological attention to openness, non-totalization, and locality. Stiegler's philosophy provides concepts that allow us to articulate this balance between totalizing judgment and openness, while his own political judgments also demonstrate the difficulty of this task. It is in this way that his work represents a combination of both ambition and modesty in which continental political thought may find ample resources for addressing the global challenges that lie ahead of it.

Notes

Introduction

1. Alongside figures like Friedrich Kittler, for example. While some might argue that Martin Heidegger's work also represents a precursor to more recent continental philosophies of technology, for Stiegler his work privileged language over technicity and therefore could not fully come to terms with the nature of technics (Stiegler 1998, 3–8).

2. This distinct methodological commitment is most clearly seen in accounts of how continental thought differs from the analytic tradition (e.g., Arnold 2020; Floyd 2016; Donahue and Ochoa Espejo 2016). While I acknowledge the value of attempts to move beyond the analytic-continental distinction (e.g., Livingston 2012), there nevertheless remain clear stylistic, argumentative, and political differences between them. As such, I hold to the existence of a set of concerns, or ways of dealing with those concerns, that are unique to continental political theory.

3. For example, these analyses have inspired and influenced the replacement of closed and exclusionary definitions of the human found in humanism with the concept of the posthuman, a figure that is non-totalizable, as it is constituted by a tendency toward perpetual change and redefinition rather than fixed a-historical attributes. See the work of Rosi Braidotti as an example of the embrace of the non-totalizing aims of poststructuralism in the shift from humanism to posthumanism (2013, 13–54).

4. See, for example, the work of Oliver Marchart (2007; 2018), Stephen White (2000), Mark Wenman (2013), and Nathan Widder (2012), among other edited collections and interventions on political ontology (Mihai et al. 2017; Tønder and Thomassen 2005; Strathausen 2009).

5. An approach that has come under sustained attack by recent realist and speculative philosophy, a position most succinctly articulated by Quentin Meillassoux (2009).

6. See the work of Henry Somers-Hall on this explicit rejection of judgment in modern French philosophy (2022).

7. For an account of this indifference and contemporary responses to it, see the work of Iain Mackenzie (2022).

8. The distinction between the political and politics derives from the French division between *le politique* and *la politique*, which are associated, respectively, with an originary human political relation and the world of power and policy (Marchart 2007, 67–69; Raynaud 2014).

9. Foundational texts include those of Jane Bennett, Diane Coole, and Samantha Frost (Bennett 2010; Coole 2013; Frost and Coole 2010). For an overview of positions within new materialism, see the work of Iris van der Tuin and Rick Dolphijn (2012) and Charles Devellennes and Benoît Dillet (2018).

10. Chin makes a similar claim to the one pursued here in his account of the shortcomings of Connolly's thought in the context of an exploration of the work of Richard Rorty (2018).

11. For the work of Ars Industrialis, see the two manifestos coauthored with other founding members of the group (Ars Industrialis 2014b; 2014a) and the site http://www.arsindustrialis.org. For the work of Plein Commune, see http://www. plainecommune.fr. For the Internation Collective, see https://internation.world.

12. A full exploration of the a-transcendental was forthcoming in a future volume of Stiegler's *Technics and Time* series (Crogan 2006, 50, n.6).

13. Stiegler's a-transcendental method also distinguishes his philosophy from approaches that sit on either side of the divide between transcendental and empirical methodologies within the philosophy of technology (Lemmens 2022).

14. From the perspective of the argument pursued here, those who seek to escape the human through ontological realism also unwittingly make assumptions about the nature of politics and the human because of the a-transcendental status of ontology. In lieu of an overview of this approach, found in speculative realism and object-oriented ontology, see the work of Peter Gratton (2014).

15. Stiegler engaged fleetingly with the work of Achille Mbembe and Édouard Glissant in his later work, but these considerations are subordinate to the relationship between locality and calculation (2019e; 2020c, 311–12).

16. There are many accounts of Stiegler's critique of contemporary capitalism (Abbinnett 2015; 2018; Barker 2012b; James 2010; G. Moore 2013) and the various topics within it, such as addiction (G. Moore 2018), the attention economy (Bueno 2017; Crogan and Kinsley 2012; Pettman 2015; Reveley 2015), automation (Crogan 2019; Crowley 2019), the culture industry (Sinnerbrink 2009), industrial temporal objects (Crogan 2013), political economy (de Beistegui 2013), proletarianization (Dillet 2017; Hutnyk 2012), and the future of work (Manche 2021; Turner 2021a). Stiegler's work has also attracted a large amount of attention within the philosophy of education, particular from those interested in the interface between technology, capitalism, and pedagogy (e.g., J. P. N. Bradley and Kennedy 2021).

17. These omissions include the work of Heidegger and Husserl in particular, as Stiegler is often read as an inheritor of the phenomenological tradition. I have published on Stiegler's relationship to Husserl elsewhere (2020), and both Tracy

Colony (2010) and Daniel Ross (2021a) have provided overviews of his reading of Heidegger. Ross has also situated Stiegler's use of both authors within a wider periodization of his work (2018).

Chapter 1

1. While the specifics of the species that comprise the evolutionary path that Leroi-Gourhan traces may be "obsolete" (Ingold 2013, 36), the intuitions behind his argument have been drawn upon by recent anthropology and archaeology (Ingold 1999; Malafouris 2013, 153–55; Tomlinson 2018, 110).

2. Brief references to the a-transcendental that characterize it as this complex of transcendental and empirical themes can be found across Stiegler's work (e.g., 1995, 247, 277–78; 2012e, 187; 2018c, 39). An unfinished, future volume of *Technics and Time* was intended to elaborate on the nature of the a-transcendental (Stiegler 2013b, n.20, 142). It is also worth noting that in the second volume of *Qu'appelle-t-on panser*, Stiegler refers to the "exo-transcendental" in the context of a discussion of the relationship between fiction and reason (Stiegler 2020c, 58). This shift derives from his adoption of the language of exosomatization in his late work, which is discussed in chapter 7. It is unclear, however, whether the concept of exo-transcendence represents a different concept entirely to that of the a-transcendental, or merely a change in terminology.

3. This understanding of the relationship between *anamnesis* and *hypomnesis* is first found in the opening volume of the *Technics and Time* series (1998, 96–100). While not explored by name in the rest of that series, the two terms become a reference for the intertwinement of thought with technicity across Stiegler's work (2006a; 2009a, 14–16; 2010d, 70–72; 2011a, 39–40; 2014f, 79–81).

4. Stiegler relies on the claim that across the chronology of Plato's dialogues they become less "Socratic" and more "Platonic." See Stiegler's reference to this point in *The Age of Disruption* (2019d, 154) and Benoît Dillet's translators note in *Philosophising by Accident* (2017c, n.2, 56).

5. The negative role of woman in both the Platonic and Hesiodic version of the Prometheus myth goes without comment, aside from Stiegler's acknowledgement that sexual difference also arrives with the fall in Rousseau (1998, 195). Despite the mythical status of the "event" of sexual difference, there are grounds to question its place in Stiegler's work that are beyond the scope of the discussion here. Deborah Withers has explored the relevance of his philosophy of technics to the transmission and inheritance of feminist archives and memory (2015); however, they do not address the broader role that feminist theory might play in the reception of Stiegler's work. I begin to consider this elsewhere with respect to his politics of work (Turner 2021a).

6. Stiegler's version of "prometheanism" differs significantly from the adoption of the language of promethean politics by figures like Ray Brassier (2014a; 2014b).

While Stiegler shares the goal of rehabilitating totalizing, large-scale, and ambitious political projects in some form, he nevertheless places a much more significant emphasis on the pharmacological fragility and uncertainty that underpins them.

7. Nancy and Lacoue-Labarthe's investigation of the political in relation to politics derives partially from Heidegger's distinction between the ontological essence of technics and the ontical nature of technology (Nancy and Lacoue-Labarthe 1997, 110). See the work of Ian James (2006, 152–201) and Oliver Marchart (2007, 61–84) for an exploration of this theme.

8. For a more extensive account of this idea, see the work of Marchart (2007, 61–67).

9. Hui himself argues that the ontological difference forms the basis of a particular understanding of technicity unique to Western cosmology. Other cosmological frameworks, such as those particular to Chinese philosophy, do not necessarily understand technicity in terms of a difference between the ontic and the ontological (Hui 2016).

10. On this point, see also Kennan Ferguson's argument that the presence of politics among pre–*Homo sapiens* may have acted as a non-biological evolutionary influence within the history of the human (2014).

Chapter 2

1. On Derrida's relationship to the *Phaedrus* more widely, see the work of Miriam Leonard (2005, 190–94).

2. The different formats and spellings of the term *différance* in the following are reproduced from the texts cited.

3. The term "pure" here is clumsy, bringing with it the implication of a metaphysical conception of life separate from technical life. Stiegler accepts, however, that "*phusis* as life was already *différance*" (Stiegler 1998, 139).

4. It is worth noting that Stiegler's approach here differs significantly from those who apply *différance* beyond life to the level of quantum physics, such as Karen Barad (2010). He explicitly rejects such gestures and refers to the principle of *différance* applying to the living and the psychosocial "but not the mineral" (Stiegler 2015a, 56).

5. The centrality of this distinction is demonstrated by Stiegler's reference to it across several texts (2003, 158; 2006a; 2008a, 32; 2010d, 74).

6. This is a common concern in the literature on Stiegler's work (Beardsworth 1998a, 81; A. Bradley 2011, 128–31; Ekman 2007, 170; Lechte 2018, 176–77; Pettman 2011, 160–72; Tuckwell 2020, 92; Van Camp 2009b, 140).

7. A point also made by several others (Brown 2014, 144; James 2010, 213–14; G. Moore 2017, 208–9; Van Camp 2009a).

8. As also expressed by several other interpreters of Stiegler's work (A. Bradley 2006; Sinnerbrink 2009; Abbinnett 2020, 151–52; Colony 2017, 80–81).

9. I explore this claim regarding the relationship between politics and phar-macological invention with respect to the links between Derrida, Leroi-Gourhan, Georges Canguilhem, and Gilbert Simondon elsewhere (B. Turner 2016).

10. The importance of the quasi-cause and stupidity here shows that while Stiegler is often thought of and read primarily as a student of Derrida, Deleuze plays an equally important role in his thought (Stiegler 2013e, 490).

Chapter 3

1. It should be recognized that Stiegler is not the only member of his generation of thinkers to take significant influence from Simondon. For example, he notes that it was François Laruelle who introduced him to Simondon's work, allowing him to formalize his early theory of the "idiotext" on the basis of the concept of individuation (Stiegler 2012a, 165–66).

2. Jason Tuckwell has argued that Hui reverses Stiegler's prioritization of "a singular genesis of technics" that "underwrites an anthropological universality," thereby correcting his neglect of cultural influences upon technological development (Tuckwell 2020, 84). In contrast, as the following demonstrates, I take Hui to further Stiegler's commitment to the co-constitution of the social, or cultural, and the technical. In doing so, he explicates a position that was already present within Stiegler's philosophy of technics.

3. For more comprehensive introductions to Simondon's philosophy, see the work of Andrea Bardin (2015), Pascal Chabot (2014), and Muriel Combes (2013).

4. A point that Stiegler makes elsewhere (Stiegler 2011c, 58; 2018c, 79–80), and that is also explored by Daniel Ross (Ross 2013, 245).

5. Stiegler first conceptualized grammatization in volume one of *Symbolic Misery* (Stiegler 2014e, 48–59) to further the understanding of the co-constitution of the interior and exterior described in the first volume of *Technics and Time*.

6. As also noted by Mark Hansen (Hansen 2017, 176–77) and Ben Roberts (Roberts 2016, 103–4). Stiegler himself makes repeated reference to the essential connection between grammatization and the pre-individual (Stiegler 2006a, 3; 2009c, 40; 2011a, 38–41; 2013a, 31–33; 2014e, 53–59; 2015b, 41–43).

7. The importance of this critique to Stiegler's work has been noted by several commentators (Abbinnett 2015, 72; Colony 2017, 72–73; Crogan 2013, 104–6; Roberts 2012, 17).

8. We might also add that Combes's criticism misses its mark because Stiegler is less concerned with an accurate representation of Simondon's position and more with a "cross-fertilization" of his ideas with those of others (Barker 2013, 260).

9. The perspective presented here is limited to Stiegler's understanding of the term organology. Others have discussed its translation from musicology to phi-losophy (Nikolić 2020) and given longer histories of the concept (Hoquet 2018; Hui 2019, 146–83).

10. Also influential here is Canguilhem's use of the term organology when discussing understandings of machines that deploy concepts usually applied to organisms (Canguilhem 2008, 75).

11. See Ross's introduction to *The Neganthropocene* (2018, 26).

12. For example, see Stiegler's 1986 piece "Technologies of Memory and Imagination," which sets out many of the themes of the later *Technics and Time* series (Stiegler 2018b, 68).

13. For example, see "Ce qui fait défaut" (1995).

Chapter 4

1. It is worth noting that sublimation is not articulated in a decisive way within the Freudian corpus, and may not even be taken fully seriously by Freud. As a result, Stiegler must be understood as working with his own definition of this term. See the work of Oliver Davis for both of these points (2013, 172–73).

2. There is not room here to fully explore Stiegler's relationship to Marx; however, he claims that Marx "lost sight of the question of ideality" (Stiegler 2020a, 66). Stiegler reads Marx and Freud together to introduce the problem of consistence into political economy. For more extensive accounts of Stiegler's reading of Marx, see the work of Ross Abbinett (2018), Richard Beardsworth (2010), and Irmak Ertuna (2009).

3. Here Stiegler develops and leans heavily on Theodore Adorno and Max Horkheimer's arguments regarding the culture industry (Adorno and Horkheimer 1972).

4. Stiegler draws heavily on Luc Boltanski and Eve Chiapello's *The New Spirit of Capitalism* to make these claims, in which they argue that the "artistic critique" of society represented by 1968 and the poststructuralists was incorporated into capitalist production (Boltanski and Chiapello 2018). He is critical of their account, however, and argues that their overview of the artistic critique that emerged from 1968 fails to engage with the philosophy underpinning it, particularly with respect to the concept of desire (Stiegler 2012a, 175–76).

5. Stiegler refers to this third dimension of knowledge as "*savoir theorizer*" (Stiegler 2010b, 30), "*savoirs théoriques*" (Stiegler 2015b, 50), and also "*savoir-conceptualiser et theorizer*" (Stiegler 2016b, 159). Unlike *savoir-faire* and *savoir-vivre*, the French is not maintained consistently in translation and is referred to here as theoretical knowledge.

6. For an exploration of Stiegler's economic proposals and his relationship to the critique of political economy, see the work of Solange Manche (2021).

7. In lieu of such an account, see the work of Robert Nichols (2020).

8. It is worth noting that Dillet recognizes a "tendency or a temptation in Stiegler's work . . . to raise the notion of proletarianization as a universal category"

(Dillet 2013, 90). My claim is that this is not just a "tendency" or "temptation," but rather central to the development of the general concept of proletarianization.

Chapter 5

1. An important exception can be found in the work of Martin Crowley, who develops an account of Stiegler's understanding of the decision in the context of his own immanent conception of agency (2022, 120–59).

2. The first is represented by John Rawls and Jürgen Habermas, whereas the latter is represented by, among others, William Connolly (Zerilli 2016, 2–5).

3. For example, Habermas (1994) and Seyla Benhabib (1996).

4. Stiegler does not articulate a historically accurate reading of the work of Aristotle or Hippocrates but instead transforms their writings to fit his conceptual apparatus (Lampe 2017). For deeper engagements with Stiegler's reading of Aristotle in particular, see the work of Conor Heaney (2020) and Daniel Ross (2009).

5. Stiegler directly links the chain of terms that he takes to be signified by Aristotle's *krinon*, "a discernment, a *krinein*, a judging, a *making-a-difference*," and that he associates with aesthetic judgment, with the singularities that Simondon claims drive a process of psychic and collective individuation (Stiegler 2012e, 191).

6. A point that Stiegler also iterates elsewhere (2011d, 231).

7. For a more extensive overview of this literature, see the work of Bruno Bosteels (2010).

8. In *Communitas*, Esposito argues that an unrepresentable being-in-common is the root of any mythological conception of community as "full" or "present," which bears the same logic as the impolitical (2010). Stiegler refers to Esposito's concept of community as expressing the logic of the default of origin in several places (Stiegler 2012b, 60–62; 2016a, 75, 128; 2019d, 53, 104, 276).

9. There is not space for an all-encompassing overview of this turn here; however, several excellent accounts exist (Charbonnier and Salmon 2014; Holbraad and Pederson 2017; J. D. Kelly 2014; Charbonnier, Salmon, and Skafish 2017).

10. I have explored this consequence of the ontological turn in anthropology in more detail elsewhere (B. Turner 2019a; 2021b).

Chapter 6

1. I have published a longer exposition of how Stiegler interprets these two terms in the work of Blanchot elsewhere (2019b).

2. Before the publication of *Automatic Society*, Stiegler had come under criticism for his claim that technological transmission had made possible the real-time dissemination of information, due to its digression from Blanchot's position

regarding the impossible (Wambacq and Buseyne 2012, 72). His more extensive references to Blanchot in *Automatic Society* can be read as a response to this problem.

3. Here Stiegler echoes Bataille: "Woe to those who, to the very end, insist on regulating the movement that exceeds them with the narrow mind of the mechanic who changes a tire" (Bataille 1988, 26).

4. The published translation reads "becoming *qua* the bringing into play of the nonprogrammed, the im-probable, and destiny *qua* nonpredestination" (Stiegler 1998, 172).

5. Lengthier examinations of the relationship between Stiegler and Foucault can be found elsewhere (Cohen 2017; de Boever 2010; Fuggle 2013; C. Turner 2010).

6. Stiegler consistently equates the meaning of the Greek term *skholē* with the Latin *otium* (e.g., Stiegler 2008b, 39; 2010e, 170; 2011a, 122; 2013b, 31).

7. Some have interpreted Stiegler's use of *otium* in terms of Christian liturgy (Du Toit and Loubser 2016; Roussouw 2016). Here my reading of *otium* suggests that Stiegler sees Christian practices for the cultivation of belief as instances of *otium* understood in a broader, anthropological sense.

8. The *otium/negotium* coupling is not replaced by the tripartite distinction between subsistence, existence, and consistence, as Erich Hörl suggests (2014, 13, n.49). Instead, each of these two conceptual constellations mutually reinforces the meaning of the other.

9. See also Christina Howells (2013, 142) and Gerald Moore (G. Moore 2017, 202) for the claim that aesthetics qua technics is constitutive of human existence.

10. This also applies to cinema. See, for example, Stiegler's assessment of the French New Wave and the director Abbas Kiarastami (Stiegler 2016c; 2014c).

11. See Crowley for a more extensive account of Stiegler's reading of Beuys (2013a).

12. Here Stiegler combines a Western, renaissance conception of art as elevation with the classical understanding of art as skill or craft (Barker 2017, 60), which represents a "neo-Hellenic fusion of technics and art" (Pettman 2011, 161). For some this reduces art to technics in a manner that erases any possibility of the autonomy of aesthetic experience from technical experience (Ieven 2012, 81–82). However, as we have seen in our consideration of Muriel Combes's critique of Stiegler's reading of Simondon, he would reject the possibility of this autonomy.

Chapter 7

1. As shown by Céline Lafontaine's exploration of the relationship between cybernetics and "French Theory" (2007).

2. Stiegler's repetition of this point (2017a, 131) and its presence in work prior to his substantive discussions of entropy (2003, 155–56) highlight its importance.

3. The ecological character of Stiegler's thought has been highlighted by several commentators (Crowley 2013a; James 2019b, 201–18; Woodward 2017).

4. See the work of Nathan Brown (2014) and Conor Heaney (2020) for more extensive explorations of Stiegler's relationship to Whitehead.

5. In lieu of an account of Stiegler's reading of Nietzsche here, see the work of Ashley Woodward (2019).

6. For an account of these problems of periodization within the context of the politics of the Anthropocene, see the work of Duncan Kelly (2019, 8–28).

7. Similar claims are also made by others (e.g., Galloway and LaRivière 2017, 135).

8. As also argued by Ulrik Ekman (2007, 48) and John Lechte (2018, 176).

9. For the former claim about the priority of the theoretical gestures of the critic, see the work of Oliver Davis (2013). For the latter claim regarding the subject of history in Stiegler's philosophy, see the work of Pettman (2011, 255, n.52).

10. I weigh in on this debate with respect to Stiegler's politics of work elsewhere (B. Turner 2021a).

Chapter 8

1. This is in addition to the political consequences of Gilbert Simondon's own work (Bardin 2015; Read 2016).

2. Dominic Smith has explored the methodological role of metaphor within Stiegler's work more widely (2021).

3. This analogy is made extensively with respect to the *polis* in *La télécratie contre la démocratie* (2006b) and with respect to education in *Taking Care of Youth and the Generations* (2010e).

4. On Clastres's influence on twentieth-century French thought and the broader consequences of his critique of totalization, see the work of Samuel Moyn (2004).

5. On Vernant as a structuralist, see the work of François Dosse (1997, 183–85).

Bibliography

Abbinnett, Ross. 2015. "The Politics of Spirit in Stiegler's Techno-Pharmacology." *Theory, Culture & Society* 32 (4): 65–80.

———. 2018. *The Thought of Bernard Stiegler: Capitalism, Technology and the Politics of Spirit*. London: Routledge.

———. 2020. "Living After Auschwitz: Memory, Culture and Biopolitics in the Work of Bernard Stiegler and Giorgio Agamben." *Theory, Culture & Society* 37 (7–8): 255–77.

Adorno, Theodore, and Max Horkheimer. 1972. *The Dialectic of Enlightenment*. London: Verso.

Alombert, Anne. 2020. "From Derrida's Deconstruction to Stiegler's Organology: Thinking after Postmodernity." *Derrida Today* 13 (1): 33–47.

Anderson, Chris. 2008. "The End of Theory: The Data Deluge Makes the Scientific Method Obsolete." *Wired*, June 23, 2008. https://www.wired.com/2008/06/pb-theory/.

Apter, Emily. 2018. *Unexceptional Politics: On Obstruction, Impasse, and the Impolitic*. London: Verso.

Arendt, Hannah. 1960. "Freedom and Politics: A Lecture." *Chicago Review* 14 (1): 28–46.

———. 1990. "Philosophy and Politics." *Social Research* 37 (1): 73–103.

———. 1998. *The Human Condition*. Chicago: University of Chicago Press.

Aristotle. 1986. *On the Soul, Parva Naturalia, On Breath*. Translated by W. S. Hett. Cambridge: Harvard University Press.

Arnold, Jeremy. 2020. *Across the Great Divide: Between Analytic and Continental Political Theory*. Stanford: Stanford University Press.

Ars Industrialis. 2014a. "Ars Industrialis: 2005 Manifesto." In *The Re-Enchantment of the World: The Value of Spirit Against Industrial Populism*, by Bernard Stiegler, 11–16. London: Bloomsbury.

———. 2014b. "Ars Industrialis: 2010 Manifesto." In *The Re-Enchantment of the World: The Value of Spirit Against Industrial Populism*, by Bernard Stiegler, 17–28. London: Bloomsbury.

Bachelard, Gaston. 1984. *The New Scientific Spirit*. Translated by Arthur Goldhammer. Boston: Beacon Press.

Bailly, Francis, and Giuseppe Longo. 2009. "Biological Organization and Anti-Entropy." *Journal of Biological Systems* 17 (1): 63–96.

Banerjee, Prathama. 2020. *Elementary Aspects of the Political: Histories from the Global South*. Durham: Duke University Press.

Barad, Karen. 2010. "Quantum Entanglements and Hauntological Relations of Inheritance: Dis/continuities, SpaceTime Enfoldings, and Justice-to-Come." *Derrida Today* 3 (2): 240–68.

Bardin, Andrea. 2015. *Epistemology and Political Philosophy in Gilbert Simondon: Individuation, Technics, Social Systems*. Dordrecht: Springer.

Barker, Stephen. 2012a. "Post-Scriptum: Pharmacodemocracy." *Derrida Today* 5 (1): 1–20.

———. 2012b. "Enchantment, Disenchantment, Re-Enchantment: Toward a Critical Politics of Re-Individuation." *New Formations* 77: 21–43.

———. 2013. "Techno-Pharmaco-Genealogy." In *Stiegler and Technics*, edited by Gerald Moore and Christina Howells, 259–75. Edinburgh: Edinburgh University Press.

———. 2017. "Unwork and the Duchampian Contemporary." *Boundary* 2 44 (1): 53–78.

Barthélémy, Jean-Hugues. 2012. "Individuation and Knowledge: The 'Refutation of Idealism' in Simondon's Heritage in France." Translated by Arne de Boever and Mark Hayward. *SubStance* 41 (3): 60–75.

Bataille, Georges. 1985. *Visions of Excess: Selected Writings, 1927–1939*. Translated by Allan Stoekl. Minneapolis: University of Minnesota Press.

———. 1986. *Eroticism: Death and Sensuality*. Translated by Mary Dalwood. San Francisco: City Lights Books.

———. 1988. *The Accursed Share: An Essay on General Economy*. Vol. I, translated by Robert Hurley. New York: Zone Books.

———. 1991. *The Accursed Share: An Essay On General Economy*. Vols. II and III, translated by Robert Hurley. New York: Zone Books.

———. 2001. *The Unfinished System of Nonknowledge*. Translated by Stuart Kendall. Minneapolis: University of Minnesota Press.

Bates, David. 2020. "The Political Theology of Entropy: A Katechon for the Cybernetic Age." *History of the Human Sciences* 33 (1): 109–27.

Beardsworth, Richard. 1996. *Derrida and the Political*. London: Routledge.

———. 1998a. "Thinking Technicity." *Cultural Values* 2 (1): 70–86.

———. 1998b. "Towards a Critical Culture of the Image." *Tekhnema* 4. http://tekhnema.free.fr/4Beardsworth.html.

———. 2010. "Technology and Politics: A Response to Bernard Stiegler." *Cultural Politics* 6 (2): 181–99.

Beiner, Ronald. 1983. *Political Judgment*. London: Methuen.

Benhabib, Seyla. 1996. *The Reluctant Modernism of Hannah Arendt*. Thousand Oaks: Sage.

Bennett, Jane. 2010. *Vibrant Matter: A Political Ecology of Things*. Durham: Duke University Press.

———. 2020. *Influx and Efflux: Writing up with Walt Whitman*. Durham: Duke University Press.

Bennington, Geoffrey. 2000. *Interrupting Derrida*. London: Routledge.

Beuys, Joseph. 1990. *Energy Plan for the Western Man: Joseph Beuys in America. Writings and Interviews with the Artist*. New York: Four Walls Eight Windows.

Bishop, Ryan, and Daniel Ross. 2021. "Technics, Time and the Internation: Bernard Stiegler's Thought—A Dialogue with Daniel Ross." *Theory, Culture & Society* 38 (4): 111–33.

Blanchot, Maurice. 1988. *The Unavowable Community*. Translated by Pierre Joris. New York: Station Hill Press.

———. 1993. *The Infinite Conversation*. Translated by Susan Hanson. Minneapolis: University of Minnesota Press.

———. 2000. "The Beast of Lascaux." *Oxford Literary Review* 22 (1): 9–18.

Boltanski, Luc, and Eve Chiapello. 2018. *The New Spirit of Capitalism*. Translated by Gregory Elliott. London: Verso.

Boltzmann, Ludwig. 1974. *Theoretical Physics and Philosophical Problems: Selected Writings*. Translated by Brian McGuinness. Dordrecht: Reidel.

Bosteels, Bruno. 2010. "Politics, Infrapolitics, and the Impolitical: Notes on the Thought of Roberto Esposito and Alberto Moreiras." *CR: The New Centennial Review* 10 (2): 205–38.

Braidotti, Rosi. 2013. *The Posthuman*. Cambridge: Polity.

Bradley, Arthur. 2006. "Derrida's God: A Genealogy of the Theological Turn." *Paragraph* 29 (3): 21–42.

———. 2011. *Originary Technicity: The Theory of Technology from Marx to Derrida*. New York: Palgrave Macmillan.

Bradley, Joff P. N., and David Kennedy, eds. 2021. *Bernard Stiegler and the Philosophy of Education*. Abingdon: Routledge.

Brassier, Ray. 2014a. "Prometheanism and Its Critics." In *#Accelerate: The Accelerationist Reader*, edited by Robin Mackay and Armen Avanessian, 467–87. London: Urbanomic.

———. 2014b. "Prometheanism and Real Abstraction." In *Speculative Aesthetics*, edited by Robin Mackay, Luke Pendrell, and James Trafford, 72–77. London: Urbanomic.

Brogan, Walter. 1989. "Plato's *Pharmakon*: Between Two Repetitions." In *Derrida and Deconstruction*, edited by J. Silverman, 7–23. London: Routledge.

Brown, Nathan. 2014. "The Technics of Prehension: On the Photography of Nicolas Baier." In *The Lure of Whitehead*, edited by Nicholas Gaskill and A. J. Nocek, 127–54. Minneapolis: University of Minnesota Press.

Bueno, Claudio Celis. 2017. *The Attention Economy: Labour, Time and Power in Cognitive Capitalism*. London: Rowman and Littlefield International.

Butler, Judith. 1999. *Gender Trouble*. London: Routledge.

Cadena, Marisol de la. 2010. "Indigenous Cosmopolitics in the Andes: Conceptual Reflections beyond 'Politics.'" *Cultural Anthropology* 25 (2): 334–70.

Candea, Matei. 2011. "'Our Division of the Universe': Making a Space for the Non-Political in the Anthropology of Politics." *Current Anthropology* 52 (3): 309–34.

Canguilhem, Georges. 1991. *The Normal and the Pathological*. Translated by Caroline Fawcett. New York: Zone Books.

———. 2008. *Knowledge of Life*. Edited by Paolo Maratti and Todd Meyers. Translated by Stefanos Geroulanos and Daniela Ginsburg. New York: Fordham University Press.

Chabot, Pascal. 2014. *The Philosophy of Simondon: Between Technology and Individuation*. Translated by Aliza Krefetz and Graeme Kirkpatrick. London: Bloomsbury.

Chakrabarty, Dipesh. 2009. "The Climate of History: Four Theses." *Critical Inquiry* 35 (2): 197–222.

———. 2012. "Postcolonial Studies and the Challenge of Climate Change." *New Literary History* 43 (1): 1–18.

Chalmers, Madeleine. 2020. "Living as We Dream: Automatism and Automation from Surrealism to Stiegler." *Nottingham French Studies* 59 (3): 368–83.

Changeux, Jean-Pierre. 2007. "Préface." In *Les neurones de la lecture*, by Stanislas Dehaene. Paris: Odile Jacob.

Charbonnier, Pierre, and Gildas Salmon. 2014. "The Two Ontological Pluralisms of French Anthropology." *Journal of the Royal Anthropological Institute* 20 (3): 567–73.

Charbonnier, Pierre, Gildas Salmon, and Peter Skafish, eds. 2017. *Comparative Metaphysics: Ontology after Anthropology*. London: Rowman and Littlefield International.

Chimisso, Cristina. 2008. "From Phenomenology to Phenomenotechnique: The Role of Early Twentieth-Century Physics in Gaston Bachelard's Philosophy." *Studies in History and Philosophy of Science* 39 (3): 384–92.

Chin, Clayton. 2018. *The Practice of Political Theory: Rorty and Continental Thought*. New York: Columbia University Press.

———. 2021. "Just What Is Ontological Political Theory Meant to Do? The Method and Practice of William E. Connolly." *Political Studies* 69 (4): 771–90.

Clastres, Pierre. 1988. *Society Against the State: Essays in Political Anthropology*. Translated by Robert Hurley and Abe Stein. New York: Zone Books.

Clifford, James, and George E. Marcus, eds. 1986. *Writing Culture: The Poetics and Politics of Ethnography*. Berkeley: University of California Press.

Cohen, Ed. 2017. "Dare to Care: Between Stiegler's Mystagogy and Foucault's Aesthetics of Existence." *Boundary 2* 44 (1): 149–66.

Colebrook, Claire. 2014. *Death of the PostHuman: Essays on Extinction*. Vol. 1. Ann Arbor: Open Humanities Press.

———. 2017. "Impossible, Unprincipled, and Contingent: Bernard Stiegler's Project of Revolution and Redemption." *Boundary* 2 44 (1): 213–37.

Colony, Tracy. 2010. "A Matter of Time: Stiegler on Heidegger and Being Technological." *Journal of the British Society for Phenomenology* 41 (2): 117–31.

———. 2011. "Epimetheus Bound: Stiegler on Derrida, Life, and the Technological Condition." *Research in Phenomenology* 41 (1): 72–89.

———. 2017. "The Future of Technics." *Parrhesia* 27: 64–87.

Combes, Muriel. 2013. *Gilbert Simondon and the Philosophy of the Transindividual*. Translated by Thomas LaMarre. Cambridge: MIT Press.

Connolly, William E. 2013. *The Fragility of Things: Self-Organizing Processes, Neoliberal Fantasies, and Democratic Activism*. Durham: Duke University Press.

———. 2017. *Facing the Planetary: Entangled Humanism and the Politics of Swarming*. Durham: Duke University Press.

Coole, Diana. 2013. "Agentic Capacities and Capacious Historical Materialism: Thinking with New Materialisms in the Political Sciences." *Millennium: Journal of International Studies* 41 (3): 451–69.

Coulthard, Glen Sean. 2014. *Red Skin, White Masks: Rejecting the Colonial Politics of Recognition*. Minneapolis: University of Minnesota Press.

Crogan, Patrick. 2006. "Essential Viewing: Review of '*La Technique et Le Temps 3: Le Temps Du Cinéma et La Question Du Mal-Être*.'" *Film Philosophy* 10 (2): 39–54.

———. 2013. "Editing (and) Individuation." *New Formations* 77: 97–110.

———. 2019. "Bernard Stiegler on Algorithmic Governmentality: A New Regimen of Truth?" *New Formations* 98: 48–67.

Crogan, Patrick, and Samuel Kinsley. 2012. "Paying Attention: Towards A Critique of the Attention Economy." *Culture Machine* 13: 1–29.

Crowley, Martin. 2013a. "Bernard Stiegler Goes Seal-Hunting with Joseph Beuys." *Forum for Modern Language Studies* 49 (1): 45–59.

———. 2013b. "The Artist and the Amateur, from Misery to Invention." In *Stiegler and Technics*, edited by Christina Howells and Gerald Moore, 119–34. Edinburgh: Edinburgh University Press.

———. 2019. "#automaticpolitics." *Diacritics* 47 (1): 136–53.

———. 2022. *Accidental Agents: Ecological Politics Beyond the Human*. New York: Columbia University Press.

Daggett, Cara New. 2019. *The Birth of Energy: Fossil Fuels, Thermodynamics, and the Politics of Work*. Durham: Duke University Press.

Davis, Oliver. 2013. "Desublimation in Education for Democracy." In *Stiegler and Technics*, edited by Christina Howells and Gerald Moore, 165–78. Edinburgh: Edinburgh University Press.

de Beistegui, Miguel. 2013. "The New Critique of Political Economy." In *Stiegler and Technics*, edited by Christina Howells and Gerald Moore, 181–91. Edinburgh: Edinburgh University Press.

de Boever, Arne. 2010. "The Allegory of the Cage: Foucault, Agamben, and the Enlightenment." *Foucault Studies* 10: 7–22.

de Boever, Arne, Alex Murray, Jon Roffe, and Ashley Woodward, eds. 2012. *Gilbert Simondon: Being and Technology*. Edinburgh: Edinburgh University Press.

Dehaene, Stanislas. 2009. *Reading in the Brain: The New Science of How We Read*. London: Penguin.

Deleuze, Gilles. 1990. *The Logic of Sense*. Translated by Mark Lester. New York: Columbia University Press.

———. 1994. *Difference and Repetition*. Translated by Paul Patton. London: Athlone Press.

———. 1995. *Negotiations, 1972–1990*. New York: Columbia University Press.

———. 1997. *Essays Critical and Clinical*. Translated by Daniel W. Smith and Michael A. Greco. Minneapolis: University of Minnesota Press.

———. 2006. *Nietzsche and Philosophy*. Translated by Michael Hardt. New York: Columbia University Press.

Deleuze, Gilles, and Félix Guattari. 1983. *Anti-Oedipus: Capitalism and Schizophrenia*. Translated by Robert Hurley, Mark Seem, and Helen R. Lane. Minneapolis: University of Minnesota Press.

Derrida, Jacques. 1976. *Of Grammatology*. Translated by Gayatri Chakravorty Spivak. Baltimore: John Hopkins University Press.

———. 1981. "Plato's Pharmacy." In *Dissemination*, translated by Barbara Johnson, 61–172. London: Athlone Press.

———. 1982. "*Différance*." In *Margins of Philosophy*, translated by Alan Bass, 1–27. Chicago: University of Chicago Press.

———. 2004. *Positions*. Translated by Alan Bass. London: Continuum.

Derrida, Jacques, and Bernard Stiegler. 2002. *Ecographies of Television*. Translated by Jennifer Bajorek. Cambridge: Polity.

Descola, Philippe. 2005. "On Anthropological Knowledge." *Social Anthropology* 13 (1): 65–73.

———. 2013. *Beyond Nature and Culture*. Translated by Janet Lloyd. Chicago: University of Chicago Press.

Dillet, Benoît. 2017. "Proletarianization, Deproletarianization, and the Rise of the Amateur." *Boundary* 2 44 (1): 79–105.

Dillet, Benoît, and Charles Devellennes. 2018. "Questioning New Materialisms: An Introduction." *Theory, Culture & Society* 35 (7–8): 5–20.

Donahue, Thomas J., and Paulina Ochoa Espejo. 2016. "The Analytical–Continental Divide: Styles of Dealing with Problems." *European Journal of Political Theory* 15 (2): 138–54.

Dosse, François. 1997. *History of Structuralism*. Vol. 1, *The Rising Sign, 1945–1966*, translated by Deborah Glassman. Minneapolis: University of Minnesota Press.

Du Toit, Calvyn C., and Gys M. Loubser. 2016. "Liturgical Pharmacology: Time of the Question, Complexity and Ethics." *HTS Teologiese Studies/Theological Studies* 72 (1): 1–8.

Dubreuil, Laurent. 2016. *The Refusal of Politics*. Translated by Cory Browning. Edinburgh: Edinburgh University Press.

Dupré, John. 2012. *Processes of Life: Essays in the Philosophy of Biology*. Oxford: Oxford University Press.

Ekman, Ulrik. 2007. "Of Transductive Speed—Stiegler." *Parallax* 13 (4): 46–63.

Ertuna, Irmak. 2009. "Stiegler and Marx for a Question Concerning Technology." *Transformations* 17. http://www.transformationsjournal.org/wp-content/uploads/2017/01/Ertuna_Trans17.pdf.

Espinoza, Tania. 2013. "The Technical Object of Psychoanalysis." In *Stiegler and Technics*, edited by Christina Howells and Gerald Moore, 151–64. Edinburgh: Edinburgh University Press.

Esposito, Roberto. 2010. *Communitas: The Origin and Destiny of Community*. Translated by Timothy Campbell. Stanford: Stanford University Press.

———. 2015. *Categories of the Impolitical*. Translated by Connal Parsley. New York: Fordham University Press.

Eze, Emmanuel Chukwudi. 1997. "The Color of Reason: The Idea of 'Race' in Kant's Anthropology." In *Postcolonial African Philosophy: A Critical Reader*, edited by Emmanuel Chukwudi Eze, 103–31. Oxford: Blackwell.

Fanon, Frantz. 2008. *Black Skin, White Masks*. Translated by Charles M. Markmann. London: Pluto Press.

Featherstone, Mark. 2020. "Apocalypse Now!: From Freud, Through Lacan, to Stiegler's Psychoanalytic 'Survival Project.'" *International Journal for the Semiotics of Law—Revue Internationale de Sémiotique Juridique* 33 (2): 409–31.

Ferguson, Kennan. 2014. "What Was Politics to the Denisovan?" *Political Theory* 42 (2): 167–87.

Floyd, Jonathan. 2016. "Analytics and Continentals: Divided by Nature but United by Praxis?" *European Journal of Political Theory* 15 (2): 155–71.

Foucault, Michel. 1997. "Self Writing." In *Ethics: Subjectivity and Truth. The Essential Works of Michel Foucault 1954–1984*, edited by Paul Rabinow, translated by Robert Hurley, 207–22. London: Penguin.

Freud, Sigmund. 1953. *The Standard Edition of the Complete Psychological Works of Sigmund Freud*. Vol. VII, *A Case of Hysteria, Three Essays on Sexuality, and Other Works*, edited and translated by James Strachey. London: The Hogarth Press.

———. 1961. *The Standard Edition of the Complete Psychological Works of Sigmund Freud*. Vol. XXI, *The Future of An Illusion, Civilization and Its Discontents and Other Works*, edited and translated by James Strachey. London: The Hogarth Press.

———. 1989. *The Ego and the Id*. Edited by James Strachey. Translated by Joan Riviere. New York: W. W. Norton and Company.

Frost, Samantha, and Diana Coole, eds. 2010. *New Materialisms: Ontology, Agency, and Politics*. Durham: Duke University Press.

Fuggle, Sophie. 2013. "Stiegler and Foucault: The Politics of Care and Self-Writing." In *Stiegler and Technics*, edited by Christina Howells and Gerald Moore, 192–207. Edinburgh: Edinburgh University Press.

Galloway, Alexander, and Jason R. LaRivière. 2017. "Compression in Philosophy." *Boundary 2* 44 (1): 125–48.

Gasché, Rodolphe. 2016. *Deconstruction, Its Force, Its Violence*. Albany: State University of New York Press.

Gayon, Jean. 2007. "The Concept of the Gene in Contemporary Biology: Continuity or Dissolution?" In *The Influence of Genetics on Contemporary Thinking*, edited by Anne Fagot-Largeault, Shahid Rahman, and Juan Manuel Torres, 81–95. Dordrecht: Springer.

Georgescu-Roegen, Nicholas. 1971. *The Entropy Law and the Economic Process*. Cambridge: Harvard University Press.

Gille, Baptiste. 2017. "Ordering What Is: The Political Implications of Ontological Knowledge." In *Comparative Metaphysics: Ontology After Anthropology*, edited by Pierre Charbonnier, Gildas Salmon, and Peter Skafish, translated by Nicolas Carter, 301–26. London: Rowman and Littlefield International.

Gordon, Jane Anna. 2014. *Creolizing Political Theory: Reading Rousseau Through Fanon*. New York: Fordham University Press.

Gratton, Peter. 2014. *Speculative Realism: Problems and Prospects*. London: Bloomsbury.

Gutting, Gary. 2011. *Thinking the Impossible: French Philosophy Since 1960*. Oxford: Oxford University Press.

Habermas, Jürgen. 1994. "Hannah Arendt's Communications Concept of Power." In *Hannah Arendt: Critical Essays*, edited by Lewis Hinchman and Sandra Hinchman, 211–30. Albany: State University of New York Press.

Hansen, Mark. 2004. "The Time of Affect, or Bearing Witness to Life." *Critical Inquiry* 30 (3): 584–626.

———. 2009. "Living (with) Technical Time: From Media Surrogacy to Distributed Cognition." *Theory, Culture & Society* 26 (2–3): 294–315.

———. 2012. "Engineering Pre-Individual Potentiality: Technics, Transindividuation, and 21st-Century Media." *SubStance* 41 (3): 32–59.

———. 2017. "Bernard Stiegler, Philosopher of Desire?" *Boundary 2* 44 (1): 167–90.

Haworth, Michael. 2016. "Bernard Stiegler on Transgenerational Memory and the Dual Origin of the Human." *Theory, Culture & Society* 33 (3): 151–73.

Hayles, N. Katherine. 1999. *How We Became Posthuman: Virtual Bodies in Cybernetics, Literature, and Informatics*. Chicago: University of Chicago Press.

Heaney, Conor. 2020. "Rhythmic Nootechnics: Stiegler, Whitehead, and Noetic Life." *Educational Philosophy and Theory* 52 (4): 397–408.

Hesiod. 1988. *Theogeny and Works and Days*. Translated by M. L. West. Oxford: Oxford University Press.

Hobbes, Thomas. 1996. *Leviathan*. Edited by C. A. Gaskin. Oxford: Oxford University Press.

Holbraad, Martin, and Morten Axel Pederson. 2017. *The Ontological Turn: An Anthropological Exposition*. Cambridge: Cambridge University Press.

Honig, Bonnie. 1993. *Political Theory and the Displacement of Politics*. Ithaca: Cornell University Press.

Hoquet, Thierry. 2018. "Cyborgs, Between Organology and Phenomenology: Two Perspectives on Artifacts and Life." In *French Philosophy of Technology: Classical Readings and Contemporary Approaches*, edited by Sacha Loeve, Xavier Guchet, and Bernadette Bensaude Vincent, 257–77. Dordrecht: Springer.

Hörl, Erich. 2014. "Prostheses of Desire: On Bernard Stiegler's New Critique of Projection." *Parrhesia* 20: 2–14.

Howells, Christina. 2013. "'Le Défaut d'origine': The Prosthetic Condition of Love and Desire." In *Stiegler and Technics*, edited by Christina Howells and Gerald Moore, 137–50. Edinburgh: Edinburgh University Press.

Howells, Christina, and Gerald Moore. 2013. "Introduction: Philosophy—The Repression of Technics." In *Stiegler and Technics*, edited by Christina Howells and Gerald Moore, 1–14. Edinburgh: Edinburgh University Press.

Hughes, Robert. 2014. "Bernard Stiegler, Philosophical Amateur, or, Individuation from Eros to Philia." *Diacritics* 42 (1): 46–67.

Hui, Yuk. 2016. *The Question Concerning Technology in China: An Essay in Cosmotechnics*. London: Urbanomic.

———. 2017. "On Cosmotechnics: For a Renewed Relation between Technology and Nature in the Anthropocene." *Techné: Research in Philosophy and Technology* 21 (2): 319–41.

———. 2019. *Recursivity and Contingency*. London: Rowman & Littlefield International.

———. 2020. "Writing and Cosmotechnics." *Derrida Today* 13 (1): 17–32.

———. 2022. "For a Cosmotechnical Event." *Foundations of Science* 27 (1): 141–54.

Hui, Yuk, and Pieter Lemmens. 2017. "Reframing the Technosphere: Peter Sloterdijk and Bernard Stiegler's Anthropotechnological Diagnoses of the Anthropocene." *Krisis* 2: 26–41.

Hutnyk, John. 2012. "Proletarianisation." *New Formations* 77: 127–49.

Ieven, Bram. 2012. "The Forgetting of Aesthetics: Individuation, Technology, and Aesthetics in the Work of Bernard Stiegler." *New Formations* 77: 76–96.

Ingold, Tim. 1999. "'Tools for the Hand, Language for the Face': An Appreciation of Leroi-Gourhan's Gesture and Speech." *Studies in the History and Philosophy of Biology and Biomedical Science* 30 (4): 411–53.

———. 2013. *Making: Anthropology, Archaeology, Art and Architecture*. London: Routledge.

Jacob, François. 1973. *The Logic of Life: A History of Heredity*. Translated by Betty E. Spillman. New York: Pantheon Books.

James, Ian. 2006. *The Fragmentary Demand: An Introduction to the Philosophy of Jean-Luc Nancy*. Stanford: Stanford University Press.

———. 2010. "Bernard Stiegler and the Time of Technics." *Cultural Politics* 6 (2): 207–27.

———. 2012. *The New French Philosophy*. Cambridge: Polity.

———. 2013. "Technics and Cerebrality." In *Stiegler and Technics*, edited by Gerald Moore and Christina Howells, 17–33. Edinburgh: Edinburgh University Press.

———. 2015. "Totality, Convergence, Synchronization." In *Concentrationary Imaginaries: Tracing Totalitarian Violence in Popular Culture*, edited by Griselda Pollock and Max Silverman, 81–96. London: I.B. Tauris.

———. 2019a. "Post-Deconstructive Thought and Criticism." *French Studies* 73 (1): 84–102.

———. 2019b. *The Technique of Thought*. Minneapolis: University of Minnesota Press.

Jenco, Leigh K. 2011. "Recentering Political Theory: The Promise of Mobile Locality." *Cultural Critique* 79 (Fall): 27–59.

Jenco, Leigh K., Murad Idris, and Megan C. Thomas. 2020. "Comparison, Connectivity, and Disconnection." In *The Oxford Handbook of Comparative Political Theory*, edited by Leigh K. Jenco, Murad Idris, and Megan C. Thomas, 1–37. Oxford: Oxford University Press.

Johnson, Christopher. 2013. "The Prehistory of Technology: On the Contribution of Leroi-Gourhan." In *Stiegler and Technics*, edited by Christina Howells and Gerald Moore, 34–52. Edinburgh: Edinburgh University Press.

Kelly, Duncan. 2019. *Politics and the Anthropocene*. Cambridge: Polity.

Kelly, John D. 2014. "Introduction: The Ontological Turn in French Philosophical Anthropology." *HAU: Journal of Ethnographic Theory* 4 (1): 259–69.

Kelly, Mark G. E. 2018. *For Foucault: Against Normative Political Theory*. Albany: State University of New York Press.

Kouppanou, Anna. 2015. "Bernard Stiegler's Philosophy of Technology: Invention, Decision, and Education in Times of Digitization." *Educational Philosophy and Theory* 47 (10): 1110–23.

Laclau, Ernesto, and Chantal Mouffe. 1985. *Hegemony and Socialist Strategy*. London: Verso.

Lafontaine, Céline. 2007. "The Cybernetic Matrix of 'French Theory.'" *Theory, Culture & Society* 24 (5): 27–46.

Lampe, Kurt. 2017. "From Metaphysics to Ethics (with Bernard Stiegler, Heraclitus, and Aristotle)." In *Contemporary Encounters with Ancient Metaphysics*, edited by Abraham Greenstine and Ryan Johnson, 323–30. Edinburgh: Edinburgh University Press.

Lechte, John. 2018. *The Human: Bare Life and Ways of Life*. London: Bloomsbury.

Lemke, Thomas. 2018. "An Alternative Model of Politics? Prospects and Problems of Jane Bennett's Vital Materialism." *Theory, Culture & Society* 35 (6): 31–54.

Lemmens, Pieter. 2022. "Thinking Technology Big Again. Reconsidering the Question of the Transcendental and 'Technology with a Capital T' in the Light of the Anthropocene." *Foundations of Science* 27 (1): 171–87.

Leonard, Miriam. 2005. *Athens in Paris: Ancient Greece and the Political in Post-War French Thought*. Oxford: Oxford University Press.

Leroi-Gourhan, André. 1993. *Gesture and Speech*. Translated by Anna Bostock Berger. Cambridge: MIT Press.

Lévi-Strauss, Claude. 1961. *Tristes-Tropiques*. Translated by Doreen Weightman and John Weightman. New York: Criterion Books.

———. 1987. *Introduction to the Work of Marcel Mauss*. Translated by Felicity Baker. London: Routledge and Kegan Paul.

Lewis, Michael. 2013. "Of a Mythical Philosophical Anthropology: The Transcendental and the Empirical in *Technics and Time*." In *Stiegler and Technics*, edited by Christina Howells and Gerald Moore, 53–68. Edinburgh: Edinburgh University Press.

Lindberg, Susanna. 2020. "Politics of Digital Learning—Thinking Education with Bernard Stiegler." *Educational Philosophy and Theory* 52 (4): 384–96.

Livingston, Paul M. 2012. *The Politics of Logic: Badiou, Wittgenstein, and the Consequences of Formalism*. New York: Routledge.

Lotka, Alfred. 1945. "The Law of Evolution as a Maximal Principle." *Human Biology* 17 (3): 167–94.

Lynes, Philippe. 2019. "After Biodeconstruction in the Neganthropocene." *CR: The New Centennial Review* 19 (3): 65–98.

MacKenzie, Iain. 2022. "Critique in the Age of Indifference." *Theory & Event* 25 (1): 47–68.

MacKenzie, Iain, and Robert Porter. 2021. "Totalizing Institutions, Critique and Resistance." *Contemporary Political Theory* 20 (2): 233–49.

Malabou, Catherine. 2008. *What Should We Do With Our Brain?* Translated by Sebastien Rand. New York: Fordham University Press.

———. 2016. *Before Tomorrow: Epigenesis and Rationality*. Translated by Carolyn Shread. Cambridge: Polity.

Malafouris, Lambros. 2013. *How Things Shape the Mind: A Theory of Material Engagement*. Cambridge: MIT Press.

Malaspina, Cecile. 2018. *An Epistemology of Noise*. London: Bloomsbury.

Manche, Solange. 2021. "The Problem is Proletarianisation, Not Capitalism: A Critique of Bernard Stiegler's Contributive Economy." *Radical Philosophy* 2 (11): 38–49.

Maniglier, Patrice. 2014. "A Metaphysical Turn? Bruno Latour's An Inquiry into Modes of Existence." Translated by Olivia Lucca Fraser. *Radical Philosophy* 187: 37–44.

———. 2016. "Signs and Customs: Lévi-Strauss, Practical Philosopher." Translated by Matthew H. Evans. *Common Knowledge* 22 (3): 415–30.

Marchart, Oliver. 2007. *Post-Foundational Political Thought: Political Difference in Nancy, Lefort, Badiou and Laclau*. Edinburgh: Edinburgh University Press.

———. 2018. *Thinking Antagonism: Political Ontology After Laclau*. Edinburgh: Edinburgh University Press.

Marcuse, Herbert. 1955. *Eros and Civilization: A Philosophical Inquiry into Freud*. Boston: The Beacon Press.

Marshall, David L. 2010. "The *Polis* and Its Analogues in the Thought of Hannah Arendt." *Modern Intellectual History* 7 (1): 123–49.

Marx, Karl. 1973. *Grundrisse: Foundations of the Critique of Political Economy*. Translated by Martin Nicolaus. London: Penguin.

Mauss, Marcel. 2002. *The Gift: The Form and Reason for Exchange in Archaic Societies*. Translated by W. D. Halls. London: Routledge.

McNay, Lois. 2014. *The Misguided Search for the Political*. Cambridge: Polity.

———. 2016. "Agency." In *The Oxford Handbook of Feminist Theory*, edited by Lisa Disch and Mary Hawkesworth, 39–57. Oxford: Oxford University Press.

Meillassoux, Quentin. 2009. *After Finitude: An Essay on the Necessity of Contingency*. Translated by Ray Brassier. London: Continuum.

Mellamphy, Dan, and Nandita Biswas Mellamphy. 2015. "*Mort à Discredit*: Otium, Negotium, and the Critique of Transcendental Miserabilism. Bernard Stiegler, *Disbelief and Discredit*, Volumes I–III." *Parrhesia* 22: 131–51.

Mihai, Mihaela, Lois McNay, Oliver Marchart, Aletta Norval, Vassilios Paipais, Sergei Prozorov, and Mathias Thaler. 2017. "Democracy, Critique and the Ontological Turn." *Contemporary Political Theory* 16 (4): 501–31.

Montévil, Maël, Bernard Stiegler, Giuseppe Longo, Ana Soto, and Carlos Sonnenschein. 2021. "Anthropocene, Exosomatization and Negentropy." In *Bifurcate: "There is No Alternative,"* edited by Bernard Stiegler and the Internation Collective, translated by Daniel Ross, 45–62. London: Open Humanities Press.

Moore, Gerald. 2011. *Politics of the Gift: Exchanges in Poststructuralism*. Edinburgh: Edinburgh University Press.

———. 2013. "Adapt and Smile or Die! Stiegler Among the Darwinists." In *Stiegler and Technics*, edited by Gerald Moore and Christina Howells, 17–33. Edinburgh: Edinburgh University Press.

———. 2017. "On the Origin of Aisthesis by Means of Artificial Selection; or, The Preservation of Favored Traces in the Struggle for Existence." *Boundary 2* 44 (1): 191–212.

———. 2018. "The Pharmacology of Addiction." *Parrhesia* 28: 190–211.

Moore, Jason W. 2015. *Capitalism in the Web of Life: Ecology and the Accumulation of Capital*. London: Verso.

Mouffe, Chantal. 2000. *The Democratic Paradox*. London: Verso.

———. 2005. *On the Political*. Abingdon: Routledge.

———. 2013. *Agonistics: Thinking the World Politically*. London: Verso.

Moyn, Samuel. 2004. "Of Savagery and Civil Society: Pierre Clastres and the Transformation of French Political Thought." *Modern Intellectual History* 1 (1): 55–80.

Mui, Constance L., and Julien S. Murphy. 2020. "The University of the Future: Stiegler after Derrida." *Educational Philosophy and Theory* 52 (4): 455–65.

Mullarkey, John. 2006. *Post-Continental Philosophy: An Outline*. London: Continuum.

Nancy, Jean-Luc. 1991. *The Inoperative Community*. Translated by Peter Connor, Lisa Garbus, Michael Holland, and Simona Sawhney. Minneapolis: University of Minnesota Press.

———. 1997. *The Sense of the World*. Translated by Jeffrey S. Librett. Minneapolis: University of Minnesota Press.

———. 2010. *The Truth of Democracy*. Translated by Pascale-Anne Brault and Michael Naas. New York: Fordham University Press.

Nancy, Jean-Luc, and Philippe Lacoue-Labarthe. 1997. *Retreating the Political*. Translated by Simon Sparks. London: Routledge.

Nichols, Robert. 2020. *Theft Is Property! Dispossession & Critical Theory*. Durham: Duke University Press.

Nikolić, Sanela. 2020. "Digital Studies and Transcontextualization of the Humanities: The Case of Organology." *Digital Scholarship in the Humanities* 35 (2): 390–98.

Oksala, Johanna. 2012. *Foucault, Politics, and Violence*. Evanston: Northwestern University Press.

Owen, David. 2016. "Reasons and Practices of Reasoning: On the Analytic/Continental Distinction in Political Philosophy." *European Journal of Political Theory* 15 (2): 172–88.

Panagia, Davide. 2009. *The Political Life of Sensation*. Durham: Duke University Press.

Pavanini, Marco. 2022. "Multistability and Derrida's *Différance*: Investigating the Relations Between Postphenomenology and Stiegler's General Organology." *Philosophy & Technology* 35 (1): 1–22.

Pettman, Dominic. 2006. *Love and Other Technologies: Retrofitting Eros for the Information Age*. New York: Fordham University Press.

———. 2011. *Human Error: Species-Being and Media Machines*. Minneapolis: University of Minnesota Press.

———. 2015. *Infinite Distraction*. Cambridge: Polity.

Plato. 1997a. "Meno." In *Complete Works*, edited by John M. Cooper and D. S. Hutchinson, translated by G. M. A. Grube, 870–97. Indianapolis: Hackett.

———. 1997b. "Phaedrus." In *Complete Works*, edited by John M. Cooper and D. S. Hutchinson, translated by Alexander Nehamas and Paul Woodruff, 506–56. Indianapolis: Hackett.

———. 1997c. "Protagoras." In *Complete Works*, edited by John M. Cooper and D. S. Hutchinson, translated by Karen Bell and Stanley Lombardo, 746–90. Indianapolis: Hackett.

———. 1997d. "Symposium." In *Complete Works*, edited by John M. Cooper and D. S. Hutchinson, translated by Alexander Nehamas and Paul Woodruff, 457–505. Indianapolis: Hackett.

Prigogine, Ilya, and Isabelle Stengers. 2017. *Order Out of Chaos: Man's New Dialogue with Nature*. London: Verso.

Rabinbach, Anson. 1992. *The Human Motor: Energy, Fatigue, and the Origins of Modernity*. Berkeley: University of California Press.

Rae, Gavin. 2020. *Poststructuralist Agency: The Subject in Twentieth-Century Theory*. Edinburgh: Edinburgh University Press.

Rancière, Jacques. 1999. *Disagreement: Politics and Philosophy*. Translated by Julie Rose. Minneapolis: University of Minnesota Press.

Randazzo, Elisa, and Hannah Richter. 2021. "The Politics of the Anthropocene: Temporality, Ecology, and Indigeneity." *International Political Sociology* 15 (3): 293–312.

Raynaud, Philippe. 2014. "Politics, Policy." In *Dictionary of Untranslatables*, edited by Barbara Cassin, translated by Emily Apter, Jacques Lezra, and Michael Wood, 803–4. Princeton: Princeton University Press.

Read, Jason. 2015. "Relations of Production: Combes on Transindividuality." *Historical Materialism* 23 (3): 201–14.

———. 2016. *The Politics of Transindividuality*. Leiden: Brill.

Rees, Tobias. 2018. *After Ethnos*. Durham: Duke University Press.

Rekret, Paul. 2016. "A Critique of New Materialism: Ethics and Ontology." *Subjectivity* 9 (3): 225–45.

Reveley, James. 2015. "School-Based Mindfulness Training and the Economisation of Attention: A Stieglerian View." *Educational Philosophy and Theory* 47 (8): 804–20.

Roberts, Ben. 2005. "Stiegler Reading Derrida: The Prosthesis of Deconstruction in Technics." *Postmodern Culture* 16 (1). http://pmc.iath.virginia.edu/issue.905/16.1roberts.html.

———. 2006. "Rousseau, Stiegler and the Aporia of Origin." *Forum for Modern Language Studies* 42 (4): 382–94.

———. 2012. "Technics, Individuation and Tertiary Memory: Bernard Stiegler's Challenge to Media Theory." *New Formations* 77: 8–20.

———. 2013. "Memories of Inauthenticity: Stiegler and the Lost Spirit of Capitalism." In *Stiegler and Technics*, edited by Gerald Moore and Christina Howells, 225–39. Edinburgh: Edinburgh University Press.

———. 2016. "An 'Exemplary Contemporary Technical Object': Thinking Cinema between Hansen and Stiegler." *New Formations* 88: 88–104.

Ross, Daniel. 2009. "Politics and Aesthetics, or, Transformations of Aristotle in Bernard Stiegler." *Transformations* 17. http://www.transformationsjournal.org/wp-content/uploads/2017/01/Ross_Trans17.pdf.

———. 2013. "Pharmacology and Critique After Deconstruction." In *Stiegler and Technics*, edited by Gerald Moore and Christina Howells, 243–58. Edinburgh: Edinburgh University Press.

———. 2018. "Introduction." In *The Neganthropocene*, by Bernard Stiegler, translated by Daniel Ross, 7–32. London: Open Humanities Press.

———. 2021a. "Care and Carelessness in the Anthropocene: Bernard Stiegler's Three Conversions and Their Accompanying Heideggers." *Cultural Politics* 17 (2): 145–62.

———. 2021b. *Psychopolitical Anaphylaxis: Steps Towards a Metacosmics*. London: Open Humanities Press.

Rousseau, Jean-Jacques. 1997. "Discourse on the Origins and Foundations of Inequality Among Men." In *The Discourses and Other Early Political Writings*, edited and translated by Viktor Gourevitch, 111–222. Cambridge: Cambridge University Press.

Roussouw, Johann. 2016. "Bernard Stiegler's Politics of the Soul and His New Otium of the People." In *The Resounding Soul: Reflections on the Metaphysics and the Vivacity of the Human Person*, edited by Eric Austin Lee and Samuel Kimbriel, 40–58. Eugene: Wipf and Stock.

Rouvroy, Antoinette, and Thomas Berns. 2013. "Algorithmic Governmentality and Prospects of Emancipation: Disparateness as a Precondition for Individuation Through Relationships?" Translated by Elizabeth Libbrecht. *Réseaux* 177 (1): 163–96.

Rouvroy, Antoinette, and Bernard Stiegler. 2016. "The Digital Regime of Truth: From the Algorithmic Governmentality to a New Rule of Law." Translated by Anaïs Nony and Benoît Dillet. *La Deleuziana* 3: 6–27.

Sahlins, Marshall. 2008. *The Western Illusion of Human Nature*. Chicago: Prickly Paradigm Press.

Schrödinger, Erwin. 1992. *What Is Life?* Cambridge: Cambridge University Press.

Simondon, Gilbert. 2015. "Culture and Technics." *Radical Philosophy* 189: 17–23.

———. 2017. *On the Mode of Existence of Technical Objects*. Translated by Cecil Malaspina and John Rosgrove. Minneapolis: Univocal.

———. 2020. *Individuation in Light of Notions of Form and Information*. Translated by Taylor Adkins. Minneapolis: University of Minnesota Press.

Simpson, Audra. 2014. *Mohawk Interruptus: Political Life across the Borders of Settler States*. Durham: Duke University Press.

Singh, Julietta. 2018. *Unthinking Mastery: Dehumanism and Decolonial Entanglements*. Durham: Duke University Press.

Sinnerbrink, Robert. 2009. "Culture Industry Redux: Stiegler and Derrida on Technics and Cultural Politics." *Transformations* 17. http://www.transformationsjournal. org/wp-content/uploads/2017/01/Sinnerbrink_Trans17.pdf.

Skeaff, Christopher. 2018. *Becoming Political: Spinoza's Vital Republicanism and the Democratic Power of Judgment.* Chicago: University of Chicago Press.

Smith, Dominic. 2021. "Stiegler's Rigour: Metaphors for a Critical Continental Philosophy of Technology." *Journal of Aesthetics and Phenomenology* 8 (1): 37–54.

Somers-Hall, Henry. 2022. *Judgement and Sense in Modern French Philosophy.* Cambridge: Cambridge University Press.

Sophocles. 2015. *Antigone.* Translated by Robert Fagles. London: Penguin.

Steinberger, Peter J. 2018. *Political Judgment.* Cambridge: Polity.

Stengers, Isabelle. 2018. "The Challenge of Ontological Politics." In *A World of Many Worlds,* edited by Marisol de la Cadena and Mario Blaser, 83–111. Durham: Duke University Press.

Stiegler, Bernard. 1995. "Ce qui fait défaut." *Césure* 8: 233–78.

———. 1996. "Persephone, Oedipus, Epimetheus." Translated by Richard Beardsworth. *Tekhnema* 3: 69–112.

———. 1998. *Technics and Time 1: The Fault of Epimetheus.* Translated by Richard Beardsworth and George Collins. Stanford: Stanford University Press.

———. 2001. "Derrida and Technology: Fidelity at the Limits of Deconstruction and the Prosthesis of Faith." In *Derrida and the Humanities: A Critical Reader,* edited by Tom Cohen, translated by Richard Beardsworth, 238–70. Cambridge: Cambridge University Press.

———. 2003. "Technics of Decision: An Interview." Translated by Sean Gaston. *Angelaki: Journal of the Theoretical Humanities* 8 (2): 151–68.

———. 2006a. "*Anamnesis & Hypomnesis.*" http://arsindustrialis.org/anamnesis-and-hypomnesis.

———. 2006b. *La télécratie contre la démocratie.* Paris: Flammarion.

———. 2006c. "Nanomutations, Hypomnemata and Grammatisation." http://arsindustrialis.org/node/2937#_ftn1.

———. 2007. "Technics, Media, Teleology: Interview with Bernard Stiegler." *Theory, Culture & Society* 24 (7–8): 334–41.

———. 2008a. *Économie de l'hypermatériel et psychopouvoir.* Paris: Mille et une nuits.

———. 2008b. "Mystagogy: On Contemporary Art." In *Thinking Worlds: The Moscow Conference on Philosophy, Politics, and Art,* edited by Joseph Backstein, Daniel Birbaum, and Sven-Olov Wallenstein, 31–46. Berlin: Sternberg Press.

———. 2009a. *Acting Out.* Translated by David Barison, Stephen Barker, and Daniel Ross. Stanford: Stanford University Press.

———. 2009b. *Technics and Time 2: Disorientation.* Translated by Stephen Barker. Stanford: Stanford University Press.

———. 2009c. "Teleologics of the Snail: The Errant Self Wired to a WiMax Network." *Theory, Culture & Society* 26 (2–3): 33–45.

———. 2009d. "The Carnival of the New Screen." In *The YouTube Reader,* edited by Pelle Snickars and Patrick Vonderau, 40–59. Stockholm: National Library of Sweden.

————. 2009e. "The Magic Skin; or, The Franco-European Accident of Philosophy after Jacques Derrida." *Qui Parle* 18 (1): 97–110.

————. 2010a. "Bernard Stiegler's Pharmacy: A Conversation." *Configurations* 18 (3): 459–76.

————. 2010b. *For A New Critique of Political Economy.* Translated by Daniel Ross. Cambridge: Polity.

————. 2010c. "Knowledge, Care, and Trans-Individuation: An Interview with Bernard Stiegler." Translated by Chris Turner. *Cultural Politics* 6 (2): 157–70.

————. 2010d. "Memory." In *Critical Terms for Media Studies*, edited by Mark B. N. Hansen and W. J. T. Mitchell, 64–87. Chicago: University of Chicago Press.

————. 2010e. *Taking Care of Youth and the Generations.* Translated by Stephen Barker. Stanford: Stanford University Press.

————. 2011a. *Disbelief & Discredit 1: The Decadence of Industrial Democracies.* Translated by Daniel Ross. Cambridge: Polity.

————. 2011b. "Pharmacology of Desire: Drive-Based Capitalism and Libidinal Dis-Economy." *New Formations* 72: 150–61.

————. 2011c. *Technics and Time 3: Cinematic Time and the Question of Malaise.* Translated by Stephen Barker. Stanford: Stanford University Press.

————. 2011d. "The Tongue of the Eye: What 'Art History' Means." In *Releasing the Image: From Literature to New Media*, edited by Jacques Khalip and Robert Mitchell, translated by Thangam Ravindranathan and Bernard Geoghegan, 222–36. Stanford: Stanford University Press.

————. 2012a. "Bernard Stiegler: 'A Rational Theory of Miracles: On Pharmacology and Transindividuation.'" *New Formations* 77: 164–84.

————. 2012b. "Five Hundred Million Friends: The Pharmacology of Friendship." Translated by Daniel Ross. *UMBR(a): Technology*, 59–75.

————. 2012c. "Interview: From Libidinal Economy to the Ecology of the Spirit." Translated by Arne de Boever. *Parrhesia* 14: 9–15.

————. 2012d. "Relational Ecology and the Digital *Pharmakon.*" *Culture Machine* 13: 1–19.

————. 2012e. "The Theater of Individuation Phase-Shift and Resolution in Simondon and Heidegger." In *Gilbert Simondon: Being and Technology*, edited by Arne de Boever, Alex Murray, Jon Roffe, and Ashley Woodward, translated by Kristina Lebedeva, 185–202. Edinburgh: Edinburgh University Press.

————. 2013a. "Die Aufklärung in the Age of Philosophical Engineering." In *Digital Enlightenment Yearbook 2013*, edited by Mireille Hildebrandt, Kieron O'Hara, and Michael Waidner, translated by Daniel Ross, 29–39. Amsterdam: IOS Press.

————. 2013b. *Disbelief & Discredit 2: Uncontrollable Societies of Disaffected Individuals.* Translated by Daniel Ross. Cambridge: Polity.

————. 2013c. *Pharmacologie du front national: suivi du vocabulaire d'Ars Industrialis.* Paris: Flammarion.

———. 2013d. "The Most Precious Good in the Era of Social Technologies." In *Unlike Us Reader: Social Media Monopolies and Their Alternatives*, edited by Geert Lovink and Miriam Rasch, translated by Patrice Riemens, 16–30. Amsterdam: Institute of Network Cultures.

———. 2013e. "The Pharmacology of Post-Structuralism: An Interview with Bernard Stiegler." In *The Edinburgh Companion to Post-Structuralism*, edited by Benoît Dillet, Iain Mackenzie, and Robert Porter. Edinburgh: Edinburgh University Press.

———. 2013f. *What Makes Life Worth Living: On Pharmacology*. Translated by Daniel Ross. Cambridge: Polity.

———. 2014a. "Afterword: Web Philosophy." In *Philosophical Engineering: Toward a Philosophy of the Web*, edited by Harry Halpin and Alexandre Monnin, 187–98. Cambridge: Wiley Blackwell.

———. 2014b. *Disbelief & Discredit 3: The Lost Spirit of Capitalism*. Translated by Daniel Ross. Cambridge: Polity.

———. 2014c. "On Abbas Kiarostami's Close Up." *Parrhesia* 20: 40–48.

———. 2014d. "Programs of the Improbable, Short Circuits of the Unheard-Of." Translated by Robert Hughes. *Diacritics* 42 (1): 70–108.

———. 2014e. *Symbolic Misery 1: The Hyperindustrial Epoch*. Translated by Daniel Ross. Cambridge: Polity.

———. 2014f. *The Re-Enchantment of the World*. Translated by Trevor Arthur. London: Bloomsbury.

———. 2015a. *States of Shock: Stupidity and Knowledge in the 21st Century*. Translated by Daniel Ross. Cambridge: Polity.

———. 2015b. *Symbolic Misery 2: The Katastrophē of the Sensible*. Translated by Barnaby Norman. Cambridge: Polity.

———. 2015c. "The Shadow of the Sublime: On Les Immatériaux." In *30 Years After Les Immatériaux: Art, Science and Theory*, edited by Andreas Broeckmann and Yuk Hui, translated by Daniel Ross, 147–57. Lüneberg: Meson Press.

———. 2015d. "The Uncanniness of Thought and the Metaphysics of Penelope." Translated by Arne de Boever, Greg Flanders, and Alicia Harrison. *Parrhesia* 23: 63–77.

———. 2016a. *Automatic Society 1: The Future of Work*. Translated by Daniel Ross. Cambridge: Polity.

———. 2016b. "The Digital, Education, and Cosmopolitanism." Translated by David Bates. *Representations* 134 (1): 157–64.

———. 2016c. "Organology of Dreams and Archi-Cinema." Translated by Daniel Ross. *The Nordic Journal of Aesthetics* 24 (47): 7–37.

———. 2016d. "Ars and Organological Inventions in Societies of Hyper-Control." Edited and translated by Colette Tron and Daniel Ross. *Leonardo* 49 (5): 480–84.

———. 2017a. "General Ecology, Economy, and Organology." In *General Ecology: The New Ecological Paradigm*, edited by Erich Hörl and James Burton, translated by Daniel Ross. 129–50. London: Bloomsbury.

———. 2017b. "Kant, Art, and Time." Translated by Stephen Barker and Arne de Boever. *Boundary 2* 44 (1): 19–34.

———. 2017c. *Philosophising by Accident*. Translated by Benoît Dillet. Edinburgh: Edinburgh University Press.

———. 2017d. "The New Conflict of the Faculties and Functions: Quasi-Causality and Serendipity in the Anthropocene." Translated by Daniel Ross. *Qui Parle* 26 (1): 79–99.

———. 2017e. "The Quarrel of the Amateurs." Translated by Robert Hughes. *Boundary 2* 44 (1): 35–52.

———. 2017f. "The Proletarianization of Sensibility." Translated by Arne de Boever. *Boundary 2* 44 (1): 5–18.

———. 2018a. *Qu'appelle-t-on panser? 1: L'immense régression*. Paris: Éditions les liens qui libèrent.

———. 2018b. "Technologies of Memory and Imagination." Translated by Ashley Woodward and Amélie Berger Soraruff. *Parrhesia* 29: 25–76.

———. 2018c. *The Neganthropocene*. Translated by Daniel Ross. London: Open Humanities Press.

———. 2018d. " 'We Have to Become the Quasi-Cause of Nothing—of Nihil': An Interview with Bernard Stiegler." *Theory, Culture & Society* 35 (2): 137–56.

———. 2019a. "Fall and Elevation: Simondon's Apolitics." Translated by David Maruzzella. *Philosophy Today* 63 (3): 585–600.

———. 2019b. "For a Neganthropology of Automatic Society." In *Machine*, by Bernard Stiegler, Thomas Pringle, and Gertrud Koch. Translated by Daniel Ross. Lüneberg: Meson Press.

———. 2019c. "Philia, Drives, Automatisms." In *To Mind Is to Care*, edited by Joke Brouwer and Sjoerd van Tuinen. Translated by Pieter Lemmens, 96–123. Rotterdam: V2.

———. 2019d. *The Age of Disruption: Technology and Madness in Computational Capitalism*. Translated by Daniel Ross. Cambridge: Polity.

———. 2019e. " 'Night Gives Birth to Day' as the 'Conquest of Imperfection.' " *Lecture, Guayaquil,* July 2019. Translated by Daniel Ross. https://www.academia. edu/40305976/Bernard_Stiegler_Night_Gives_Birth_to_Day_as_the_Conquest_ of_Imperfection_2020_.

———. 2020a. *Nanjing Lectures 2016–2019*. Edited and translated by Daniel Ross. London: Open Humanities Press.

———. 2020b. "Noodiversity, Technodiversity: Elements of a New Economic Foundation Based on a New Foundation for Theoretical Computer Science."

Translated by Daniel Ross. *Angelaki: Journal of the Theoretical Humanities* 25 (4): 67–80.

———. 2020c. *Qu'appelle-t-on panser? 2: La leçon de Greta Thunberg.* Paris: Éditions les liens qui libèrent.

———. 2020d. "Elements for a General Organology." Translated by Daniel Ross. *Derrida Today* 13 (1): 72–94.

———. 2021a. "Afterword: Positive Pharmacology." In *Psychopolitical Anaphylaxis: Steps towards a Metacosmics*, by Daniel Ross. Translated by Daniel Ross, 357–68. London: Open Humanities Press.

———. 2021b. "Elements for a Neganthropology of Automatic Man." Translated by Daniel Ross. *Philosophy Today* 65 (2): 241–64.

———. 2022. "The Ordeal of Truth: Causes and Quasi-Causes in the Entropocene." Translated by Daniel Ross. *Foundations of Science* 27 (1): 271–80.

Stiegler, Bernard, Paolo Vignola, and Mitra Azar. 2021. "Introduction—Decarbonization and Deproletarianization: Gagner sa vie in the Twenty-First Century." In *Bifurcate: 'There is No Alternative,'* edited by Bernard Stiegler and the Internation Collective, translated by Daniel Ross, 18–44. London: Open Humanities Press.

Strathausen, Carsten, ed. 2009. *A Leftist Ontology: Beyond Relativism and Identity Politics.* Minneapolis: University of Minnesota Press.

Strathern, Marilyn. 2001. *The Gender of the Gift: Problems with Women and Problems with Society in Melanesia.* Berkeley: University of California Press.

Tomlinson, Gary. 2018. *Culture and the Course of Human Evolution.* Chicago: University of Chicago Press.

Tønder, Lars, and Lasse Thomassen, eds. 2005. *Radical Democracy: Politics Between Abundance and Lack.* Manchester: Manchester University Press.

Tsao, Roy T. 2002. "Arendt Against Athens: Rereading the Human Condition." *Political Theory* 30 (1): 97–123.

Tuckwell, Jason. 2020. "Technics and Agency: The Pluralism and Diversity of *Technē.*" *Angelaki: Journal of the Theoretical Humanities* 25 (4): 81–96.

Tuin, Iris van der, and Rick Dolphijn. 2012. *New Materialism: Interviews & Cartographies.* Ann Arbor: Open Humanities Press.

Turner, Ben. 2016. "Life and the Technical Transformation of *Différance*: Stiegler and the Noopolitics of Becoming Non-Inhuman." *Derrida Today* 9 (2): 177–98.

———. 2017. "Ideology and Post-structuralism after Bernard Stiegler." *Journal of Political Ideologies* 22 (1): 92–110.

———. 2019a. "Affinity and Antagonism: Structuralism, Comparison and Transformation in Pluralist Political Ontology." *Philosophy & Social Criticism* 45 (1): 27–49.

———. 2019b. "From Resistance to Invention in the Politics of the Impossible: Bernard Stiegler's Political Reading of Maurice Blanchot." *Contemporary Political Theory* 18 (1): 43–64.

———. 2020. "Politicising the Epokhé: Bernard Stiegler and the Politics of Epochal Suspension." In *The Subject(s) of Phenomenology*, edited by Iulian Apostolescu, 341–54. Dordrecht: Springer.

———. 2021a. "'Above and Beyond the Market': The Family, Social Reproduction, and Conservatism in Bernard Stiegler's Politics of Work." *Angelaki: Journal of the Theoretical Humanities* 26 (6): 68–85.

———. 2021b. "The Limits of Culture in Political Theory: A Critique of Multiculturalism from the Perspective of Anthropology's Ontological Turn." *European Journal of Political Theory* 20 (2): 252–71.

Turner, Chris. 2010. "Kant Avec Ferry: Some Thoughts on Bernard Stiegler's *Prendre Soin: I. De La Jeunesse et Des Générations.*" *Cultural Politics* 6 (2): 253–57.

Vaccari, Andrés. 2009. "Unweaving the Program: Stiegler and the Hegemony of Technics." *Transformations* 17. http://www.transformationsjournal.org/wp-content/uploads/2017/01/Vaccari_Trans17.pdf.

Van Camp, Nathan. 2009a. "Animality, Humanity, and Technicity." *Transformations* 17. http://www.transformationsjournal.org/wp-content/uploads/2017/01/VanCamp_Trans17.pdf.

———. 2009b. "Stiegler, Habermas and the Techno-logical Condition of Man." *Journal for Cultural Research* 13 (2): 125–41.

———. 2011. "Negotiating the Anthropological Limit: Derrida, Stiegler, and the Question of the Animal." *Between the Species: A Journal for the Study of Philosophy and Animals* 14 (1): 57–80.

Vernant, Jean-Pierre. 1980. *Myth and Society in Ancient Greece.* Translated by Janet Lloyd. Brighton: Harvester Press.

———. 1986. "At Man's Table: Hesiod's Foundation Myth of Sacrifice." In *The Cuisine of Sacrifice Among the Greeks*, edited by Jean-Pierre Vernant and Marcel Detienne, translated by Paula Wissing, 21–86. Chicago: University of Chicago Press.

Vernant, Jean-Pierre, and Pierre Vidal-Naquet. 1990. *Myth and Tragedy in Ancient Greece.* Translated by Janet Lloyd. New York: Zone Books.

Vesco, Shawna. 2015. "Collective Disindividuation and/or Barbarism: Technics and Proletarianization." *Boundary* 2 42 (2): 85–104.

Viriasova, Inna. 2018. *At the Limits of the Political: Affect, Life, Things.* London: Rowman and Littlefield International.

Vitale, Francesco. 2018. *Biodeconstruction: Jacques Derrida and the Life Sciences.* Translated by Mauro Senatore. Albany: State University of New York Press.

Viveiros de Castro, Eduardo. 2011. "Zeno and the Art of Anthropology: Of Lies, Beliefs, Paradoxes, and Other Truths." *Common Knowledge* 17 (1): 128–45.

———. 2014. *Cannibal Metaphysics: For a Post-Structural Anthropology.* Translated by Peter Skafish. Minneapolis: Univocal.

Vlieghe, Joris. 2014. "Education in an Age of Digital Technologies: Flusser, Stiegler, and Agamben on the Idea of the Posthistorical." *Philosophy & Technology* 27 (4): 519–37.

Voela, Angie, and Louis Rothschild. 2019. "Creative Failure: Stiegler, Psychoanalysis and the Promise of a Life Worth Living." *New Formations* 95: 54–69.

Wambacq, Judith, and Bart Buseyne. 2012. "The Reality of Real Time." *New Formations* 77: 63–75.

Warren, Calvin L. 2018. *Ontological Terror: Blackness, Nihilism, and Emancipation.* Durham: Duke University Press.

Watt, Calum. 2016. "The Uses of Maurice Blanchot in Bernard Stiegler's *Technics and Time.*" *Paragraph* 39 (3): 305–18.

Wenman, Mark. 2013. *Agonistic Democracy: Constituent Power in the Era of Globalisation.* Cambridge: Cambridge University Press.

White, Stephen K. 2000. *Sustaining Affirmation: The Strengths of Weak Ontology in Political Theory.* Princeton: Princeton University Press.

———. 2011. "Contemporary Continental Political Thought." In *The Oxford Handbook of the History of Political Philosophy*, edited by George Klosko, 480–500. Oxford: Oxford University Press.

Whitehead, Alfred North. 1929a. *Process and Reality: An Essay in Cosmology.* New York: The Free Press.

———. 1929b. *The Function of Reason.* Princeton: Princeton University Press.

Widder, Nathan. 2012. *Political Theory After Deleuze.* London: Continuum.

Wiener, Norbert. 1989. *The Human Use of Human Beings: Cybernetics and Society.* London: Free Association Books.

———. 2019. *Cybernetics: or Control and Communication in the Animal and the Machine.* Cambridge: MIT Press.

Winnicott, Donald W. 2005. *Playing and Reality.* Abingdon: Routledge.

Withers, D.-M. 2015. *Feminism, Digital Culture and the Politics of Transmission: Theory, Practice and Cultural Heritage.* London: Rowman & Littlefield International.

———. 2019. "Diabolic Marks, Organs, and Relations: Exiting Symbolic Misery." *Angelaki: Journal of the Theoretical Humanities* 24 (5): 88–103.

Wolf, Maryanne. 2008. *Proust and the Squid: The Story and Science of the Reading Brain.* Cambridge: Icon Books.

Woodward, Ashley. 2016. *Lyotard and the Inhuman Condition: Reflections on Nihilism, Information and Art.* Edinburgh: Edinburgh University Press.

———. 2017. "Circuits of Desire: Cybernetics and the Post-Natural According to Lyotard and Stiegler." In *Philosophy after Nature*, edited by Rosi Braidotti and Rick Dolphijn, 121–35. London: Rowman and Littlefield International.

———. 2019. "Nihilism, Neonihilism, Hypernihilism: 'Nietzsche aujourd'hui' Today?" *Nietzsche-Studien* 48 (1): 244–64.

Wynter, Sylvia. 2003. "Unsettling the Coloniality of Being/Power/Truth/Freedom: Towards the Human, After Man, Its Overrepresentation—An Argument." *CR: The New Centennial Review* 3 (3): 257–337.

Zerilli, Linda M. G. 2005a. *Feminism and the Abyss of Freedom*. Chicago: University of Chicago Press.

———. 2005b. " 'We Feel Our Freedom': Imagination and Judgment in the Thought of Hannah Arendt." *Political Theory* 33 (2): 158–88.

———. 2016. *A Democratic Theory of Judgment*. Chicago: University of Chicago Press.

Index

www.ingramcontent.com/pod-product-compliance
Lightning Source LLC
Chambersburg PA
CBHW020343270326
41926CB00007B/293